WITHDRAWN FROM
TSC LIBRARY

D1560275

All Hell Broke Loose

ALL HELL BROKE LOOSE

*American Race Riots from the Progressive
Era through World War II*

Ann V. Collins

Praeger Series on American Political Culture
Jon L. Wakelyn and Michael J. Connolly, Series Editors

 PRAEGER

AN IMPRINT OF ABC-CLIO, LLC
Santa Barbara, California • Denver, Colorado • Oxford, England

Copyright 2012 by Ann V. Collins

All rights reserved. No part of this publication may be reproduced, stored in a retrieval system, or transmitted, in any form or by any means, electronic, mechanical, photocopying, recording, or otherwise, except for the inclusion of brief quotations in a review, without prior permission in writing from the publisher.

Library of Congress Cataloging-in-Publication Data

Collins, Ann V.
   All hell broke loose : American race riots from the Progressive Era through World War II / Ann V. Collins.
       p. cm. — (Praeger series on American political culture)
   Includes bibliographical references and index.
   ISBN 978-0-313-39599-4 (hardcopy : acid-free paper) —
ISBN 978-0-313-39600-7 (ebook)
1. Race riots—United States—History—19th century.   2. Race riots—United States—History—20th century.   3. United States—Race relations—History—19th century.   4. United States—Race relations—History—20th century.
5. United States—Race relations—Case studies   I. Title.
   HV6477.C65 2012
   363.32'3097309041—dc23   2011053125

ISBN: 978-0-313-39599-4
EISBN: 978-0-313-39600-7

16   15   14   13   12   1   2   3   4   5

This book is also available on the World Wide Web as an eBook.
Visit www.abc-clio.com for details.

Praeger
An Imprint of ABC-CLIO, LLC

ABC-CLIO, LLC
130 Cremona Drive, P.O. Box 1911
Santa Barbara, California 93116-1911

This book is printed on acid-free paper ∞

Manufactured in the United States of America

To Carter and Elizabeth

CONTENTS

SERIES FOREWORD

In describing the development of American literature from colonial settlement to the early 20th century, Harvard Professor Barrett Wendell noted that Britain and America began as one, particularly in shared language. "A common language, one grows to feel, is a closer bond than common blood," he wrote in *The Temper of the Seventeenth Century in English Literature* from 1904. "For at heart the truest community which men can know is community of ideals; and inextricably interwoven with the structure of any language—with its words, with its idioms, with its syntax, and nowadays even with its very orthography—are ideals which, recognized or not, have animated and shall animate to the end those who instinctively phrase their earthly experience in its terms." But after initial 17th-century settlement, the two diverged, leading ultimately to the 18th-century American Revolution. That divergence came from a lack of shared experience. While Britain rolled through the turbulence of urban growth, economic distress, and political revolution, America experienced "a period of almost stationary national temper" and retained its 17th-century idealism (what Wendell termed a delicate balance of common law rights with a sense of biblical right) long after Britain's had passed. Thus, one common language came to be spoken in two entirely different nations. This divergence marked the creation not only of American literature, which emerged in full flower in the 19th century, but also of a uniquely American political culture, a culture that Wendell could still see operating in the United States of William McKinley, Theodore Roosevelt, and Woodrow Wilson. This task of understanding just what constitutes American political culture, what makes it unique from other nations as well as similar, and how that affects our current understanding of national development continues to fascinate American historians.

American political culture itself is a diverse concept, but at its base marks the boundaries, constructed over 400 years, of political discourse and understanding. We understand political change through a particular, historically developed, American lens, unique from other nations and their collective experience. How we learn political culture is also multifaceted: from friends and family, schools and universities, media sources, religious leaders and texts, or the community institutions that shape our daily experiences of life. Daniel Walker Howe, in his seminal *Political Culture of the American Whigs* (1979), defined political culture as "an evolving system of beliefs, attitudes, and techniques for solving problems, transmitted from generation to generation and finding expression in the innumerable activities that people learn; religion, child-rearing customs, the arts and professions, and, of course, politics." Jean Baker in *Affairs of Party: the Political Culture of Northern Democrats in the Mid-Nineteenth Century* (1983) noted that "Political Culture assumes that attitudes, sentiments, and cognitions that inform and govern politics are not random arrangements, but represent (if only we could see them as an anthropologist does the tribal rites of Tikopia) coherent patterns that together form a meaningful whole." This collection of impressions and attitudes we call American political culture, distinct from other national traditions, is framed by the intellectual debates, party clashes, partisan disputes, religious difficulties, economic distress, and attitudes toward governance experienced since the 18th century and earlier. In a major work of political culture, *Revolutionary Backlash* (2007), Rosemarie Zagarri shows that though Alexander Hamilton and Thomas Jefferson have been dead since the early 19th century, their clash over politics shaped the role of women in the political culture of their time. James T. Kloppenberg, the distinguished student of political culture, in his *Reading Obama* (2010), maintains that in order to understand the meaning of this new president's political values, we must continue to use that early political struggle of Hamilton and Jefferson. Their battles help frame contemporary political disputes, as does a close reading of political texts by authors like Kloppenberg aid in understanding the political culture of contemporary times. No debate over health care, environmental issues, foreign affairs, economic policy, the nature of governance, or the education of our youth occurs in a historical vacuum divorced from precedent, nor can be understood without unearthing structures of political culture with roots stretching back hundreds of years.

The guiding theme of the Praeger Series in American Political Culture is explaining how cultural factors (education, family, community, etc.)

and economic change (technological innovation, depressions, prosperity, market alterations, etc.) intersect with political methods and ideas (elections, strategies, laws, policies, institutions, etc.) to shape human actions throughout American history. While the series exhibits a theme, it is understood broadly to encourage a wide array of new projects and scholars from many disciplines—history, politics, law, and philosophy, for example. We welcome diversity in approach to historical topics, such as biography, institutional history, history of ideas, policy history, and the development of political structures, among others, but this series works within the discipline of history, not political science. We interpret political culture from a strictly historical perspective.

We are pleased to offer another volume in our series, Ann Collins's *All Hell Broke Loose,* a major work on race riots in 20th-century United States. She believes those riots to have been acts of political violence revealing much about American cultural attributes of freedom and repression. Like the important works by Paul Gilje, *Rioting in America* (1996), and George Rable, *But There Was No Peace* (1984), Collins grasps the political utility of violent reaction. She adopts Gilje's theory that one must study race riots in the context of white violence, or counterviolence, as whites attempted to undermine black desire for a better life. Violent forms of political oppression thus contested the cultural values of black freedom. Riots, states Collins, became symbols of demand for change, as well as forms of reactionary political protest with cultural overtones.

Collins develops her argument by first dissecting the nightmare 1921 race riots in Tulsa, Oklahoma. With that event as a model, she details the history of 12 other riots, their causes, and results, covering the period 1898–1945. The riots took place in sites from Chicago to New Orleans, thus were not geographic specific, but revealed similar characteristics of black protest and white response with violent rioting in black communities. In all of the riots she studies, local circumstances created extralegal and mercifully short white riots. Collins then focuses on the specific activities of each riot or what she calls its cultural form. Collins finds a pattern after 1919 of increased white violence toward black property and people. She concludes with an examination of the records of various political commissions (state and national) formed to investigate those riots. Each of these commissions' analyses of cause and result of riots confirms her theory. In doing so, Collins makes an important contribution to the political culture of those race riots that so marked the American landscape in the drive for black freedom and resultant white repression during the first half of the 20th century. As such, she points toward a reconsideration of the black civil rights movement and white violence of the 1950s and 1960s, and, alas, thereafter.

ACKNOWLEDGMENTS

This book came together with the help of many people, and I am deeply appreciative of them all. The editors I worked with to complete this project had just the right combination of gentle prodding and urgent motivation. Michael Millman proved to be especially effective at this balancing act, as well as exceedingly patient. Individuals at the following institutions provided quick responses to my queries about riot images in their collections: the Arkansas History Commission; McFarlin Library, Department of Special Collections, the University of Tulsa; the Nebraska State Historical Society; and the New Hanover County (North Carolina) Public Library. I also had the advantage of working with excellent mentors throughout my undergraduate and graduate studies, particularly Lisa Baldez, Dennis Dunn, Stanley Hilton, and Gary Miller. I thank them for their guidance and for their outstanding example both inside and outside of the classroom. They shared with me the tools I needed to write this book.

I have the best job in the world, not only because of the subject I teach—all aspects of American politics—but also because of the people I interact with on a daily basis. The students, staff, administration, and faculty make McKendree University in Lebanon, Illinois, a special place to work. The friends that I have made throughout my life have made it enriching, and I am thankful for my good fortune. Finally, my family has shown great enthusiasm and interest during the research and writing of this book (and in all my endeavors). My parents, Luan and Kent Haynes and the late Bill Brunson, as well as my parents-in-law, Joyce and Ged Collins, have cheered me along the whole way. My husband, Steve, has offered much-needed support in numerous ways throughout this process. His knowledge and passion for history have helped me greatly. I dedicate this book to my children, Carter and Elizabeth, who consistently give me perspective and insight into life and love. I hope that they and future generations will learn from the past and find ways to embrace one another and work together for the common good of humankind.

INTRODUCTION

An angry crowd of Tulsa, Oklahoma's white residents congregated in front of the city's courthouse on the evening of May 31, 1921. Inside, Dick Rowland, a 19-year-old African American shoeshine, sat detained for an alleged infraction that struck fear into whites across the country during the late 19th and early 20th centuries—attempted sexual assault. As in many other instances, it did not matter that the charges later proved false completely exonerating the young man. The gathering throng avowed that Rowland must pay with his life. The mob intended to lynch him.[1] When a group of men from Tulsa's black community converged on the courthouse to protect Rowland, a scuffle ensued. A shot rang out, and then, according to a sheriff, "all hell broke loose."[2] One of the worst race riots in American history was under way. When the violence stopped, Greenwood, Tulsa's once thriving black community, lay in ruins.

Unfortunately, the events in Tulsa were not unique. Race riots of this kind—characterized by white aggression toward blacks and their property (see the discussion that follows for what constitutes a race riot in this study)—cropped up over and over again in the United States during the late 19th century and into the middle of the 20th century. This work explores the riots that occurred during that time period, beginning with Wilmington, North Carolina, in 1898, and those that followed until the end of World War II, with the 1943 riot in Beaumont, Texas, serving as the last major white-on-black riot in this study. From 1898 to 1945, at least 50 significant race riots flared throughout the United States, with more than 25 occurring in the Red Summer of 1919 alone.[3] Not solely a southern, northern, eastern, or western trend, these riots appeared in geographical locales as diverse as Atlanta, Georgia; Washington, D.C.; Detroit, Michigan; Chicago, Illinois; Omaha, Nebraska; Longview, Texas; and rural Arkansas.

One scholar of riots contends that "an examination of confrontations in selected American cities throughout the nineteenth and early twentieth centuries demonstrates that there is *no clearly discernable pattern* to this country's race riots." Instead, according to this author, distinctive origins and local community history provide the crucial variables for explaining American racial violence during this era.[4] Although unique in some respects, upon closer inspection, these riots do share common characteristics that can be highlighted within the broader context in which they occurred. Against the backdrop of white radicalism, Jim Crow laws, political unrest, economic turmoil, labor strife, two world wars, African American assertions for equality at home as they fought for democracy abroad, and demographic change and its resultant effect on such issues as housing, race riots plagued the American landscape for most of the first half of the 20th century. A discernable pattern can be found among them, and one of the contributions that this volume provides is that it makes a connection between these national concerns and local circumstances.

Through this window of American history—the Progressive Era through World War II—my research examines the conditions that allowed race riots to occur. Although riot violence existed both before and after these decades, this particular era lacks a thorough assessment of these incidents.[5] Most studies that do examine race riots during these years focus on one riot,[6] or a narrower chronological time span of one or two years.[7] Other scholars include these riots within a larger framework.[8] This work, therefore, explores the race riots that occurred during a crucial period of American history and fills a long-neglected gap in the literature.

Attentive to the research of previous collective violence social scientists, I define the race riots of this era as rational, extralegal, relatively short eruptions of white-on-black violence aimed at influencing social change.[9] Like Paul Brass, an expert on collective violence and riots in India,[10] I avoid labeling these acts completely spontaneous because white individuals mired in a culture committed to hate, destruction, and the annihilation of the African American race carried them out so deliberately. In the case of race riots from the late 1890s through World War II, whites intended to thwart—by any means necessary—economic, political, or social progress that African Americans strove to make.

Indeed, "much of our nineteenth- and twentieth-century violence," as Richard Maxwell Brown contends, "has represented the attempt of established Americans to preserve their favored position in the social, economic, and political order."[11] The violent actions of white rioters, therefore, hinged on the rational goal of impeding any steps that might advance America's black population. Moreover, whites possessed a virtual carte blanche to carry out this agenda. As other scholars conclude, vigilantism propels "established groups to preserve the status quo at times when the formal system of rule enforcement is viewed as ineffective or irrelevant."[12] In many instances during the era of white riots, the local, state, and national authorities openly supported or condoned these atrocities. As I explain in the pages that follow, these factors and others allowed "all hell to break loose."

In Chapter 1, I place the white-on-black riots that occurred during the Progressive Era through World War II in historical context by providing a general history of race riots in the United States up until that period. I then lay out a conception of how race riots erupt. The next chapters explain the structural factors, cultural framing, and precipitating events for the riots that occurred from the Progressive Era through World War II, the time frame analyzed in this work. I also present 12 case studies—6 racial pogroms during the Progressive Era through World War II (Wilmington, North Carolina; New Orleans, Louisiana; Atlanta, Georgia; East St. Louis, Illinois; Tulsa, Oklahoma; and Beaumont, Texas) and 6 riots from the Red Summer of 1919 (Longview, Texas; Washington, D.C.; Chicago, Illinois; Knoxville, Tennessee; Omaha, Nebraska; and Phillips County, Arkansas), a particularly vicious year and the apex of white-on-black race riots. I conclude with a broad outline of my arguments and examine the changing nature of race riots at midcentury with an overview of the 1943 race riot in Detroit. Finally, I include an epilogue addressing riot commissions set up in the immediate aftermath of various 20th-century race riots, as well as modern-day truth commissions established for some of the riots examined in this study.

My journey into race riot research actually began in Latin America (albeit intellectually, not physically). While working on my master's degree in American and Latin American History at Louisiana State University, I became interested in the truth commissions set up in Latin America after the military dictatorships of the 1960s, 1970s, and 1980s. This topic led me to the commission organized in 1997 by the Oklahoma state legislature for the purpose of airing the atrocities that occurred during the 1921 Tulsa race riot. As I further explored this subject during my doctoral studies in political science at Washington University in St. Louis, the more I realized that this significant and critical story needed to be told. Dozens of white-on-black race riots marred the country, and they need to be analyzed to explain why.

Race relations continue to play a large role in the social fabric of the United States, most recently with the election of the first African American to the presidency. And while race riots have lain dormant for many decades now, racism continues to thrive in the United States. According to one study, for example, hate groups proliferated in response to President Barack Obama's inauguration.[13] Moreover, communities such as Atlanta, Georgia; Springfield, Illinois; Wilmington, North Carolina; and Tulsa, Oklahoma, have established organizations or commissions in recent years to grapple with the race riots that plagued their cities over 100 years ago. Clearly, the atrocities continued to haunt them. Indeed, while the wholesale, overt slaughter of black communities has not occurred in more than half a century now, the United States must understand its history of racial violence and racism in order to comprehend its present situation and to work for the betterment of society for future generations. It is my hope that *All Hell Broke Loose* helps shed some light on that endeavor.

Chapter 1

RACE RIOTS: STRUCTURAL FACTORS, CULTURAL FRAMING, AND PRECIPITATING EVENTS

HISTORICAL PERSPECTIVE

The United States has long carried on a tradition of violent group conflict.[1] White viciousness caused African Americans to suffer unimaginable hardships and violence of every stripe during their years under slavery. White-on-black race riots began in earnest in the 1830s and persisted throughout the antebellum period primarily in response to abolitionists' push for emancipation. In the most well-known cases, whites in Cincinnati, New York City, and Philadelphia forced blacks from their homes, razed black churches and schools, and beat or killed any African American they could find.[2] During the Civil War, this brand of violence continued, with the most famous instance erupting in New York City in July 1863, when whites vented their condemnation of the black-aligned Republican Party and the Civil War draft in the form of vicious attacks against African Americans. The riot marked an escalation of white savagery as mobs mutilated and strung up unsuspecting blacks and targeted a black orphanage. More than 100 people, mostly rioters and at least 11 blacks, died. Even more suffered injuries, and property damage was immense.[3] Rioting also broke out in other parts of the state—Buffalo and Troy—as well as Newark, New Jersey, during the war.[4] In these incidents and others, many whites assumed that the draft would force them into a war that would free the slaves, who would subsequently usurp their jobs and assail their women,[5] dimensions that would take on particularly significant proportions by the end of the century.

Unfortunately, the war's end did not stem the violence. "For the South," as historian George Rable echoes Clausewitz's renowned maxim, "peace became war carried on by other means."[6] Reconstruction did usher in an era of hope for African Americans, but whites, particularly in the South, redoubled their efforts—with the aid of the newly minted Ku Klux Klan and other vigilante groups[7]—to quash any progress toward securing equal racial protection under the law, as well as social and economic advancements.[8] Of course, "the Klan's birth did not initiate that tradition nor did the Klan's disappearance terminate it," avers historian Edward Ayers. "Honor, kinship, isolation, localistic republicanism, and poverty—along with hatred for blacks—fed group violence in the southern hills for generations."[9] But while the Klan generally focused its wrath on rural targets, race riots, typically a northern phenomenon before and during the Civil War, exploded in southern cities immediately after the war. Charleston and Norfolk in 1865, Memphis and New Orleans in 1866, New Orleans again in 1868, Colfax, Louisiana, in 1873, and Charleston again in 1876 experienced intense racial conflagrations.[10] Race riots eventually broke out in northern cities (Philadelphia, for example) after the war as well.[11] According to one study, 33 major race riots took place during Reconstruction, most often for political control, but also because of white concerns over labor, social mores, and supposed black uprisings.[12]

With the end of Reconstruction, as southern whites enacted de facto and later de jure segregation and disfranchisement without the veil of federal authorities over them, racial violence continued with a vengeance. But white terror did not stay confined to the South after 1877. As in the antebellum era, racial violence reappeared in the North, and now also in the East and the West, as well as rural and urban locales.[13] Fueled by a white radical ideology that cast blacks as naturally savage and bestial and envisioned no place for the African American in the United States,[14] white fear focused especially on the supposed black threat to white womanhood.[15] With the Industrial Revolution and the subsequent agricultural depression in the 1890s, white males lost control of their economic independence. This occurrence, in conjunction with the loss of unfettered sexual accessibility to black women after emancipation, dealt a serious blow to their manhood.[16] Unable to provide for their household, white men turned their attention to enforcing Victorian principles designed to shield their women from the concocted "black beast rapist."[17] In response to these and other threats, genuine or invented, a particularly sadistic form of aggression emerged, mainly in the South. Between 1882 and 1937, 5,112 Americans were lynched—strung up, tortured, mutilated, and charred, or any combination thereof—with 3,657 of them being African Americans.[18] By the turn of the century, racial animosity reached a fever pitch, and a new wave of race riots erupted across America, often in tandem with lynchings. This book focuses on these riots and those that followed through the end of World War II.

A CONCEPTION OF RACE RIOTS

Although people may conceive of riots as spontaneous and purely irrational, the individuals who carried out the race riots of the late 19th and the first half of the 20th centuries proved both purposeful and strategic—in the words of Donald Horowitz, possessing "lucid madness," not "blind fury."[19] Perhaps more aptly described as massacres or pogroms,[20] particularly during the early part of this study, the racial violence that occurred in the United States fits the definition that Horowitz constructs in his study on riots:

> The deadly ethnic [based on ascriptive differences] riot is an intense, sudden, though not necessarily wholly unplanned, lethal attack by civilian members of one ethnic group on civilian members of another ethnic group, the victims chosen because of their group membership. . . . The riot is not an unstructured mêlée, in which it is impossible to disentangle attackers from their victims. Rather, the ethnic riot consists of a series of discernible actions, identifiable initiators and targets, attacks and (rarely) counterattacks. Riots spring from highly patterned occurrences and conditions, and they reflect clear-cut structures of ethnic-group relations.[21]

Horowitz's conception of riots captures much of the racial tension that permeated the United States between 1898 and 1945. Some 50 race riots erupted across the country, and in each incident, whites targeted individual blacks not because they knew them but because of their skin color and the political, economic, and social threat that it represented to them.[22]

In his book on riots, revolts, and insurrections, Raymond Momboisse paints a dramatic picture of mob behavior and accurately reflects the descriptions provided in newspapers and other accounts detailing the race riots of the Progressive Era through World War II:

> Mobs . . . do not suddenly spring into full bloom. They are the product of a process of evolution. Individuals who constitute a mob always have certain common interests and needs. . . . These individuals are preconditioned, for tension conditions do not as a rule arise abruptly. There may be a series of irritating events or a deluge of vicious rumors which create a climate of tension. Frustrations are built up.
> The first step in the transformation of a preconditioned and responsive group of individuals into a mob is some climatic [sic] event. . . . It causes a crowd to gather at the scene. Its members mill about like cattle. The gathering

of a crowd automatically causes more onlookers to accumulate. . . . Rumors
are numerous and spread rapidly. . . . As an incident proceeds to attract
numbers of individuals, they are pressed together. . . . They initiate con-
versations with strangers. . . . [T]hey "mill" about. . . . Through the milling
process, the crowd excites itself more and more. . . . More and more people
appear on the scene. . . .

As tension mounts, individuals become less and less responsive to stimu-
lation arising outside the group and respond only to influences from within
the crowd itself. . . . Brutalized emotions rise and receive the sanction of the
mob. . . . Such overt behavior is, of course, always violent and destructive. . . .
Once action has begun, it usually spreads quickly, engulfing even the more
intelligent and self-controlled. . . . To the members of a rebellious group,
violence of whatever order provides an outlet for those feelings.[23]

This work identifies the existing conditions and factors that produce the
specific instances in time at which race riots coalesce in this process, causing all hell to break loose. The tipping point model also provides a use-
ful and effective way to explore the proximate process that leads to riots.
Fleshed out by Thomas Schelling in his analysis of neighborhood racial
segregation,[24] scholars use tipping to study any number of phenomena.[25]
Schelling concludes that a tip occurs in a neighborhood once a certain
threshold of nonwhites emerges causing large numbers of whites to leave.
The likelihood that any particular person joins in this group action hinges
on his or her perception of what others seem likely to do.[26]

The tipping model, then, relies on the conception of how individuals
react to those around them, highlighting the significance of *perception* in
spurring mobilization. Recent scholars, moreover, use this model to explain how movement organizers use cultural norms—common customs
and values within a society—to spur on collective behavior.[27] Mobilization
based on race, as in the case of this study, would mean framing actions
through the prism of racial cultural norms. During the late 19th century
and first half of the 20th, newspaper editors and politicians particularly
served as the agents in this quest for white racial supremacy and, alternatively, black equality. But as Lisa Baldez suggests in her study of women's
movements in Chile, movement leaders cannot presume that individuals
will automatically step into place once an appeal for action sounds forth.
Instead, a political entrepreneur's call will resonate only if specific conditions exist.[28]

Like Baldez, I also examine the *macro* conditions that allow tipping to
occur. Specifically, my work focuses on the factors that prompted whites
to unite violently under racial terms against their black neighbors. While
previous collective behavior scholars use the tipping point model to explain the *micro*-level decisions that prompt individuals to coordinate

into collective action, Baldez and I differ from others in our approach of employing this model.[29] For race riots to occur, and therefore for a tipping point to be reached, three conditions must exist: certain *structural factors*—primarily demographic, economic, labor, political, legal, social, and institutional features; *cultural framing*, or actions and discourse by both whites and blacks to further their own causes; and a *precipitating event*, the immediate spark that ignites the violence.

Structural Factors

Some social scientists attribute the emergence of collective action to structural features within a society. In this scholarship, overarching political, social, and economic conditions play a large role in explaining when collective behavior occurs. Forces such as urbanization, the growth of capitalism, and industrialization exemplify this line of research. Structural factors make up one component of race riots; the violence that occurred from the Progressive Era through World War II erupted under specific societal conditions.

Beginning in the 1890s, for example, American blacks started to leave the rural South for the hope of better opportunities. Some went to southern cities, while others made their way to the North and the West. A Great Migration saw an outflux of 500,000 African American southerners between 1916 and 1919 and close to one million more the following decade. Chicago's black population swelled from 44,103 in 1910 to 109,458 some 10 years later. Detroit saw a similar demographic change in the same decade, from 5,741 black residents in 1910, to 40,838 by 1920. New York's black community also grew, from 91,709 in 1910 to 152,467 in 1920.[30] This influx of people resulted in strains on housing, public transportation, and food, contributing to often already tense racial relations. In the South, white leaders began to undertake de jure measures to separate the races. And as more blacks left this Jim Crow South, they asserted their rights for equality in the North, often to the chagrin of the whites there. Indeed, African Americans faced deep racism and long-established patterns of residential segregation in the North.

Other structural factors apparent during this era featured economic, labor, and political issues, as well as the neglect of authorities. Economic fluctuation, at both the local and the national level, commonly left workers unemployed for weeks or months at a time.[31] When jobs became scarce, whites resented competition from black workers. The labor strife of the late 19th century carried forward well into the 20th as workers tried to organize and businesses resisted, often with violence. Adding fuel to the fire of racial resentment, businesses also used blacks as strikebreakers. Moreover, the agrarian revolt of the 1880s and 1890s that for a short time offered a class-based cooperative environment between the races broke down as white agrarian radicals began to use strident racist rhetoric to win elections and set up a segregated society.[32] Furthermore, white authorities also often ignored or displayed open hostility toward African Americans. Some policemen and militia members, for example, turned a blind eye toward race riots or even actively participated in them themselves. The cities that suffered race riots during this era featured one or more of these structural factors.

Cultural Framing

While these structural factors existed in riot cities during the 50-year span of my study, many of them appeared in nonriot cities as well.[33] It remains insufficient, therefore, to simply uncover the structural factors that allowed riots to erupt. It also proves necessary to clarify why whites perceived these factors as demanding them to act. Cultural framing provides this answer. Aaron Wildavsky and his colleagues conceptualize culture not only as "ideas, values, and beliefs, as is commonly done, or as patterns of social relations, but [also] as values justifying relationships indissolubly bound together." Moreover, they contend, political culture passes through generations, but in an altered form. "A first step in this direction," they aver, "is to allow for the importance of adult, rather than only childhood experience in shaping individual orientations."[34] This mind-set helps explain the growing assertion of African Americans of their fundamental rights and also whites' gradual acceptance of this fact throughout the 1940s, 1950s, and 1960s.

As David Snow and Robert Benford contend, framing provides "an interpretive schema that signifies and condenses the 'world out there' by selectively punctuating and encoding objects, situations, events, experiences, and sequences of action in one's present or past environment."[35] This framing, they assert, proves crucial to building a consensus and a motivation for action. "By constructing a compelling sense of injustice and collective identities for the protagonists and their targets," Marc Steinberg echoes, "frames provide a diagnosis and prognosis of a problem and a call to action to resolve it."[36] The structural conditions that inflamed racial tensions during the first half of the 20th century, therefore, existed within a cultural framework that allowed race riots to erupt.

Moreover, the 1890s were crucial years in terms of cultural framing, influencing race relations for decades to come. As Joel Williamson argues, a radical ideology emerged that incorporated social Darwinism and scientific racism, which fed views of white supremacy. This ideology led to a paranoid fear of sexual attacks on the sanctity of white womanhood. In combination with vitriolic political rhetoric, yellow journalism, and racist literature, this mentality resulted in hundreds of lynchings and the codi-fication of segregation and disfranchisement.[37] Jeff Davis, the governor of Arkansas from 1901 to 1907 and later a U.S. senator, for example, an-nounced in one campaign speech, "[W]e may have a lot of dead niggers in Arkansas, but we shall never have negro equality, and I want to say that I would rather tear, screaming from her mother's arms, my little daughter and bury her alive than to see her arm in arm with the best nigger on earth." In another screed he declared "that 'nigger' domination will never prevail in this beautiful Southland of ours, as long as shotguns and rifles lie around loose, and we are able to pull the trigger."[38] Not surprisingly, black Arkansans felt the weight of those words. In Harrison, Arkansas, for in-stance, between 1900 and 1910, the town's black population dwindled from 115 to 1, after two "instances of racial cleansing in 1905 and 1909, in which white mobs forced black persons out their homes, giving them twenty-four hours to leave."[39] Overwhelmingly, newspapers served as the medium for spreading this white fear and paranoia. In this study, therefore, I examine newspapers, literature, and rhetoric to reveal how cultural faming played such a powerful role in creating an environment ripe for violence.

In addition, as whites strove to shut down black political and social rights, African Americans fought against this tidal wave in the courts, in elections, and in day-to-day interactions. A younger generation of blacks born after the Civil War resented their parents' acquiescence to white supremacy. In the 20th century, leadership in the African American community began to shift from Booker T. Washington's Atlanta Compromise position to a more assertive push for civil rights articulated by W.E.B. Du Bois. Using organi-zations, such as the Niagara Movement and the NAACP, Du Bois stressed the need for immediate civil rights through federal intervention and the courts. Moreover, blacks created their own music, art, and literature that expressed their aspirations for their place in American society.

International events also played a large role in domestic racial politics. The Spanish-American War heightened whites' views of racial solidarity and the white man's burden. Almost two decades later, Woodrow Wilson argued that the United States entered World War I "to make the world safe for democracy." Self-determination for all people became a key ingredi-ent in this formulation. African Americans clearly saw possibilities for do-mestic reform based on Wilson's rhetoric during the war. Instead, the war unleashed xenophobia, racial resentment, and violence. Similarly, during World War II, blacks launched the Double Victory campaign pushing for civil rights and equal economic opportunities at home as they fought doc-trines of racial superiority overseas. In each of these wars, whites attacked

African Americans in response to their demands for equality. These cultural faming ideas, in tandem with certain structural factors, created an environment for riot mobilization.

Precipitating Events

It remains possible (even probable), however, that structural factors and cultural framing occurred in nonriot locales as well. Precipitating events provide the third element necessary for race riots to occur. While structural factors and cultural framing set the scene for collective behavior, these precipitating events spark the immediate cause for people to mobilize.[40] "The precipitating factor," Neil Smelser stresses, "confirms the existence, sharpens the definition, or exaggerates the effect of [existing] conditions."[41] Moreover, "it provides adherents of a belief with more evidence of the workings of evil forces. . . . A precipitating factor, then, links the generalized belief to concrete situations."[42] Horowitz echoes, "In the view of participants, precipitants render aggression both appropriate and necessary. . . . They supply a shorthand recollection of group qualities and relations, as well as guidance for a course of action."[43]

Similarly, Schelling highlights the role of precipitating events, or what he calls incidents, in riot activity, especially in the absence of organized leaders:

> It is usually the essence of mob formation that the potential members have to know not only where and when to meet but just when to act so that they act in concert. Overt leadership solves the problem; but leadership can often be identified and eliminated by the authority trying to prevent mob action. In this case the mob's problem is to act in unison without overt leadership, to find some common signal that makes everyone confident that, if he acts on it, he will not be acting alone. The role of "incidents" can thus be seen as a coordinating role; it is a substitute for overt leadership and communication. Without something like an incident, it may be difficult to get action at all, since immunity requires that all know when to act together.[44]

Not surprisingly (due to the white radical and racist ideology that permeated the country), the overwhelming majority of precipitating events resulting in race riots from the 1890s through the mid-1940s stemmed from charges of real or alleged instances of interracial sexual assault or murder. Other infractions, such as blacks acting as strikebreakers or encroaching into white public facilities, also served as precipitating events. Moreover, rumors often exaggerated and distorted the reality of these events, stoking an already heated environment, and newspapers help spread their destruction.[45]

But newspapers proved only partially responsible for spreading rumors. Audiences had to be willing to accept them, and then to act on that information. As Horowitz suggests,

> A rumor is a short-lived, unverified report, usually anonymous in its origin. No rumor that is disseminated widely enough to help precipitate collective violence can be understood as merely a chance falsehood or, as is commonly thought, a bit of misinformation that gains currency because official news channels have been remiss in putting out the truth. Concealed threats and outrages committed in secret figure prominently in pre-riot rumors. . . .
>
> Rumors form an essential part of the riot process. They justify the violence that is about to occur. Their severity is often an indicator of the severity of the impending violence. Rumors narrow the options that seem available to those who join crowds and commit them to a line of action. They mobilize ordinary people to do what they would not ordinarily do. They shift the balance in a crowd toward those proposing the most extreme action. They project onto the future victims of violence the impulses entertained by those who will victimize them. They confirm the strength and danger presented by the target group, thus facilitating violence born of fear. Rumors, then, are not stray tales. They perform functions for the group and for individuals in it. . . .
>
> [B]ut a rumor will not take hold unless there is a market for it, a need in an emerging situation; and rumors change in the telling, becoming sharper in their factual assertions and more meaningful to recipients. . . . Moreover, the same rumors recur across widely different contexts, suggesting that an evolutionist, rather than a creationist, view of them is warranted.[46]

Brass stresses the role of leaders in using rumors to incite action. In many cases, "[t]here is . . . little or nothing that is either arbitrary or spontaneous about the occurrence of . . . rumor[s]. . . . Rumors serve the purpose of mobilizing members of a community for attack or defense."[47] Recurrent rumors did come into play—quite prominently—before, during, and after the race riots that erupted during the Progressive Era through World War II.[48] Indeed, white leaders used these rumors to great effect. And white society often proved ready to accept them.

Between the Progressive Era and World War II, therefore, structural factors, cultural framing, and precipitating events combined to prompt white Americans to riot against blacks over and over again in a wide variety of geographical locations. This conceptualization is drawn out in Figure 1.1.

This work, then, provides an analysis of the causes leading to the numerous race riots that occurred during the Progressive Era through World War II. Drawing partially on collective behavior, collective violence, and riot literature, this conception of race riots demonstrates the conditions that led whites to riot against blacks during this period. As I reveal, for

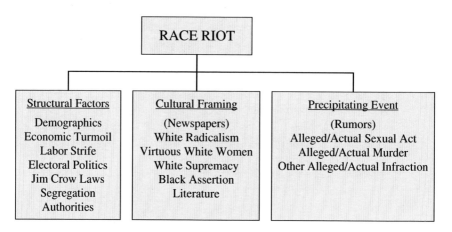

Figure 1.1. A model of race riots

these riots to erupt, structural factors, cultural framing, and precipitating events coalesced to provide a tipping point for white Americans to riot. It is important to note, however, that riots did *not* occur in most of the United States during this period. Critical components of the model must be missing in those instances that could have tipped into riots but that did not. After the July 1919 Chicago race riot, for example, many people feared that another riot would occur. However, the police force and local press took an aggressive stand against racial conflict, in sharp contrast to their behavior before.[49]

Therefore, this work provides an understanding of the crucial ingredients that allowed race riots to occur. Structural factors, such as demographic change, economic turmoil, labor strife, and electoral politics provided an overarching societal backdrop. Cultural framing stirred these structural embers. Newspaper editors and politicians especially played an important role in spreading white radical and racist ideology. Meanwhile, African Americans organized to assert their rights and to expose the hypocrisy of white Americans. Finally, precipitating events, such as actual or alleged sexual attacks or murder, created the immediate spark for rioting.

In the chapters that follow, I explore these topics more in-depth and provide 12 case studies that illustrate my conception of race riots.[50] In Chapters 2 and 3, I examine the structural factors, cultural framing, and precipitating events in the riots that occurred in Wilmington (1898), New Orleans (1900), Atlanta (1906), East St. Louis (1917), Tulsa (1921), and Beaumont (1943). These six riots exemplify the racial pogroms that erupted from the Progressive Era through World War II. In Chapters 4 and 5, I analyze the 1919 Red Summer riots that all occurred within months of each other, but in geographically diverse locales. Longview, Washington, D.C., Chicago, Knoxville, Omaha, and Phillips County—six of the seven major race riots that year—provide a good representation of the riots that exploded in the aftermath of World War I. In my conclusion, I use Detroit (1943) to illustrate the changing nature of race riots at midcentury. The Detroit riot has characteristics of the earlier riots (that I examine in this study) and foreshadows the so-called black ghetto race riots of the 1960s.

Chapter 2

RACIAL POGROMS

After Reconstruction, southern whites moved to consolidate their control of society politically, economically, and socially, and to impose white supremacy.[1] By the 1890s, the promise of equality once held out by the 14th and 15th Amendments had all but been lost. Most African Americans toiled in the economically depressed South as sharecroppers, tenant farmers, and wage laborers. Those who moved up the economic ladder faced constant threats to their lives and property. Whites used any means necessary to consolidate their power, including race riots. In this chapter and the next, I examine the structural factors, cultural framing, and precipitating events that created the racial pogroms from the Progressive Era through World War II. I also provide six case studies of these types of riots—Wilmington, New Orleans, Atlanta, East St. Louis, Tulsa, and Beaumont. The riots share similar features—the precipitating events stemmed from perceived black violations against sacred facets of white society (assaults against white women or authorities); black resistance existed but proved largely futile; and the outcome left whites securely in control.

STRUCTURAL FACTORS

At the turn of the century, 90 percent of African Americans lived in the rural South.[2] However, a tremendous demographic shift had begun. Many blacks moved to southern cities, and increasingly northern cities, looking for better jobs, schools, and opportunities.[3] In regard to this migration, "something new seemed to be happening from the mid-1880s, and especially from the early 1890s," historian Steven Hahn explains, "as to volume, direction, composition, and political meaning."[4] Whites met this

movement with fear and trepidation. Moreover, younger African Americans, the first generation "born and bred in freedom," made up a large
contingent of these new urban migrants. They wanted to form new communities and expand not only their economic advantage but also their social position in society.[5] Paranoid whites viewed this younger generation as
a threat to their supremacy. "The generation of Negroes which have grown
up since the war," stated a white Memphis newspaper editorial in 1892,
"have lost in large measure the traditional and wholesome awe of the white
race which kept the Negroes in subjection."[6]

Indeed, this urban migration during the late 19th and early 20th centuries brought blacks and whites into contact in new ways that often created
challenges to whites' conceptions of racial separation and social control.
When a wealthy black farmer drove his new car to a nearby town in Georgia in 1917, for example, a white mob set the car on fire and warned him,
"From now on, you niggers walk into town, or use that ole mule if you
want to stay in this city."[7] Housing and job competition, as well as political concerns, often spurred this racial animosity. Whites feared that blacks
would work for lower wages and undermine their economic position in
society. Economic fluctuations, such as the Panic of 1893, led to increased
tensions both economically and politically. In the late 19th century, both
black and white farmers suffered under the strain of low agricultural prices
and looked for political solutions to their economic crisis.

The Populist Party emerged in the 1890s, especially in the South and
Midwest, to provide a voice for agrarian anger. For a moment, some historians argue, class outweighed race. Black and white Farmers' Alliances
formed and sometimes worked in tandem. This cooperation worried the
more conservative elements in the Democratic Party committed to white
supremacy. Southern Democrats also feared fusion between Republicans
and Populists. Indeed, political considerations played a considerable role
in many of the American race riots from the Progressive Era through
World War II. As soon as black men garnered the right to vote with the
15th Amendment in 1870, many whites began to take measures to thwart
them from doing so. As Horowitz suggests, "Groups constituting a political threat . . . have a greater likelihood than others do of becoming victims
of violence."[8] And, not surprisingly, the agrarian revolt of the 1880s and
1890s that for a short time offered a class-based cooperative environment
between the races broke down as white radicals began to use strident racist
rhetoric to win elections.[9]

The 1898 Wilmington, North Carolina, race riot, for example, erupted
directly as a result of the Democratic Party's efforts to prevent blacks from
maintaining any sort of political power in the region as they had done
in the previous two elections by aligning with the Populists. In speeches

leading up to the November 8 election that year, Colonel Alfred Moore Waddell, a former U.S. congressman and officer in the Confederate cavalry, avowed, "We will never surrender to a ragged raffle of negroes, even if we have to choke the current of the Cape Fear with carcasses." In a screed to the white denizens of Wilmington on the eve of the election, he directed, "Go to the polls tomorrow, and if you find the negro out voting, tell him to leave the polls, and if he refuses, kill him."[10] His words proved prophetic. Although the election passed with no violence in Wilmington and some African Americans turned out to vote, in the days that followed, the city's democratically elected officials resigned under pressure and fled town, Democrats appointed themselves to the vacated offices, and the black population suffered death, injury, and exile. After the riot, which broke out two days after the election, one woman's recollection of the Democrat's white supremacy campaign relayed, "It is pitiful to hear the accounts of reliable eye-witnesses to the harrowing scenes. 'We are just shooting to see the niggers run,' they cried as the black men began to fall in every direction. . . . [The] whole thing was with the object of striking terror to the [black] man's heart, so that he would never vote again."[11] White supremacy had indeed reigned supreme.

In addition to outright violence, whites used other means to prevent blacks from attaining the power they secured through the 14th and 15th Amendments. While this Jim Crow mentality existed earlier (Jim Crow Cars—or segregated cars—started running on some northern railroads even before the war), southern states began passing legislation in the late 1890s to enact de jure measures relegating African Americans to second-class status.[12] By 1910, every former Confederate state had securely enacted this system of discrimination—primarily blocking black males from voting and segregating the races in public places. Beginning in the 1870s and culminating in 1896 with *Plessy v. Ferguson,* the U.S. Supreme Court gave its consent.

Southern states passed such measures as poll taxes, literacy tests, white primaries, and grandfather clauses to disfranchise black citizens. They also hung segregated signs marking public restrooms, water fountains, courthouses, theaters, libraries, or any public building.[13] In their *White Man's Declaration of Independence* revealed on November 8, 1898, Wilmington, North Carolina's whites trumpeted:

[T]he Constitution of the United States contemplated a government to be carried on by an enlightened people . . . , not . . . the enfranchisement of an ignorant population of African origin. . . . We declare that we will no longer be ruled, and will never again be ruled, by men of African origin . . . [in part because] . . . the negro has demonstrated, by antagonizing our interest in

every way, and especially by his ballot, that he is incapable of realizing that
his interests are and should be identical with [ours].[14]

Between 1865 and 1967, over 400 city ordinances, state laws, and constitutional amendments ensured this mentality took hold throughout the
country.[15]

Local, state, and federal authorities contributed to how race riots played
out from the late 1890s through the mid-1940s as well. At least 17 states
passed statutes against mob violence by 1890, and 24 states did so by the
mid-1930s, reacting to "such activities as lynchings, labor confrontations,
civil disturbances, and demonstrations involving religious feelings."[16] But
the victims of race riots often found themselves either ignored by authorities during the violence or blamed afterward. Officials sometimes even
joined in the brutality themselves. On August 17, 1900, for example, the
editors of the *New York Times* responded with disgust to the role of the
police in that city's riot:

> The record of the police in the riotous attacks on negroes in their quarter
> on Wednesday night may briefly be summed up. They stood idly by for the
> most part while the negroes were being beaten except when they joined
> savagely in the sport, until the rioting threatened to extend dangerously;
> then they gradually dispersed the crowds, arresting almost no whites and
> many blacks, most of the latter being clubbed most unmercifully. . . . It
> discloses several vices both in the individual policemen who established
> the record and in the system under which they act. It tells of cruelty, of
> the brutal cowardice of armed men assaulting helpless men and women,
> of violent racial prejudice, but especially of the open and brazen violation
> of the first duties of policemen. And it tells of implicit confidence on the
> part of the offending officers that they will not be called to account by their
> superiors.[17]

Shortly after the 1921 Tulsa, Oklahoma, race riot, rumors circulated—
"apparently well-founded," according to Alfred Brophy—"that the entire
bench of the Tulsa district court, the court clerk, the county sheriff, and all
jury commissioners" belonged to the Ku Klux Klan.[18]

The national government often did little in the way of riot intervention,
and not until Franklin Roosevelt's administration did federal authorities
begin to move toward ensuring blacks' rights. William McKinley, for example, opted not to send federal troops into Wilmington, North Carolina,
during the 1898 riot. He did convene his cabinet to discuss the situation
and, in the end, decided against intervention since the governor had not
asked for it.[19] After the riot, a number of African Americans sent pleas
to the president for assistance. One Denver writer reminded McKinley

that blacks fought bravely on behalf of the United States in the Spanish-American War, yet continued to face hostilities at home:

> My race stands loyal to this government and to the Stars and Stripes. When the call came for the negro to pick up arms and go face a foreign foe, leaving their own country, wives and children, they never faltered but went willingly to the field of battle and have shown to the world that they were no cowards. . . . [W]hat is this country in the South doing for their brothers[?] Is it possible we must leave our homes and go fight a foreign foe and not get any protection at home by the government we are defending? We see at Wilmington, N.C. and Greenwood, S.C. the negroes shot down like dogs and deprived of the right of ballot. . . . The outrages of the negro in the South if left to continue will spread to the North and West, and then what is left for us to do but prove disloyal to our government. In the name of God and humanity lend us a helping hand![20]

A Wilmington woman echoed these sentiments: "I call on you the head of the American Nation to help. . . . We are loyal we go when duty calls us. And are we to die like rats in a trap? Will you for God sake in your next message to Congress give us some releif [*sic*]? . . . The laws of our state is [*sic*] not good for the negro."[21] A New Yorker besieged, "Please do all in your power to stop [the violence], if there needs to be a standing army, please send one there. Lynching has been going on in the Southern States ever since President Hayes removed the Standing army from the South."[22]

Structural factors, therefore, helped set the stage for these racial pogroms to occur. Demographic concerns, such as black migration to cities; economic factors, namely recessions and depressions that constricted jobs; political alliances between blacks and Populists, much to the Democrats' dismay; de facto and de jure segregation; and the failure of local, state, and national authorities to protect blacks against white violence exemplify the structural factors that allowed race riots to erupt. Cultural framing played an important role as well.

CULTURAL FRAMING

The Progressive Era proved crucial in terms of shaping race relations for decades to come. As Joel Williamson argues, a white radical ideology emerged that incorporated social Darwinism, scientific racism, and (probably most important to the outbreak of race riots) the fear of sexual attacks on the sanctity of white womanhood, all in conjunction with vitriolic political rhetoric and yellow journalism.[23] This racist mind-set resulted in thousands of lynchings and numerous race riots and helped solidify the codification of segregation and disfranchisement.

So-called experts, such as Paul Barringer, a professor of medicine at the University of Virginia, suggested at the turn of the century, for instance, that only enslavement had truly protected blacks and that "all things point to the fact that the Negro as a race is reverting to barbarism with the inordinate criminality and degradation of that state. It seems, moreover, that he is doomed at no distant day to ultimate extinction."[24] Echoing this sentiment, Professor William Smith of Tulane University published *The Color Line* in 1905, concluding, "The vision . . . of a race vanishing before its superior is not at all dispiriting, but inspiring rather. . . . The doom that awaits the Negro has been prepared in like measure for all inferior races."[25]

White politicians also weighed in on the supposed subordination of the black race. Senator Wade Hampton of South Carolina, for example, labeled black suffrage "a crime against civilization, humanity, constitutional rights, and Christianity."[26] Moreover, he and others proposed a complete schism between the races. "I unhesitatingly assert," Senator James Vardaman of Mississippi declared in 1913,

> that political equality for the colored races leads to social equality. Social equality leads to race amalgamation, and race amalgamation to deterioration and disintegration. . . . I expect to favor and urge the enactment of laws that will make perfect the social and political segregation of the white and colored races. We cannot follow the idea of Lincoln and send the colored man away to a country of his own. The next best thing, therefore, is to bring about complete segregation.[27]

Others beat the Darwinian drum, as studies suggested that black birthrates fell below death rates as African Americans began migrating to cities. "God's law of evolution, the survival of the fittest, and the extinction of the unfit," declared Senator John Sharp Williams of Mississippi in 1907, "is operating."[28]

To white radicals, however, this supposed black degeneracy came at a steep price—the peril that it put white women and girls in as a result. "The single most significant and awful manifestation of black retrogression [in the radical mind-set]," asserts historian Joel Williamson, "was an increasing frequency of sexual assaults on white women and girl children by black men. Above all else, it was this threat that thrust deeply into the psychic core of the South, searing the white soul, marking the character of the Southern mind radically and leaving it crippled and hobbled in matters of race long after the mark itself was lost from sight."[29] With the end of slavery, white radicals suggested, black males could roam the country unchecked in their quest to satisfy their thirst for white women.[30] Moreover, the Industrial Revolution and economic uncertainty undermined the white man's control over his own household (women and children began to work more and more outside the home) and weakened his economic independence, further accentuating his insecurities.[31] Countless southern politicians, such as Senators James Vardaman, Pitchfork Ben Tillman, and Coleman Blease, made their name by capitalizing on this angst and stressing the vast danger of—and the remedies for—this conjured black male beast.[32]

"I have three daughters," Tillman pronounced on the Senate floor in 1907, "but so help me God, I had rather find either one of them killed by a tiger or a bear and gather up her bones and bury them, conscious that she had died in the purity of her maidenhood, than to have her crawl to me and tell me the horrid story that she had been robbed of the jewel of her womanhood by a black fiend."[33] Tillman sounded this theme regularly. Southerners "have never believed [African Americans] to be equal to the white man," he thundered before his Senate colleagues seven years earlier, "and we will not submit to his gratifying his lust on our wives and daughters without lynching him."[34] White radical politicians, writers, journalists, preachers, and scholars saw that this threat loomed all around them, and they spread the message of fear every opportunity they could.

And with this crescendo of radical thinking, Tillman's pronouncement on lynching came true. "The sudden and dramatic rise in the lynching of black men in and after 1889," historian Joel Williamson asserts, "stands out like some giant volcanic eruption on the landscape of Southern race relations. There was, indeed, something new and horribly palpable on the earth. It was signalized by the mob, the rushing, swelling fury of a mass of struggling men, the bloody and mangled bodies, and the smell of burning flesh. It would be some years before anyone would earnestly contend that actually only about one-third of the lynchings were committed for 'the new crime' (the rape of white women by black men), and many more years before Southerners at large would acknowledge that lynching itself was itself a crime."[35] Indeed, many whites did feel justified in using lynching as a weapon to tame the supposed black beast.

Southern white newspapers constantly promoted this racist theme. "It is the spontaneous outburst of emotions long felt and long smothered," *Atlanta Constitution* columnist Bill Arp wrote in 1897, "and those emotions are based upon love—love for home and wife and children, love and respect for the wives and daughters of the neighbors. Lynching negroes for this crime is no evidence of lawlessness among our [white] people. . . . How many more outrages there would be if these lynchings should stop we can only conjecture."[36] And Georgian Rebecca Latimer Felton invoked this most hideous form of violence when she trumpeted, "if it takes lynching to protect woman's dearest possession from drunken, ravening human beasts—then I say lynch a thousand a week if it becomes necessary."[37] Yet protecting the virtue of white women proved not to be solely relegated to the South. In Urbana, Ohio, in June 1897, for example, a white mob charged the local jail to capture a black man accused of assaulting a white woman. Before the National Guard could quell the crowd, they strung the man up from a tree in the town square, only a short distance from a Union soldier monument.[38]

People who spoke out against the atrocity of lynching became "nigger lovers" or the victims of violence themselves. One activist, Jessie Daniel Ames, received an anonymous letter in 1926 stating, "God will burn . . . the Big African Brute in Hot Hell for molesting our God-like pure snowwhite angelic American Women." And Ames's local newspaper, the Williamson County (Texas) *Sun,* avowed, "Abstractly we are against mob violence, but negro rapists, North or South, must die; by the law if possible; without the law if need be."[39] Moreover, as one attendee of the 1900 Montgomery race conference declared, the white man "regards the rape of white women by Negroes not as ordinary criminality, [but as] an attack on the integrity of the race."[40] Nothing struck condemnation or anxiety into whites more than this largely imagined threat, and many white men capitalized on this fear through violence.

Moreover, white women also played a role—and not always altogether passive—in promoting racial violence at the turn of the century and beyond. Some simply turned a blind eye on the brutality elicited in their names. But others took a more active approach. Rebecca Cameron, cousin of Wilmington's white supremacists' leader Alfred Waddell, chided him in a letter during the days leading up to the 1898 election and subsequent race riot: "Where are the white men and shotguns! It is time for the oft quoted shotgun to play a part, and an active one, in the elections. It has reached the point where blood letting is needed for the hearts of the common man and when the depletion commences *let it be thorough*! Solomon says, 'There is a Time to Kill.' "[41] Ten years later, Kate Howard, the Springfield, Illinois, "Joan of Arc," led a group of irate whites to destroy the restaurant of a white man who assisted police in escorting two alleged black rapists out of town. "What the hell are you fellows afraid of?" she rebuked the mob, "Women want protection, and this seems to be the only way to get it." And during World War II, witnesses saw white women in Mobile, Alabama, striking black male shipyard workers with bricks and iron bars after a riot broke out there because of labor strife and rape rumors.[42]

Other white leaders, however, took a more accommodationist (although often still racist) stance on race relations. "[The African American] is naturally docile and peaceable" asserted Julius Dreher, president of Roanoke College in Virginia in 1889, "and if we treat him with anything like fairness, justice, and consideration we claim for ourselves as men, we shall hear less of race antagonism in the future."[43] Other paternalistic racists went further. "The Negro race," declared Charles T. Hopkins, head of those prominent whites who gathered in Atlanta to discuss the 1906 race riot there, "is a child race. We are a strong race, their guardians. We have boasted of our superiority and we have now sunk to this level—we have shed the blood of our helpless wards. Christianity and humanity demand that we treat the Negro fairly. He is here, and here to stay. He only knows those things we teach him to do; it is our Christian duty to protect him."[44]

Of course, much of what whites taught blacks consisted of degrading rules of etiquette. Before the modern civil rights era, whites expected blacks to be deferential (move out of the way on a sidewalk, remove their hat when speaking to them), address them with respect ("Boss" or "Cap'n" for men or "Miss" for women), and separate from them in public capacities (different entrances to public buildings, even separate hospital wards and staffs). "The whole intent of Jim Crow etiquette boiled down to one simple rule," concludes historian Ronald Davis, "blacks must demonstrate their inferiority to whites by actions, words, and manners."[45] Infractions by blacks to these codes of behavior frequently led to violent outbursts. The *Shreveport Times* reminded African Americans of this fact:

> We venture to say that fully ninety percent of all the race troubles in the South are the result of the Negro forgetting his place. If the black man will stay where he belongs, act like a Negro should act, work like a Negro should work, talk like a Negro should talk . . . there will be very few riots, fights or clashes. Instead of the "societies" and "unions" floating propaganda to . . . lift them up to the plane of the white man, they should foster education that will instill in the Negro the desire, and impress upon him the NECESSITY of keeping his place.[46]

In addition to scholars and politicians, contemporary writers also explored the relationships between blacks and whites. Some harkened back to their turn-of-the-century childhoods years later and elaborated on their eventual realization of racial hierarchies. In *Making of a Southerner*, Katherine Lumpkin recalls:

> We can be certain that from the time I could sit in my high chair at table or play about the parlor floor while others conversed, my ears saturated with words and phrases at all times intimately familiar to Southern ears and in those years of harsh excitement carrying a special urgency: "white supremacy," . . . "inferiority," "good darkey," "bad darkey," "keep them in their place." As time passed, I myself would learn to speak these words perhaps with special emphasis . . . even before I had the understanding to grasp all they

stood for. Of course I did come to comprehend. When I did, it was a sharp awakening.[47]

Lillian Smith, in her 1949 autobiography *Killers of the Dream,* recounts how white children in the early 20th century learned about racial distinctions. "We were given no formal instruction in these difficult matters but we learned our lessons well. We learned the intricate systems of taboos, of renunciations and compensations, of manners, voice modulations, words, feelings, along with our prayers, our toilet habits, and our games."[48] Other writers, both black and white, who penned novels and other literary works played a large role in framing discourse at the time of these women's childhoods.

North Carolinian Thomas Dixon, for example, wrote a trilogy of novels—made into a stage play in 1905 and the film *The Birth of a Nation* in 1915—that promoted the myths of white supremacy and the black male beast. In *The Leopard's Spots: A Romance of the White Man's Burden, 1865–1900* of 1902, he addresses distortions to his view of southern history, especially in response to Harriet Beecher Stowe's 1852 novel *Uncle Tom's Cabin,* which he saw dramatized in a play in 1901.[49] Using some of her characters, he completely recasts the roles that whites and blacks play—namely to become the heroic saviors in the Ku Klux Klan and the dastardly black male rapists. The book sold over one million copies, a testament to the resonance of Dixon's words and views.[50]

He also responds to a character thinly disguised as (black Wilmington editor) Alexander Manly and his editorial challenging the idea of white supremacy as "defaming the virtue of the white women of the community" and views his actions as just more "Negro insolence."[51] For Dixon, the resulting white violence in response to the black editor's words stems from a natural impulse, and he deems it completely justifiable to preserving white supremacy and the purity of white womanhood. Penning a letter to a friend, Dixon quotes a review of *The Leopard's Spots*:

> No other book yet printed has given such a graphic presentation of the Southern view of the Negro problem. . . . [T]he book will slow up sectional prejudices. It will be read with more than passing interest in the North. . . . It is the best apology for lynching, it is the finest protest against the mistakes of reconstruction—The South has been silent when books like this might have made their position clearer.[52]

In addition to the virtues of violence, Dixon also focuses—almost obsessively—on miscegenation and racial purity in *The Leopard's Spots*: "One drop of Negro blood makes a Negro. It kinks the hair, flattens the nose, thickens the lip, puts out the light of intellect, and lights the fires of brutal passions. The beginning of Negro equality as a vital fact is the beginning of the end of this nation's life. There is enough Negro blood here to make mulatto the whole Republic."[53] In *The Clansman* (1905) and *The Traitor* (1907), he sees the Klan through in preventing this calamity and in attaining white supremacy, and he then disbands the Klan after it achieves its glorious mission.[54]

Dixon's views tie in closely with other white radicals of the time who suggested that emancipation caused African Americans to retrogress to the point of being unable to fit into American society. According to historian Glenda Gilmore, this new generation of whites emerging in the 1890s—"The New White Man"—"stated bluntly that the prerogatives of manhood—voting, sexual choice, freedom of public space—should be reserved for him alone."[55] Dixon served as a prominent voice in this group. Indeed, historian Joel Williamson labels *The Leopard's Spots* "virtually an encyclopedia of Radicalism."[56]

Dixon combined his first two novels into a play, *The Clansman,* in 1905, and two stage companies performed it to enthusiastic audiences throughout the United States.[57] Interestingly, several months before the 1906 Atlanta riot, an audience there hailed Dixon after opening night (he often attended the performances and gave a speech afterward) with an ovation lasting several minutes.[58] Clearly the racist themes resonated with white Atlantans and other white southerners, as Dixon reveals in an interview with the *Atlanta Constitution*:

> Words cannot express my gratitude and love to the southern people for the enthusiasm with which my play has been everywhere received. Thus far it has been presented in thirty cities to crowds that have broken the record of each house. But the thing that pleased me most has not been merely the size of the crowds, but the passionate approval they have given to every sentiment expressed. . . . This approval of a play from the hearts and heads of an audience is the final decision of the supreme court of public opinion.[59]

He also responds to critics of the play's racist sentiments:

> The voice of a hostile critic here and there cuts no figure against it. . . . Only six papers out of the forty-three published in thirty cities where the play has been given have attacked it. . . . One editor, who, I imagine, ate a Welsh rabbit and had a nightmare after seeing "The Clansman," gravely warned the world that the play would leave a trail of lynchings behind it. We have thus far safely passed thirty southern towns without a lynching and in one of them, on the night of the performance, a negro was caught and put in jail for an attempted assault on a beautiful white girl.[60]

Ironically, according to one source, his play *had* incited a lynching in Bainbridge, Georgia, only the week before.

According to an October 30, 1905, *Chicago Daily Tribune* story, the violence began after a local sheriff died from a gunshot wound inflicted by a black man.

> Wrought up to a high pitch of anger against negroes by the presentation of Thomas A. [*sic*] Dixon's play "The Clansman," last week, a mob of 300 men stormed the jail [where authorities incarcerated the suspect]. . . . The terrified captive was dragged through the streets to the Flint river bridge in the suburbs and suspended to a beam, where the body remained hanging all day, and object of grim curiosity to hundreds. . . . The feeling against negroes, never kindly, has been imbittered [*sic*] by the Dixon play, since when stories of the deeds of negroes during the period of reconstruction have been revived and the whites have been wrought up to a high tension.[61]

Moreover, others credit his play with contributing to race riots that broke out in cities where it appeared, such as Atlanta (several months later) and Philadelphia (in direct response to the play).[62] African Americans and progressive whites reacted strongly against Dixon's novels and their renditions on stage and screen. In a 21-page letter, Kelly Miller of Howard University lambasted Dixon for his "evil propagandism of race animosity" in *The Leopard's Spots*. "You have become," he continued, "the chief priest of those who worship at the shrine of race hatred and wrath. . . . You stir the slumbering fires of race wrath into an uncontrollable flame."[63] In reaction to the stage play, Len Broughton, a Baptist pastor and college friend of Dixon, preached from his pulpit:

> His whole show is a disgrace to southern manhood and womanhood. To claim that it is necessary today for him to go girating [*sic*] about over the south, stirring up such passions of hell, to keep the races apart and thus prevent, what he imagines, and impending amalgamation of the whites and blacks into one race of mixed bloods, is a slander of the white people of the south—a slander so vile, especially coming from a man who is posing as the friend of the south. . . . I deny that the south needs a traveling troup [*sic*] of masked men and women, from God knows where and what, to keep our men chivalrous, our women pure, and our children free from the blood of blacks. . . . I call upon the south to resent it. I call upon the north to disbelieve it and to boycott it. . . . It is unAmerican; it is unchristian; it is unsound; and it is unsafe.[64]

Several times during his speech, the 4,500-member congregation broke into "prolonged applause."[65]

The black press spoke out in response to these vitriolic words and violent actions from whites as well. According to one source, more than 1,200 black newspapers appeared throughout the country between 1895 and

1915.[66] As racial violence rose and whites grew more openly strident after Reconstruction, black editors often became circumspect in their coverage. But those who dared to criticize the prevailing white racist mentality and actions suffered at the hands of weapon-toting white arsonists ready to kill them and destroy their presses. Before the 1898 Wilmington, North Carolina, riot, for instance, Alexander Manly, black editor of the Wilmington *Daily Record*, lambasted lynching, so-called white supremacy, and white hypocrisy. Responding to a speech by Rebecca Latimer Felton, a women's rights advocate and native Georgian (and later the first woman to serve as a U.S. senator), Manly suggested that "our experience among poor white people in the country teaches us that women of that race are not any more particular in the matter of clandestine meetings with colored men than are the white men with the colored women."[67] Not long after, a white mob burned his press to the ground, as he narrowly escaped with his life.

Moreover, author Richard Wright explains some of the options available to African Americans at the beginning of the 20th century:

> They could accept the role created for them by the whites and perpetually resolve the resulting conflicts through the hope and emotional catharsis of Negro religion; they could repress their dislike of Jim Crow social relations while striving for a middle way of respectability, becoming—consciously or unconsciously—the accomplices of the whites in oppressing their brothers; or they could reject the situation, adopt a criminal attitude, and carry on an unceasing psychological scrimmage with the whites, which often flared forth into physical violence.[68]

People such as Ida B. Wells, Alexander Manly, William Monroe Trotter, Booker T. Washington, W.E.B. Du Bois, James Weldon Johnson, Mary Church Terrell, Jessie Daniel Ames, Claude McKay, Marcus Garvey, and countless other African American men and women employed these tactics and more to strike out a life of their own "behind the veil."[69] Using newspaper articles and editorials, books, statistics, grassroots organizations, and sometimes their own blood, black Americans fought back against the ignorance and fear that white radicals and their offspring sewed into the social fabric of American life.

Perhaps no one did more in the early years of lynching to speak out against it than Wells. Born in Mississippi during the Civil War in 1862, she learned firsthand the injustices and atrocities carried out by whites. In 1884, the conductor of the Chesapeake & Ohio Railroad Company in Memphis, along with other workers, forcibly removed her from a train—to the applause of the white passengers—when she refused to move out of the ladies coach into the smoking coach as she returned home from teaching one day. She recounts the event in her autobiography:

When the train started and the conductor came along to collect tickets, he took my ticket, then handed it back to me and told me that he couldn't take my ticket there. I thought that if he didn't want the ticket I wouldn't bother about it so went on reading. In a little while when he finished taking tickets, he came back and told me I would have to go in the other car. I refused, saying that the forward car was a smoker, and as I was in the ladies' car I proposed to stay. He tried to drag me out of the seat, but the moment he caught hold of my arm I fastened my teeth on the back of his hand.

I had braced my feet against the seat in front and was holding to the back, and as he had already been badly bitten he didn't try it again by himself. He went forward and got the baggagemen and another man to help him and of course they succeeded in dragging me out. They were encouraged to do this by the attitude of the white ladies and gentlemen in the car; some of them even stood on the seats so that they could get a good view and continued applauding the conductor for his brave stand.[70]

She hired a lawyer to sue the railroad, but, after an initial victory in the circuit courts, Tennessee's Supreme Court ruled against her.[71]

Undeterred, Wells went on to build a career in journalism after her white school board dismissed her when she publicly accused it of taking advantage of black female teachers.[72] Asked to recount her train experience in a Baptist weekly, she soon found a voice under the pen name Iola, and numerous black newspapers printed her words of outrage and calls for justice. In her own newspaper, the *Memphis Free Speech,* she highlighted topics such as white hypocrisy—namely white women who lured black men into relationships—violence against blacks, and the substandard conditions that blacks endured.[73] Her call to end lynching in earnest came when her good friend Thomas Moss and his two associates felt its brutal effects in March 1892. Their offense consisted of running a successful Memphis grocery store. When a white competitor organized a group to demolish the store, the black men shot three of the whites. Although authorities hauled Moss and his colleagues off to jail, a white mob wrenched them from their cells and killed them. This atrocity caused Wells to deduce that lynching provided "[a]n excuse to get rid of Negroes who were acquiring wealth and property' and thus keep the race terrorized and 'keep the nigger down.' . . . This is what opened my eyes to what lynching really was."[74]

Indeed, her friends' lynchings spurred her to look more deeply into why whites used this heinous method to kill blacks. Not convinced that black men raped white women on a regular basis, she instead revealed that whites could not abide legitimate interracial affairs. "Nobody in this section of the country," she asserted, "believed the threadbare lie that Negro men rape white women. If southern white men are not careful . . . a conclusion will be reached which will be very damaging to the moral reputation of their women." She bought a gun and urged other African Americans to do so, "when the truth dawned upon us that protection of the law was not ours." "A Winchester rifle should have a place of honor in every home," she advised in one editorial.[75] "I felt that one had better die fighting against injustice than to die like a dog or a rat in a trap," she later recalled. "I had already determined to sell my life as dearly as possible if attacked. I felt if I could take one lyncher with me, this would even up the score a little bit."[76]

Wells also urged African Americans to leave Memphis, since its environs obviously did not bode well for their future.[77] "There is . . . only one thing left that we can do," she recommended in her editorials, "save our money and leave a town which will neither protect our lives and property, nor give us a fair trial in the courts, but takes us out and murders us in cold blood when accused by white persons."[78] Foreshadowing the strategies that African Americans would use a half century later, Wells organized a streetcar boycott for those African Americans who stayed. It became so successful that the company owners made a personal appeal to her to end it.[79] Memphis's white papers reacted to her words and actions with a white call to arms. "Tie the wretch who utters these calumnies to a stake at the intersection of Main and Madison Sts.," one demanded, "brand him [sic] in the forehead with a hot iron and perform upon him a surgical operation with a pair of tailor's shears."[80] A group of white leaders took heed, demolishing the *Free Speech* office with the intention of killing its occupants as well. They also advised Wells, then on a trip through the East, not to return. Convinced to stay in New York, she joined the staff of the *New York Age* and continued her mission to end racial violence and expose white hypocrisy.[81]

In the years that followed, Wells toured other countries and published works revealing the truth about lynching. She helped organize groups instrumental in the fight for African American rights and justice, including the National Association of Colored Women in 1896, the Anti-Lynching League in 1899, and the National Association for the Advancement of Colored People (NAACP) in 1909. Outspoken in her beliefs, she grew frustrated with other black leaders' caution in race relations. Indeed, by the turn of the century, influential African Americans began a heated discussion in earnest over how best to deal with their role in the United States. Accommodationists, such as Booker T. Washington, born under slavery and founder of Tuskegee Institute, subscribed to the idea that working hard and learning skills for self-sufficiency and economic independence would do more to advance their race than resistance against white hegemony. In his famous Atlanta Exposition speech on September 18, 1895, he declared,

> The wisest among my race understand that the agitation of questions of so-
> cial equality is the extremest [sic] folly and that progress in the enjoyment

of all the privileges that will come to us, must be the result of severe and constant struggle, rather than of artificial forcing. . . . It is important and right that all privileges of the law be ours, but it is vastly more important that we be prepared for the exercise of these privileges. The opportunity to earn a dollar in a factory just now is worth infinitely more than the opportunity to spend a dollar in an opera house.[82]

These sentiments appealed to many whites and blacks, and Washington came to be considered a safe black man who would not cause trouble in race relations, consulted and praised by presidents and other powerful whites.[83] "Your words," President Grover Cleveland commended, "cannot fail to delight and encourage all who wish well for your race."[84] Some black leaders like Wells, however, shunned this approach, asserting that they must fight back in order for blacks to achieve equality and justice.

"Prof. B. T. or Bad Taste Wash. has made a speech," condemned one black newspaper. "[I]f there is anything in him except the most servile type of the old Negro we fail to find it."[85] The well-known schism between Washington and W.E.B. Du Bois, teacher, author, intellectual, and leader of the New Negro movement, received much scrutiny in subsequent years. Although generally in agreement with Washington's philosophy during the 1890s, Du Bois, born in New England just after the end of the Civil War, grew increasingly opposed to a gradualist approach to race relations.[86] While Washington focused on industrial education for blacks, Du Bois stressed the need for higher education (he was the first African American to earn a doctorate from Harvard). And as Washington called for self-help, Du Bois suggested that a "Talented Tenth," or the top 10 percent of blacks, should use their expertise to pull the rest of the race up out of poverty and oppression.[87]

Du Bois later revealed his thoughts toward Washington at the turn of the century:

> At a time when Negro civil rights called for organized and aggressive defense, he broke down that defense by advising acquiescence or at least no open agitation. During the period when laws disfranchising the Negro were being passed in all Southern states, between 1890 and 1909, and when these were being supplemented by "Jim Crow" travel laws and other enactments making color caste legal, his public speeches, while they did not entirely ignore this development, tended continually to excuse it, to emphasize the short comings of the Negro, and were interpreted widely as putting the chief onus for his condition upon the Negro himself.[88]

Du Bois's time in Nashville as an undergraduate at Fisk University during the 1880s had a profound effect on his views of racism in the United

States, where he saw its effects around him. And the brutal murder of Sam Hose outside Atlanta in 1899, as well as the death of his toddler son the same year, particularly hardened his resolve to fight for African American rights.[89] By his 1903 publication *The Souls of Black Folk,* Du Bois had become an outspoken critic of Washington and white America.

Two years later, he, William Monroe Trotter, and other black leaders in discord with Washington's philosophy formed the all-black Niagara Movement as a mighty current to push for—among other basic rights—freedom of speech, a free press, manhood suffrage, the elimination of racial and color distinctions in the United States, and equal access to education and housing.[90] "We are men," the group proclaimed; "we will be treated as men. . . . And we shall win."[91] At their second annual conference, held at Harpers Ferry, West Virginia, in 1906, they declared the following to the country:

> In the past year the work of the Negro hater has flourished in the land. Step by step the defenders of the rights of American citizens have retreated. The work of stealing the black man's ballot has progressed and the fifty and more representatives of stolen votes still sit in the nation's capital. Discrimination in travel and public accommodation has so spread that some of our weaker brethren are actually afraid to thunder against color discrimination as such and are simply whispering for ordinary decencies.
>
> Against this the Niagara Movement eternally protests. We will not be satisfied to take one jot or tittle [*sic*] less than our full manhood rights. We claim for ourselves every single right that belongs to a freeborn American, political, civil and social; and until we get these rights we will never cease to protest and assail the ears of America. . . . Never before in the modern age has a great and civilized folk threatened to adopt so cowardly a creed in the treatment of its fellow-citizens, born and bred on its soil. Stripped of verbiage and subterfuge and in its naked nastiness, the new American creed says: Fear to let black men even try to rise lest they become the equals of the white.[92]

The Brownsville, Texas, riot in August 1906, and the Atlanta riot the following month prompted the group to redouble their efforts at attaining racial justice, and its members wrote letters appealing to President Theodore Roosevelt himself.[93] By 1910, however, the Niagara Movement had dwindled to only a trickle. Lack of funds and the opposition of *The Tuskegee Machine,* as Washington and his supporters came to be known, proved too much for the struggling organization.[94] But Du Bois and his fellow Niagarans laid the groundwork for a group that would prove quite successful in many of its endeavors to fight injustices and violence over the following decades.

Indeed, Du Bois, Wells, Terrell, and other outspoken African Americans joined white leaders, such as Jane Addams, Moorfield Storey, and Mary White Ovington, to form the integrated NAACP in 1909. Du Bois urged the members of the fading Niagara Movement to enroll, too. To commemorate its five-year anniversary, Ovington wrote how the organization began, largely in response to the Springfield, Illinois, race riot:

> In the summer of 1908, the country was shocked by the account of the race riots at Springfield, Illinois. Here, in the home of Abraham Lincoln, a mob containing many of the town's "best citizens," raged for two days, killed and wounded scores of Negroes, and drove thousands from the city. Articles on the subject appeared in newspapers and magazines. Among them was one in the *Independent* of September 3rd, by William English Walling, entitled "Race War in the North." After describing the atrocities committed against the colored people, Mr. Walling declared:
>
>> "Either the spirit of the abolitionists, of Lincoln and of Love-joy must be revived and we must come to treat the Negro on a plane of absolute political and social equality, or Vardaman and Tillman will soon have transferred the race war to the North." And he ended with these words, "Yet who realizes the seriousness of the situation, and what large and powerful body of citizens is ready to come to their aid?"
>
> It so happened that one of Mr. Walling's readers accepted his question and answered it. For four years I had been studying the status of the Negro in New York. I had investigated his housing conditions, his health, his opportunities for work. I had spent many months in the South, and at the time of Mr. Walling's article, I was living in a New York Negro tenement on a Negro Street. And my investigations and my surroundings led me to believe with the writer of the article that "the spirit of the abolitionists must be revived."[95]

In addition to the NAACP's efforts, African Americans found other outlets to make their way in the United States during this era of racial violence. Just as literature sounded racial themes with white Americans, blacks used literature and music for their advantage as well. Not surprisingly, the brutality directed against them played a central role in the books they published and the music they created.[96] Following the 1898 Wilmington race riot, for instance, David Bryant Fulton (under the pseudonym Jack Thorne), penned *Hanover; or, The Persecution of the Lowly: A Story of the Wilmington Massacre,* and Charles Waddell Chesnutt wrote *The Marrow of Tradition,* fictional accounts of the violence engineered by the city's white men after the November election, as well as black reaction to it. The riot profoundly affected Chesnutt, a school teacher, businessman, and author, who lived a substantial portion of his life in North Carolina, and Fulton, a journalist and an author, and a native of North Carolina who had ties to Wilmington.[97] "[I am] deeply concerned and very much depressed," Chesnutt wrote the day after the riot, "at the condition of affairs in North Carolina." The violence represented "an outbreak of pure, malignant and altogether indefensible race prejudice, which makes me feel personally humiliated, and ashamed for the country and the state."[98] These sentiments and others pour out into their fiction, as Fulton expresses the responses of black men and women to the riot, portraying them as brave and bold in their resistance to the white violence, while Chesnutt explores more fully the complicated relationships between the races.[99]

As well, black writers pointed with pride to the achievements of their race. When the indomitable and pompous Jack Johnson knocked out Jim Jeffries (the "Great White Hope," who whites lured out of retirement to teach the "haughty" black boxer a lesson) on July 4, 1910, not only did violence ensue outside the ring, but African Americans took pleasure in their man's accomplishments.[100] Poet William Waring Cuney wrote a poem to commemorate the occasion. After black boxer Joe Louis beat German Max Schmeling (who symbolized Hitler's idea of Aryan superiority) in New York in 1938, a blues musician sang a tune in his honor.[101] Athlete, singer, and actor Paul Robeson fought Jim Crow in many arenas. His stage premier in 1924, when he performed as part of an interracial couple in a Eugene O'Neill play, infuriated whites. But he used *Show Boat* and concerts during the 1930s "to speak his mind about Jim Crowism on stages all over America and Europe." By the mid-1930s, he stressed the power of identifying with his African roots. "[I]n my music, my plays, my films," he wrote in 1935, "I want to carry always this central idea—to be African."[102] "Strange Fruit," a poem popularized in song by Billie Holiday beginning in the late 1930s, expressed the horrors of lynching.[103] These black assertions of equality did not occur in a vacuum. Whites often took umbrage with these ideas and sentiments. Signs of black assertion or pride, therefore, often led to violence.

Moreover, as they had in every American war, African Americans served bravely during the Spanish-American War in 1898. And as Frederick Douglass had stated during the American Civil War, the military uniform symbolized equality. "Once let the black man get upon his person the brass letters, U.S.," he declared, "let him get an eagle on his button, and a musket on his shoulder and bullets in his pocket, and there is no power on earth which can deny that he has earned the right to citizenship."[104] Southern whites met this assertion with hostility and violence. As black soldiers from the West traveled by train to southern ports of embarkation during the "splendid little war," interracial gatherings hailed them with support until they reached Kentucky and Tennessee.[105] There, whites glumly looked on and met the trains with resentment. "It mattered not if we were soldiers of the United States," a black sergeant noted, "we were 'niggers' as they called us and treated us with contempt."[106] Violence erupted as blacks and whites came into contact. When members of a white Ohio regiment used a black child as target practice in Tampa, for instance, black troops "fired pistols freely, wrecked saloons and cafes that had refused them service, and crashed into a white brothel." Numerous black and white soldiers suffered injuries.[107] As well, imperialism, social Darwinism, and the Spanish-American War all contributed to uniting southern whites with northern whites. As historian Edward Ayers asserts,

> The war against the Spanish, which so many black Americans thought might be a turning point in race relations in this country, in fact accelerated the decline, the loss of civility, the increase in bloodshed, the white arrogance. The major effect of the war seems to have been to enlist the North as an even more active partner in the subjugation of black Americans. The war brought Southern and Northern whites into contact with one another. They discovered, much to their delight, that they had grown more alike than they had expected. The war also brought blacks and whites in all regions into contact. They discovered, much to the dismay of the blacks, that they were even farther apart than they had imagined.[108]

As blacks articulated again later in World War I and World War II, the irony that they fought for a nation that denied them their rights did not escape them.

Indeed, during World War II, the black-owned *Pittsburgh Courier* launched the Double Victory campaign pushing for the defeat of Germany and Japan at the same time stressing civil rights and equal economic opportunities at home.[109] According to one source, the United States witnessed six civilian riots, more than 20 military mutinies and riots, and dozens of lynchings between 1941 and 1945. Moreover, a government study during this time stated that blacks perceived "an important change" and "a feeling of discontent and a growing consciousness of exclusion from social, economic, and political participation." Black leaders, the report continued, appeared "fearless and ready to state what they believe to be the basic rights of the group." Black ministers took an important role, and "it is actually coming to pass," the government concluded, "that the Negro church has become the means here and there for encouraging Negroes to resist. . . . Ideas about 'rights' are being introduced."[110]

Cultural framing, then, amplified the already strained conditions produced by structural factors. A radical ideology that trumpeted white supremacy and upheld the virtuous white woman emerged with ferocity during the late 19th century. Its vestiges could still be felt during World War II, as the race riots in Beaumont, Texas, and Mobile, Alabama, attest. White newspapers and politicians particularly preyed upon the fears unleashed by this radical mind-set. White literature also served as a powerful conveyer of this racist and deadly message. And when black leaders and newspaper editors organized or exposed the hypocrisy of white society, they only inflamed whites' impassioned hatred even more. Moreover, American wars abroad provided blacks an opportunity to assert their equality at home. When they wore the uniform, as Frederick Douglass maintained, it signified to the world that they were true Americans. Many whites could not abide this mentality. Indeed, whites paid attention to the actions and words of African Americans. Violence often erupted as a result.

PRECIPITATING EVENTS

Structural factors and cultural framing probably existed in many cities around the country that did not experience race riots. Thus, a precipitating event provides the tipping mechanism that activates this type of violence. These events confirm the existence of structural and cultural concerns, and they supply the immediate motivation to act on this anxiety. In racial pogroms, the precipitating events, often fueled by the violent rhetoric of white newspaper editors and rumors, centered on sacred aspects of white society and supremacy. As elaborated in the case studies in the next chapter, alleged or actual attacks on white women or white authorities provided the tipping points into the riots. When blacks attacked these sacred symbols of white virtue or authority, whites decided they must act. "Conversion specialists," to use Brass's term, played a leading role in imputing significance on these black infractions against white society. Authorities, particularly local police, failed to stop—and often encouraged—the onslaught.

Chapter 3

"IF WE HAVE TO CHOKE THE CURRENT OF THE CAPE FEAR WITH CARCASSES": CASE STUDIES OF SIX RACIAL POGROMS

In the case studies that follow, I demonstrate that structural factors, cultural framing, and precipitating events coalesced to create race riots. In Wilmington, New Orleans, Atlanta, East St. Louis, Tulsa, and Beaumont, all of these ingredients appeared. Demographic shifts, political wrangling, Jim Crow measures, segregation, economic turmoil, labor strife, and ineffective authorities had a hand in setting the structural scene from which the violence emerged. Moreover, white newspapers, writers, and politicians acted as fire tenders[1] to spread the gospel of white supremacy and virtuous white womanhood, and held the black male up as someone who constantly attacked these ideals. Meanwhile, blacks strove to push for equality and a decent chance at being a true American citizen with all its benefits. Each race framed these struggles to help and advance their own cause—whites in order to keep blacks down, and blacks for a chance to move up in society. Finally, a precipitating event, such as an alleged or actual infraction against something sacred in the white mindset, provided the immediate spark that resulted in numerous deaths and widespread destruction. These very one-sided incidents—unlike the riots that erupted in the wake of World War I—appeared more as massacres or pogroms. Although African Americans fought back as best they could,

whites maintained social, political, and economic dominance when the
riots had ended.

WILMINGTON—1898

Wilmington provided blacks many opportunities during the decade leading up to the riot in 1898. The 1890 census placed the city's black population at 11,324, some 2,500 more than the white populace.[2] And unlike
in many southern cities during this era, blacks in Wilmington frequented
the same shops as whites, lived in many of the same neighborhoods, and
used the same streets to get around town. Moreover, the city's blacks held
a number of important political offices, both elected and appointed. The
coalition that Republicans and Populists forged in the early 1890s to rid the
state of the Democratic Party domination of the previous decades allowed
blacks to attain positions on the board of aldermen (elected) and the board
of audit and finance (appointed by Governor Daniel Russell, a Republican), and as justice of the peace, superintendent of streets, deputy clerk of
court, and coroner. Wilmington's African Americans also organized two
black fire departments and an all-black board of health, and many served
as policemen and letter carriers. Significantly, President William McKinley appointed African American John Campbell Dancy as the highly paid
collector of customs for the Port of Wilmington in 1897, an action that
aroused the ire of many whites.[3] Blacks also owned and ran many of Wilmington's thriving businesses.

   As they saw their own power dwindle and that of Wilmington's black
citizens grow, leaders of the Democratic Party decided that they must act.
"The Secret Nine," a group of prominent white citizens, began meeting
clandestinely to devise a plan to overturn the blacks' control of the city.
Furnifold Simmons, a future U.S. senator and chair of North Carolina's
Democratic Executive Committee, helped mastermind the campaign for
white supremacy (throughout the state, but with a special emphasis on
Wilmington as well). As "a genius in putting everybody to work—men
who could write, men who could speak, and men who could ride," Simmons set numerous individuals and organizations in motion (quote from
Simmons's friend Josephus Daniels, editor of the Raleigh *News and Observer* and later secretary of the navy under President Woodrow Wilson).[4]
Pro-Democratic newspapers, the Raleigh *News and Observer,* the Wilmington *Evening Star,* and the *Wilmington Messenger,* became mouthpieces
for promoting the notions of white superiority and black degeneracy.
Headlines blared such sentiments as "White Supremacy," "Russell's Devil-
try," and "The Negroized East" throughout the months leading up to the
election, and scores of articles emphasized supposed instances of black

impudence, unproductive government, graft, and threats posed by black beast rapists.[5]

Simmons also coaxed gifted speakers to ride circuit around the state to sound the trumpet for white supremacy. Charles B. Aycock (who became governor in 1900 for his efforts), Robert Glenn (also later a governor), Wilmington's own Alfred Moore Waddell, a former U.S. congressman and officer in the Confederate cavalry (who became mayor after the coup d'état), and others urged the state's whites to join together to purge North Carolina's political system of its impurities (i.e., African Americans). "[T]he salvation of society depends on the outcome of this election," Waddell declared in a speech two weeks before the vote. He then went on to suggest that although he hoped violence would not be required, if it came to that, "I trust that it will be rigidly and fearlessly performed." He ended with the prediction that whites would prevail even "if we have to choke the current of the Cape Fear with carcasses."[6] Other individuals and groups directed their attention to riding around the state to lure prodigal whites back to the Democratic Party and intimidate blacks. The White Government Union and the Young Men's Democratic Club staged an all-out get-out-the-vote effort to persuade whites how imperative voting would be to them.

While these forces preached their diabolical message around the state, the members of the Secret Nine looked for an opportune moment to spur Wilmington's whites into action. They got their chance when black editor Alexander Manly responded to a speech given the year before (but printed again recently in one of Wilmington's white newspapers) by Rebecca Latimer Felton, who had expressed concern over white women's increasing interactions with black men. "If it needs lynching to protect women's dearest possession from the ravening human beasts," Felton proposed, "then I say lynch; a thousand times a week if necessary."[7] In his rebuttal, Manly exposed the hypocrisy of Felton and many of her white contemporaries. "[E]very Negro lynched is called a 'big, burly, black brute,'" he asserted, "when in fact many of those who have thus been dealt with had white men for their fathers and were not only not 'black' and 'burly' but were sufficiently attractive for white girls of culture and refinement to fall in love with them."[8] His editorial, as historian H. Leon Prather suggests, "had the effect of pouring gasoline on the embers of white discontent."[9]

Newspapers in Wilmington and across the South had a field day in response. They featured such headlines as "Negro Editor Slanders White Women," "Negro Defamer of White Women," "Infamous Attack on White Women," and "A Horrid Slander of White Women."[10] Manly's words set off a firestorm in Wilmington itself as well. White business owners who had placed advertisements in the *Daily Record* summarily pulled them out, and whites across the city muttered such sentiments as "the impudent nigger ought to be horsewhipped and run out of town."[11] Leaders of the white supremacy campaign, however, counseled caution. "It required the best efforts we could put forth [to] prevent the people from lynching him," one white Wilmington resident later stated. "Senator Simmons, who was here at the time, told us that the article would make it an easy victory for us and urged us to try and prevent any riot until after the election."[12]

Although Simmons and his henchmen remained successful in this mission, the Red Shirts and others, "effectively [serving as] a terrorist arm of the Democratic Party," did use rallies and intimidation to convey the message of white supremacy to blacks and their white allies.[13] They became so successful that the Populist and Republican candidates grew too terrified to speak at events in Wilmington, and Democratic leaders soon called for the Republican candidates in New Hanover County to drop out of the race altogether. "[The election] threatens to provoke a war between the black and white races," a textile owner wrote Republican Governor Daniel Russell two weeks before the election, "[and] will precipitate a conflict which may cost hundreds, and perhaps thousands of lives, and the partial or entire destruction of the city. We declare our conviction that we are on the brink of a revolution which can only be averted by the suppression of the Republican ticket."[14] A week later, on November 2, the Red Shirts and other white supremacist groups marched in a "White Man's Rally" through Wilmington and then feasted on barbecue. To demonstrate that this assembly resembled no ordinary party, however, the leaders of this movement bought a new, rapid-firing Gatling gun for the astronomical price of $1,200.[15] Preparations for the revolution were securely under way.

Rumors also spread among whites that Wilmington's blacks had acquired shipments of guns and ammunitions. "The negroes [in Wilmington] have no scruples in giving it out that when the riot begins," the *Atlanta Constitution* reported in early November, "they expect to spare none, but to kill from the cradle up." The article went on to claim, "They retire to the woods at night in squads to practice drilling, while hundreds of their women meet in their churches to discuss the situation."[16] In reality, although Wilmington's African Americans did attempt to buy weapons to protect themselves, the city's white merchants thwarted these efforts by refusing to sell to them or blocking the shipments from elsewhere.[17]

When Election Day finally arrived, some blacks simply stayed home to avoid confrontation. Both the lower turnout and "a significant degree of election fraud" turned a Republican majority of 5,000 in 1896 into a Democratic majority of 6,000 two years later.[18] No blood was shed that day even though white Democrats had been threatening violence to Wilmington's blacks if they and their white supporters turned out to vote (nonetheless many blacks remained undeterred in some polling places). But "a

[D]emocratic cyclone" swept through the state, with Wilmington as the focal point, as the Republican and Populist coalition—strong in the previous two elections—collapsed, and as the Democratic Party bullied its way into the vast majority of congressional, state legislature, and state judicial offices. "Negro domination," the *Atlanta Constitution* trumpeted, "will be succeeded by white supremacy."[19]

Emboldened by their success at the polls, the Democrats then essentially staged a coup d'état, forcing the city's white and black Fusionist leaders—the mayor, aldermen, police chief, and other officials—not only out of office, but also out of the state. The Secret Nine called the city's white men to the courthouse the next morning and had Waddell—to much applause—read aloud a "Wilmington Declaration of Independence." "We, the undersigned citizens of the City of Wilmington and County of New Hanover," the screed declared in part, "do hereby declare that we will no longer be ruled, and will never again be ruled by men of African origin. . . . [T]he time has passed for the intelligent citizens of the community owning 90% of the property and paying taxes in like proportion, to be ruled by negroes."[20] It ended with a call for Manly—who had already fled the city—to leave within 24 hours or suffer dire consequences. After this gathering, Waddell convened a committee of 25 of some of Wilmington's most prominent men to organize how to carry out the declaration's resolutions. This committee then met with 32 of the city's black leaders, read them the declaration, and issued them an ultimatum. Wilmington's blacks had to obey the authority of whites, and Manly must leave the city. They had until 7:30 the next morning (November 10) to respond to these demands.

They composed the following letter in response:

> We, the colored citizens to whom was referred the matter of expulsion from the community of the person and press of A. L. Manly, beg most respectfully to say that we are in no way responsible for, nor any way condone, the obnoxious article that called forth your actions. Neither are we authorized to act for him in this manner; but in the interest of peace we will most willingly use our influence to have your wishes carried out. Very respectfully, The Committee of Colored Citizens.[21]

They entrusted the letter to a black attorney and directed him to hand deliver it to Waddell immediately. Wary to travel to that part of the city unescorted at night, he instead placed it in the mail.

Early the next morning, throngs of weapon-toting whites gathered at the Armory to hear what the black leaders had decided. Although Waddell knew the response and that the letter had been mailed, he did not give this knowledge to the gathering mob. At approximately 8:30 A.M., on November 10, he led the angry throng (estimates range between 500 and

2,000 people) toward the building that housed the printing press of Manly's newspaper. Within minutes of the mob's arrival, the remains of the structure lay in a smoldering heap. After destroying the building, Waddell led the mass of people back to the Armory and advised them, "Now you have performed the duty you called on me to lead you to perform. Now let us go quietly to our homes and about our business and obey the law, unless we are forced in self-defense to do otherwise."[22] Unfortunately, these words of restraint came too late. Waddell and the other leaders of the white supremacy campaign had unleashed a force of hate and devastation that they could no longer control.

Clusters of white men had already started traveling around the city. When one group made their way into Brooklyn, the predominantly black section of Wilmington, a gunfight broke out (some blacks did have guns), and the race riot began in earnest. As news circulated that the riot had erupted, whites poured into the area to aid their comrades. At first, some of the whites targeted specific blacks whom they deemed especially harmful to white society. Eventually, however, they began to "kill every damn nigger in sight," according to one riot participant.[23] Witnesses later indicated that black corpses could be seen in the Cape Fear River—fulfilling Waddell's macabre premonition—or being buried in shallow graves. Although no final official death count ever surfaced (since many blacks were buried or disposed of surreptitiously), most likely dozens of blacks met a brutal

Destruction of Alexander Manly's printing press, Wilmington, North Carolina, 1898. (Courtesy New Hanover Public Library, Wilmington, NC)

end. "Wagon loads of Negro bodies," one resident asserted, "were hauled through the streets of Wilmington." "[I] saw carts pass" a teacher wrote to a relative, "with men thrown up there like dead animals they were taking . . . out to bury."[24] Whatever the death toll, Wilmington's blacks understood the message. "The roads were lined with [blacks]," a Raleigh newspaper reported, "some carrying their bedding on their heads and whatever effects could be carried."[25] While some left the city permanently, others hid in the surrounding woods and swamps (where some died from exposure) until they could be sure the threat to them had passed.[26]

As the riot raged, Waddell met with other white leaders to discuss the overthrow of the city's legitimately chosen Fusionist officials. They sent a delegation to city hall to order the mayor, aldermen, and police chief to resign. Seeing the danger in store for them if they refused, the Republicans and Populists all stepped down. Democrats quickly filled the vacant offices, and the new board chose Waddell as mayor. Waddell called for peace and order in the city and later even claimed that he had magnanimously prevented blacks from being lynched by unruly whites and that he had sent rescue parties to the woods to reassure the hiding black population.[27] At the same time, however, Waddell and the other Democratic leaders singled out specific white and black Republicans to be banished from Wilmington and had them escorted to the train station to assure their exit from the city. One former white Republican congressman and postmaster even had a noose thrown around his neck, but cooler heads prevailed and he fled to catch an outgoing train.[28] With these evictions complete, the Democrats and other white supremacists could be assured that Wilmington had at last been redeemed from "negro domination." They had now successfully set the stage for the de jure measures established in North Carolina's laws and constitution in the years to come.

NEW ORLEANS—1900

Approaching 300,000 residents by the end of the last decade of the 19th century, New Orleans stood as the largest city in the South. Blacks made up more than a quarter of the population by the turn of the century, close to 80,000.[29] During the 1880s, although unruly, dirty (New Orleans suffered the distinction of being the one sizable community in the Western world without a sewage system), oppressively humid, and politically corrupt, the city held a special appeal for both blacks and whites in the surrounding areas looking for adventure and employment. Housing remained fairly integrated among the laboring class, and Jim Crow legislation had not yet affected New Orleans streetcars. Despite this outward appearance of racial tranquility, tensions brewed below the surface. The national depression of the 1890s exacerbated the problem. Although during the 1880s, black and white labor unions joined efforts in New Orleans in the quest for mutual advancement, a decade later the lack of jobs and the threat of declining wages pitted black and white laborers against each other. Moreover, the largest city employers tended to reject whites over black workers, who usually agreed to lower pay.[30] By 1900, New Orleans seethed with racial animosity.

Moreover, the political situation in Louisiana in the 1890s created hostility between the races. African Americans played a significant role in the Fusionist movement between the Populists and the Republican Party statewide and in New Orleans. The Democratic Party moved to crush this alliance. "We are not in a condition now to permit dissention," threatened the *Baton Rouge Advocate* in 1892. "The breaches must be closed and strengthened preparatory to a vigorous assault all along the line. An active, enthusiastic campaign must be at once inaugurated in order to carry the principles of Democracy victorious over the combined assaults of the Republicans and Populists."[31] By the 1896 election, Democrats used white supremacy as their campaign platform and promised that they would disfranchise blacks in a constitutional amendment. That year the Democrats used violence and intimidation to keep African Americans from voting and fraud to stuff the ballot boxes.[32] This illegitimate election ushered in a Democratic administration that carried out its pledge to disfranchise blacks through new laws and the Constitution of 1898. Black registration quickly plunged statewide. Concomitantly, in 1896, Louisiana recorded 21 lynchings, surpassing any other state's annual total up to that time. "This 1896 election," scholar William Hair asserts, "engendered more racial feeling and violence than the state had known in any campaign since Reconstruction."[33]

Transportation in the urban South also became contested terrain. In 1891, Georgia passed the first law that segregated streetcars. By 1900, several southern cities followed Georgia's lead and started passing ordinances to segregate their streetcars.[34] New Orleans proved no different. The city's whites began pushing for streetcar segregation in 1900. "When one of these light colored mulatresses flounces in the car, dressed in all of her finery, and almost sits down on some white woman," wrote a white woman to the New Orleans *Daily Picayune* on July 2, 1900, "it does indeed make one's blood boil."[35] In May 1900, the state legislature debated a bill to segregate the New Orleans streetcars. One legislator argued that the bill would be a "demonstration of the superiority of the white man over the negro."[36]

The New Orleans press also played a critical role in the deteriorating race relations. The white radical Henry J. Hearsey, editor and publisher of the *States,* the city's foremost afternoon daily, proved especially vitriolic. A former Confederate army major, Hearsey for decades suggested that extreme measures might be required to settle "the negro problem." In one editorial he used the term "nigger" 28 times. By the summer of 1900, he trumpeted "extermination" as his "final solution." "The negro," he declared, "must be ruled down with an iron hand."[37] A series of stories in the *Times-Democrat* in June and July 1900 captured the divergent agendas of New Orleans's blacks and whites, concluding that "the fact we are on the threshold of a race war cannot be denied."[38]

Into this atmosphere of economic turmoil and inflamed racist rhetoric, Robert Charles made his way to New Orleans in late 1894 at the age of 28. Born and raised in Copiah County, Mississippi, Charles burned some bridges in his native state. Two years earlier, in 1892, he engaged in a gun-fight with a white train flagman and shortly thereafter assumed the alias Curtis Robertson. The year he left for the Crescent City, he also pled guilty to selling alcohol in his dry home county, a conviction that a jury found him innocent of two years later during one of his trips home from New Orleans. During his six years in Louisiana, Charles pieced together an as-sortment of jobs but never found steady employment. To supplement his income, he also distributed literature for two back-to-Africa causes—one espoused by the International Migration Society, a Birmingham, Alabama, group organized to send interested blacks to Liberia, and one promoted by Atlanta Bishop Henry M. Turner, an African Methodist Episcopal Church leader who published *Voice of Missions*. Charles's acquaintances also maintained that the especially grisly April 1899 lynching of Sam Hose in Newnan, Georgia, sent him into a fury.[39]

It was against this backdrop that he and his roommate, Lenard Pierce, encountered three New Orleans police officers in the late, muggy hours of July 23, 1900. As the men waited around 11:00 P.M. on a white family's doorstep for the chance to visit two women friends, Sergeant Jules C. Aucoin of the New Orleans Police Department called for Patrolmen August Mora and Joseph Cantrelle to help him investigate two suspicious men in the area. According to Mora, after the police approached the two African Americans and asked them what they were doing, Charles stood up after a vague response. Mora grabbed him. As the men began to struggle, Mora struck Charles with his billet, and they then pulled their guns on each other (Mora later changed his story on who pulled his gun first). Both Mora and Cantrelle fired shots at Charles, who fell to the ground, but managed to get up and run, leaving a trail of blood behind him. Mora took a bullet in the right thigh, and another one hit his fingers, but the other two officers remained unharmed. Meanwhile, Patrolman Aucoin leveled his pistol at Pierce's face. The police discovered that Charles eventually stopped bleed-ing, but Captain John Day of the Sixth Precinct soon learned from Pierce where to look for the missing suspect—their room of a rundown cottage at 2023 Fourth Street. By 3:00 A.M., Day and four of his men made their way to Charles's room and demanded to be admitted. As the door opened, Charles immediately aimed a bullet through the captain's heart.[40]

As the police stood in disbelief, Charles shot another patrolman through the head. Two policemen now lay dead in his front yard. Two remaining lawmen began to fire back, but Charles retreated into his room to reload his weapon, and the officers ran to a neighbor's room and stayed there until daybreak. At 4:30 A.M., Charles fired at a corporal on the street, grazing his cap. As the corporal and a colleague fled (claiming to go telephone for help), Charles made his escape to a house 14 blocks away where he knew the residents. Soon practically the whole New Orleans Police force gathered at 2023 Fourth Street. Summoning a bloodhound, the group discovered Charles had disappeared and a massive manhunt began. As the day of July 24 progressed, groups of whites could be heard plotting revenge, and poor, young blacks could barely contain their delight at what Charles had done. White crowds gathered at the house on Fourth Street, the Sixth Precinct stationhouse, where Lenard Pierce remained, and outside the city morgue, where the two killed policemen had been taken.[41]

In some part incited by the four major New Orleans newspapers, tensions rose. Throughout the riot and in its aftermath, the city's white newspapers described Charles as, among other things, a "bad nigger," "a monster," a "worthless crapshooting negro," a "ruthless black butcher," and a "bloodthirsty champion of African supremacy."[42] Hearsey's States blared, NEGRO MURDERERS in its July 25 afternoon edition headline. The editorial underneath read,

> Under the dark, seething mass of humanity that surrounds us and is in our midst, all appears peaceful and delightful; we know not, it seems, what hellish dreams are arising underneath; we know not what schemes of hate, of arson, of murder and rape are being hatched in the dark depths. We are, and we should recognize it, under the regime of the free negro, in the midst of a dangerous element of servile uprising, not for any real cause, but from the native hatred of the negro, inflamed continually by our Northern philanthropists.[43]

This paranoia preyed on whites' fears. "A vigorous course," the Times-Democrat declared, "[should] be adopted now."[44] Many of New Orleans's citizens took heed, as the white mob grew stronger.

On the night of the 25th, a crowd of some 2,000 men and teenagers, mostly of the laboring class, began their rampage. Heading for downtown, the crowd first focused their attention on passengers from nearby streetcars. They shot or beat the few unfortunate black passengers on board.

By 9:30 P.M., the mob had grown to more than 3,000 and aimed their wrath toward the Parish Prison with the intentions of lynching Lenard Pierce. Rebuffed by the police, the group then proceeded to the red light district, particularly to businesses that featured black or mixed-blood prostitutes. But by this time, most of the houses had been deserted. After midnight, the crowd began to diminish, but sporadic beatings and shootings continued throughout the night. By daybreak on July 26, three blacks died and six others suffered serious injuries. More than 50 more people, primarily blacks, required some form of medical assistance.[45] The shorthanded and poorly trained New Orleans police force had little ability—and in some cases, little desire—to stop the riot. The *New York Times* reported that the police did little to contain the riot:

POLICE ENCOURAGE RIOTERS

The police have been practically helpless during the disturbance. The force consists of some 300 men, including clerks and telegraph operators, and this is manifestly inadequate to the preservation of the peace of a city of 310,000 people. But aside from this, the fierce indignation among the members of the department of the ruthless murders of Capt. Day and Patrolman Lamb by the negro Robert Charles, to some extent made the police sympathetic with the mobs in their pretended efforts to avenge the murders. Several instances are reported where the police actually encourage the rioters in their work.

Not a single arrest was made by the police throughout the night, nor were any of the rioters, taken into custody up to noon to-day. The fact that there has been a strong feeling on the part of the working people against steamship agents and contractors employing negro labor to the exclusion of whites on public works and on the levee fronts also contributed to the disinclination of the police to do their full duty.[46]

Mayor Paul Capdevielle, who had been recovering from an illness in Mississippi, returned the morning of the 26th and put out a call for 500, and later in the day 1,500, citizens to act a special police force in suppressing the mob. Within an hour of each notice, he had plenty of volunteers. Louisiana Governor William Heard activated all state militia units in the area for Capdevielle's to use at his discretion.[47]

By sundown both the special police and the state militia protected dangerous areas, such as downtown. Unfortunately, 12 hours passed before they stood in place, and 2 more black men died and 15 others suffered severe injuries as the riot continued. The last of the rioters killed one other black woman late that night. Meanwhile, Robert Charles remained in hiding at 1208 Saratoga Street. Just before noon on July 27, the police received the information they wanted to hear from a black informer. When a patrol wagon with four policemen arrived at the residence, Charles hid in a closet on the bottom floor. As two officers entered the house, Charles killed one instantly, shooting him through the heart. The other died of a gunshot wound to the abdomen the following day. Charles then retreated to the second floor, but most of the remaining police and gathering white crowd presumed he fled. But Charles began to take aim, indiscriminately shooting any white he could, the first one being an unarmed 19-year-old civilian. For the next hour or so, he killed 2 others and wounded another 19. Beginning with his encounter with Patrolman Mora on the 23rd, Charles shot 27 whites. As news spread of his discovery, masses of white men and teens swarmed the scene. By 5:00 P.M., between 10,000 and 20,000 people congregated on or near Saratoga Street. The mayor ordered the state militia units to the site with their two Gatling guns should the white mob need subduing.[48]

Finally a fire patrol captain and a few volunteers slipped into the bottom floor of the residence around 5:00 P.M. and lit an old mattress on fire near the stairs. Five minutes later, Charles fled the inferno. Charles Noiret, a medical student and one of the mayor's special police, met him with a bullet, and then three others as Charles began to move. Shortly thereafter, a shooting free for all commenced. The crowd then pulled his body into the muddy street, where more bullets, kicks, and invectives riddled the corpse. Finally, before the mob could completely annihilate Charles's body, a patrol wagon came and delivered it to the city morgue. Still hungry for vengeance, a crowd gathered outside the morgue, while other bands of whites went in search of more African Americans. Two more black men met their fate this way. Around midnight, another crowd of whites burned down the renowned Lafon Institute, the best black school in Louisiana. Not until the next morning, Saturday, July 28, did the mob finally subside. The next day, an unmarked grave held the remains of Robert Charles. Of the some two dozen whites and blacks indicted in the whole New Orleans race riot, all but one eventually walked free. Lewis Forstall, a black admirer of Robert Charles, served seven years of hard labor for killing the informant who disclosed Charles's Saratoga Street hideout.[49]

In the four days of violence, 7 whites, including 4 law officers, died at the hands of Charles, and another 20 suffered serious or slight injury. Five other policemen soon left the force in disgrace, branded cowards for their responses to Charles's actions. The white mobs sought out and killed at least 12 African Americans and seriously wounded some 69 others.[50] In the aftermath of the riot, a former black Massachusetts state legislator argued that the riot had been controlled by elite whites in New Orleans.

The *Boston Globe* reported his beliefs. "Although many contend that the poorer element alone is taking part in the riots, he maintains that the better element has the poorer element completely under control and is allowing this thing to go on with perfect willingness." Moreover, he averred that riots would recur if rioters believed they could continue to act with impunity.[51]

ATLANTA—1906

Atlanta held the distinction of being one of the few cities in the South to experience economic prosperity at the turn of the 20th century. While other population centers languished, Atlanta became a commercial, railroad, and industrial hub for the region. Banks in the city netted $96 million in 1900 and about two and a half times that amount six years later.[52] Some 150,000 people lived in Atlanta by the time of the 1910 census, over 60,000 more than the previous census and at a growth rate second solely to Los Angeles. Approximately one-third of the residents were black. Indeed, the black population tripled between 1880 and 1910 from 16,300 to 51,900 (the white population grew at a staggering 500 percent during that same period).[53] To accommodate this close proximity of the races, the city's white leaders promoted a New South ideal of race relations and economic success by including African Americans in the market, but by relegating them to the lower rungs of the economic ladder. Whites would serve as managers, while blacks provided the labor.[54]

White leaders, including Henry Grady, editor of the *Atlanta Constitution* during the 1880s, reasoned that by incorporating blacks (albeit in a subordinate position), northerners would be more willing to invest in the city, whites would maintain their sense of superiority, and African Americans would feel included. This system worked especially well for whites, as long as they continued to maintain their supposed higher station in society.[55] By 1906, however, Atlanta's African American community included a healthy middle class, and they had carved out a thriving business and cultural community with their own restaurants, funeral parlors, grocery stores, and pharmacies. The *Atlanta Independent,* a weekly black newspaper, served as their mouthpiece in the community.[56] Moreover, if blacks did not work in the middle-class colored-only establishments, they could find ample opportunities in the working-class sector: restaurants, hotels, warehouses, freight yards, and private households. Prominent black leaders also led active congregations at black churches and taught black students in Atlanta's African American institutions of higher learning, including Spelman Seminary and Atlanta University. National black leaders, including W.E.B. Du Bois and Henry McNeal Turner, called Atlanta home during this period.

"The white man and the Negro have lived together in this city more peace-fully and in better spirit than in any other city," a 1902 Atlanta Chamber of Commerce publication boasted, "in either the North or the South."[57]

On the surface, the races appeared to be coexisting in peace. Behind the scenes, however, an undercurrent of racial strife churned in the city. Since the end of the Civil War, Atlanta's white leaders enforced a number of Jim Crow laws intending to tamp down any progress African Americans might strive for, including where they could sit on streetcars and what clothing they could be dressed in (blacks could not wear capes).[58] In addition to legitimate businesses that catered to state workers and visitors, downtown Atlanta—primarily along Decatur Street—provided illicit entertainment in the form of pool halls, dance joints, gambling houses, and brothels, a "breeding ground of Negro lust and crime."[59] Atlanta's police patrolled the area with an iron fist, and an arrest usually led to a conviction—a fate no one wanted to endure as prisoner death rates climbed to 10 percent per year.[60] Yet the crime rate soared in Atlanta in 1906, when police logged in more than 21,000 arrests (by comparison, Milwaukee had just one-fourth the arrests that year and three times the population).[61] Both the press and politicians played up the predominance of African Americans' involve-ment in Atlanta's delinquency. And in the summer of 1906, the press and politicians proved to be overlapping forces in the city.

As Clark Howell, the *Atlanta Constitution* editor, and eventual winner Hoke Smith, the former owner of the Atlanta *Journal,* vied to be the Demo-cratic candidate for governor that summer, they used race baiting for their main talking points and their newspapers as their medium.[62] Smith won the support of Populist Tom Watson with his push for black disfranchise-ment, one of the last remaining civil rights that blacks enjoyed in Georgia. Howell, while also forwarding a racist agenda (this is a white man's coun-try, and it must be governed by white men), criticized Smith's proposal of literacy tests as being a punishment against poor whites and an incentive for African Americans to educate themselves.[63] Smith, however, suggested that allowing blacks to vote only encouraged and enabled them to flout racial social norms. James Gray, Smith's campaign manager and editor of the *Journal,* played up these prejudices in an August 1 editorial (just three weeks before the Democratic primary) after the latest in a series of alleged area summer assaults on white women by black men:

> Political equality being thus preached to the Negro in the papers and on the stump, what wonder that he makes no distinction between political and so-cial equality. He grows more bumptious on the street, more impudent in his dealing with white men; and then, when he cannot achieve social equality as he wishes with the instinct of a barbarian to destroy what he cannot attain

to, he lies in wait, as that dastardly brute did yesterday near this city, and assaults the fair young girlhood of the South.[64]

While the two politicians' newspapers, the *Journal* and the *Constitution*, worded their racist screeds in political terms, Atlanta's evening newspapers—the *Atlanta Evening News* and the *Atlanta Georgian*—held no pretense of restraint.[65]

Between the months of June 1905 and September 1906, white newspapers featured 12 horrendous alleged attacks on the area's white women (a journalistic investigation by Ray Stannard Baker revealed that only two were actual assaults).[66] After a July 31, 1906, accusation by Annie Laurie Poole that a black man named Frank Carmichael attacked her and coerced her into the woods, however, the *News* ratcheted up its sensationalist, racist diatribes. A group of white men took it upon themselves to declare Carmichael guilty and killed him in "a roar of powder." During the following two months, the tabloid took every opportunity (issuing extra editions when necessary) to recount the latest activities of black beast rapists on the prowl. Lynching, of course, was the paper's prescription for this malady.[67] Further reports of alleged assaults throughout August prompted Atlanta's other newspapers to join in this campaign of "Negrophobia," a term coined by blacks to describe whites' irrational fears. By mid-September, the city had reached a fever pitch, and newspapers emphasized an epidemic of Negro crime.[68] Black leaders publicly denounced the alleged attacks. The Ministers Union of the African Methodist Episcopal Church, for example, approved resolutions late in the summer calling for law and order and counseling blacks "to be sober, industrious, and economical."[69] Behind the scenes, however, the black elite, unable to secure weapons from white-owned enterprises, surreptitiously smuggled arms and ammunition into their community just in case they came under attack.[70]

On September 20, William Jennings Bryan came to Atlanta on a presidential campaign stop. As Bryan's supporters gathered at the Piedmont Hotel that evening, officials notified the governor that another assault had occurred near the city. After a man had been arrested for the alleged attack, a mob began forming first around nearby Fort McPherson and then in the city as officers moved the suspect for his safety. Meanwhile, another incident had developed near the Piedmont when around 9:15 P.M. an inebriated, partially clothed black man, Luther Frazier, barged into the home of Reverend Thomas L. Bryan, who was away at a meeting. His wife and daughters, however, were home but managed to get away. Soon neighbors and then the police secured the invader. Upon Reverend Bryan's return home and again the next day at the suspect's hearing, Bryan charged at Frazier and called for his lynching.[71] Hundreds of white men stood ready to help Bryan carry out his command.[72] Indeed, white Atlantans had violence in the forefront of their minds when the *Atlanta Georgian* led the September 21 morning edition with "Men of Fulton, What Will You Do to Stop These Outrages against Women?"[73] Two more alleged assaults and a press intent on peddling their ware ensured that soon Atlanta could no longer promote the notion that it was a city where the two races lived in peace.

During his hearing, Frazier himself unwittingly helped focus renewed attention on Atlanta's black vice joints. "I got drunk with another Negro," he tried to explain his actions, "and the last thing I remember was when I was in a barroom on Decatur Street. I don't remember anything about taking off a part of my clothes."[74] The city's license inspector, Richard Ewing, sprang into action, met with the media to declare forthcoming raids, and both the *Journal* and the *Georgian* led with headlines on September 21 that suggested a link between the attacks on white women and the black underworld.[75] On Saturday, September 22, as authorities continued their sweep on black clubs, white men and boys congregated on the streets and deliberated about the recent attacks. Around 4:00 P.M., the *Journal* issued an extra edition and newsboys bellowed throughout downtown, "Negro Attempts to Assault Mrs. Mary Chafin Near Sugar Creek Bridge." As the *Journal's* report made its way through Atlanta's white restaurants and bars, the *Evening News* came out with its own extra edition announcing a *Two Assaults*. Only an hour later, the *Evening News* published another extra edition proclaiming a "Third Assault" by a "fiendish Negro."[76]

Almost 8:30 P.M. now, milling whites began targeting random African Americans on the street. "Let's kill all the Negroes," one man shouted to the crowd, "so our women will be safe." Mayor James Woodward dashed to the scene and implored the growing mob to disperse and to allow the law to run its course. "I beseech you not to cause this blot on the fair name of our most beautiful city," he begged.[77] "Go home, Jim!" someone in the crowd replied, "We're going to get some niggers!"[78] The riot was under way, even though all of the so-called attacks were simply cases of a white woman being frightened—not actually assaulted—by a black man.[79] At around 9:30 P.M., yet even more extra editions circulated throughout downtown about news of a "Fourth Assault" after an elderly woman reported seeing a black man peering at her through her window on Magnolia Street.[80] By this time, thousands of area whites (estimates suggest as many 10,000) were out on the city streets. Many of them headed toward Decatur Street, the center of black vice. At 10:00 P.M., several theaters and bars started emptying, adding more chaos to the rowdy mob. Mayor Woodward again appealed for order, but when none came, he called for fire hoses to be trained on the horde.[81] This act only caused the throng to splinter into smaller mobs and to leave the heart of downtown in all directions: north toward Darktown,

Atlanta's black neighborhoods; south to the central train depot; east into the vice district on Decatur Street; and west toward other black businesses and homes. Other rioters targeted the city's streetcars, many filled with blacks unaware of the unfolding violence.[82]

For hours the white mob used every weapon imaginable to hunt down, attack, brutalize, and kill any African American they could find. Numerous blacks were tortured to differing extents and left dead or dying in the streets. Although rioters consisted mainly of younger and lower class white men, people who saw the violence firsthand recognized storeowners, students, and white-collar members of society among the throng. Even some of the city's white women and children cheered them on.[83] The police and other city officials offered varying degrees of protection to Atlanta's blacks, and witnesses suggested that some officers actually joined the rioters.[84] The city's riot alarm finally went off near midnight, signaling to the governor that the time had arrived to bring in the state militia. By 2:00 A.M., heavy rain scattered many of the rioters; 30 minutes later the first troops reached the city. As Atlantans headed to church that Sunday morning, many just learning of the violence, it appeared as if another mob might gather. Soldiers tamped down the threat, but the governor called in more troops anyway. By the end of the day on September 23, some 600 militiamen secured the city, primarily to ease whites' anxiety over a black reprisal rather than to protect African Americans.[85]

The city's white newspapers blamed African Americans, of course. The *Journal* called the rioting "an inevitable harvest of unbridled crime," and Atlanta's blacks braced themselves for more violence as night fell on Sunday. "That it is possible for one of these black devils to assault and almost kill a white woman, practically within a stone's throw of the heart of the city, and make good his escape seems incredible," the *News* averred. "It is enough to fill the heart of every white citizen of this community with a desire for vengeance."[86] The national media picked up the story of the riot, and when the *New York World* asked Mayor Woodward (the same man who had begged the white mob to allow the law to run its course) what actions he planned on taking in response to the violence, he retorted, "The only remedy is to remove the cause. As long as black brutes attempt rape upon our white women, just so long will they be unceremoniously dealt with."[87] And, again, whites did take it upon themselves to carry out their version of justice. Although authorities jailed a black man on the afternoon of September 23 in a southern suburb for bearing a concealed weapon, a group of white men escorted him to the woods that night and lynched him.[88] Several scuffles broke out throughout the city.[89] It finally became clear to authorities that stricter actions would be necessary to prevent more violence.

On Monday, September 24, orders went out that no more weapons would be sold in the city, saloons would be closed until further notice, any police officer discovered shirking his duty would be fired, and no males could be on the streets after 5:00 P.M.[90] Militia commander Clifford Anderson also attempted to prevent Atlanta's newspapers from issuing extra editions.[91] That same day, W.E.B. Du Bois (who had been in Alabama doing census research when he learned of the riot) arrived back in Atlanta so he could stand guard over his wife and daughter, as well as the community at Atlanta University, where he served on the faculty.[92] The campus sat on the outskirts of Brownsville, a wealthy black suburb of Atlanta, where rumors began to circulate late Monday that it would be the next target of white rage. The community of 1,500 maintained relative independence and stayed largely out of the sphere of white Atlanta with its own school, post office, restaurants, and businesses.[93] Brownsville was also home to Clark College and Gammon Theological Seminary, which both offered refuge to residents on Monday.[94]

That evening, a group of white men did approach the black suburb. Fulton County officer James Heard led them into homes to confiscate any weapons that the black residents might own. Unfortunately, to the people of Brownsville, the group appeared to be just more roughs intent on violence, not a crew of deputized citizens carrying out the orders of a law official. A scuffle broke out, Heard was shot and killed, and a few other white men were injured.[95] The remaining whites arrested six blacks and took them back to Atlanta (two of the six attempted to escape and were met with a volley of gunfire). In response to the events in Brownsville, troops headed there early the morning of Tuesday, September 25, to finish what Heard and his men had started the evening before. At least five more blacks were killed, and the president of Gammon Theological Seminary was struck over the head with a rifle and arrested. In all, the militia detained some 100 blacks from the community, charging many of them with murder.[96] While this drama unfolded in Brownsville, Atlanta's white and black leaders decided the time had come to meet.

Tuesday's *Constitution* announced that a meeting would take place at 11:00 A.M. in the city council chambers and that "only those invited may attend."[97] The mayor and other white officials promised the black elites—a group of seven religious and business leaders—that they would provide safety for the city's black community if they would convince their fellow African Americans to follow the law. In other words, it would be up to Atlanta's blacks to ensure more violence did not occur. Blacks had the "power to stop trouble or bring on a war of extermination," asserted the *Constitution*. "If the negroes will stop their attacks," the story went on, quoting the commander of the militia, "no attacks will be made on them. . . . It is to the interest of the negroes even more than to the interest of the whites to stop the present conflict at once. It is hoped they will see this and act accordingly."[98] In response to the meeting, Atlanta's black ministers issued a resolution to the city's newspapers that urged black citizens not to resist white authorities and offered their support for the law.[99] Later Tuesday afternoon, the Chamber of Commerce, keenly aware of the financial impact the riot had on Atlanta (many businesses were destroyed and others were empty as people stayed away from downtown, and by now the national media had picked up on the riot in Atlanta), called another meeting at the county courthouse for the city's best citizens.[100] Most of the 1,000 or so who showed up were white, but several black leaders, including W.E.B. Du Bois, appeared at the gathering as well. The group passed a resolution critical of the violence of the last few days, and they gathered over $3,700 for riot victims and their relatives. The group also appointed a Committee of Ten (dubbed the Committee of Safety by the press) to work with authorities in maintaining order.[101]

No real violence broke out Tuesday night, and on Wednesday morning (September 26), the *Constitution* declared, "Atlanta Is Herself Again; Business Activity Restored and the Riot Is Forgotten."[102] Of course, the black community would not forget. Between 26 and 47 African Americans died, and more than 1,000 fled Atlanta during the carnage and its aftermath.[103] The *Washington Post* likened the violence to the New York City draft riot of 1863 and asserted, "The Atlanta riot is the most deplorable exhibition of race ferocity and savagery that this country has seen for many years."[104] Two whites also died during the riot—Officer Heard and a woman who reportedly died of a heart attack after witnessing from her home a brutal attack on a black man.[105] The mayor laid much of the blame on an irresponsible press. "I do not believe that violence would have been resorted to," he announced at a September 28 city council meeting, "if it had not been for the inflammatory, sensational newspaper extras that were continually flooding the streets."[106] Only 22 whites received indictments for assault and attempted murder on Saturday night, and only 2 were convicted.[107] Scores of white men received misdemeanor charges and were served with a 30-day sentence in the stockade or a $100 fine. A police board also accused a few officers of misconduct during the riot.[108] The 60 or so black men arrested for Officer Heard's shooting slowly secured release from prison, and only 1 was convicted for his death (he was sentenced to life in prison).[109]

The city released its official report on the riot on December 9, when both black and white leaders revealed its findings in public forums. It put the death count at 12—10 black and 2 white—and pinned the riot on Atlanta's tougher elements, exonerating both races' better classes.[110] Booker

T. Washington visited the city that night and spoke at the First Congrega-
tional Church. He praised Atlanta's leaders for focusing on getting past the
riot and continued his mantra that the races should be engaged in civic and
business activities together but not in social or political ones.[111] He also
suggested that the riot would serve a bigger cause. "What is being done by
the Civic League [a society established in November to foster understanding between the races and to maintain law and order] and other organizations that have grown out of the Atlanta riot," he predicted, "will not only
serve a higher purpose in the city of Atlanta and the state of Georgia, but I
believe the movement will spread throughout the south."[112] Unfortunately,
these lofty claims failed to materialize. Washington had repeatedly proclaimed that hardworking and upstanding African Americans would not
suffer at the hands of whites. The Atlanta riot proved him wrong; white
rioters besieged any black in sight, respectable or supposedly otherwise.[113]
Some black elites left the city over the next few years, and one black editor
fled Atlanta after it became known that he blamed the riot on "sensational
newspapers and unscrupulous politicians."[114] Du Bois, disheartened by
race relations in Atlanta, moved north in 1910.[115] As for Atlanta's whites,
they remained firmly in command. Two years after the riot, Hoke Smith's
campaign platform of black disfranchisement became institutionalized in
the 1908 state constitution.[116]

EAST ST. LOUIS—1917

By the 1910 census, East St. Louis, Illinois—just across the Mississippi River
from the fourth biggest city in the United States, St. Louis, Missouri—had a
population of 58,000; approximately 10 percent of the residents were black.
Five years later, the black community had grown to some 7,900 residents
or about 11 percent of the city's population.[117] By 1917, a year of severe
racial strife in East St. Louis, some estimates place the black population
at more than 10,600.[118] As part of the exodus from the South during the
Great Migration, African Americans flocked to the city in search of work.
Known as the "Pittsburgh of the West" and the "Hoboken of St. Louis," East
St. Louis by this time served as a bustling industrial center with a network
of 27 railroads crossing it. Inexpensive land and readily available coal drew
corporations to East St. Louis (at least to its outskirts where they did not
have to pay city taxes), and by 1917, thousands of laborers worked in the
stockyards, manufacturing companies, and packing plants.[119] This influx
of African Americans created tension in the city, particularly on housing
and labor issues, and a sensationalist press made a point of highlighting
any racial conflict. Political conditions also contributed to the volatile
situation.[120]

Moreover, a city nationally renowned for its history of vice, East St. Louis teemed with crime and corruption. Prostitutes and pimps—both predominantly white—freely advertised their trade in an area of the city called the Valley in clear sight of city hall. Although regularly arrested, they simply paid the appropriate official a bribe and went back to work.[121] Indeed, the police were widely considered to be above the law themselves. During the summer of 1916, for example, Frank Florence, the assistant chief of detectives, shot and killed a member of the police vice squad (who had his hands in the air) who had been intent upon closing down a gambling operation that Florence happened to own partially. Florence was acquitted of the murder even though a number of people witnessed the killing.[122] While whites (and some authorities at that) carried out much of the city's crime and vice, however, the *East St. Louis Daily Journal*—a mouthpiece for the Democratic Party—played up racial tensions and prominently featured black-on-white transgressions, real or imagined.[123]

Indeed, it was into this environment that black migrants arrived by the hundreds between 1915 and 1917, hearing about job opportunities from friends, relatives, newspaper advertisements, and even recruiters.[124] A series of strikes beginning in the summer of 1916 caused fiery interactions between labor and management in East St. Louis, and when companies brought in African Americans as strikebreakers, many whites became even more disgruntled. In July, for example, more than 4,000 laborers for the three largest meatpackers went on strike when some workers were fired for attempting to put together a union. The companies used hundreds of African Americans to fill in as strikebreakers, but soon welcomed back the previous workers (except the organizers), who had quickly deserted the idea of a union in favor of employment. Another strike followed in October 1916—this time 600 workers from the Aluminum Ore Company— and again black strikebreakers stepped in to work.[125] One of the company's assistant superintendents readily admitted the enmity this action created among whites in the city. "Labor unrest," he asserted, "engendered bitterness against the negroes who came in here."[126]

The scene in the city soon turned political, when also in the fall of 1916, Democrats used race as a wedge issue to win a nastily fought election, charging the city's Republicans of bringing in African Americans from the South ("colonizing" the city) to guarantee electoral success.[127] As the November 7 election drew closer, the *East St. Louis Daily Journal* ran numerous articles about black colonizers riding a crime wave.[128] Then three weeks before the election, rumors circulated throughout East St. Louis that Dr. Leroy Bundy, a prominent black dentist and civil rights leader, had plotted an Election Day scam that would shepherd numerous blacks between Chicago and East St. Louis to vote in both cities as well as in a third town in between. Another group would leave East St. Louis and head for Chicago to vote three times in that direction. Chicago officials arrested Bundy on charges that he had illicitly registered some 300 people on the west and south sides of the city, but he was let go due to inadequate proof. The *East St. Louis Daily Journal,* however, splashed Bundy's arrest all over its front page.[129] Democratic incumbent President Woodrow Wilson won St. Clair County and East St. Louis itself (the state of Illinois as a whole went Republican), and Democrats won local elections as well. The city's whites feared too much political power wielded by their black neighbors.[130]

Whites continued to fear African Americans in other ways as well. In the early months of 1917, the *East St. Louis Daily Journal* featured more alleged black-on-white crime. One mid-February headline trumpeted, "Negro Brute Seizes White Girl of 19," even though the woman was not injured and a suspect never located. Just a few days later, *The Birth of a Nation* played at the Majestic theater downtown to full audiences. The racist film no doubt played on the racial anxieties already palpable in the city. On April 3, 1917, incumbent East St. Louis mayor, Fred Mollman, won reelection handily after promising to clean up the city. He also assured black support by promising to hire black police officers and to erect a new fire house in one of the black neighborhoods, and drew white ire when he threw a postelection party for hundreds of his black supporters.[131] By this time, blacks had become a strong voting bloc in the city, encouraged by people such as black physician Dr. Lyman Bluitt to vote for candidates, not along party lines.[132] On April 17, workers at the Aluminum Ore Company decided to go on strike the next day. And even though mostly whites served as strikebreakers over the next week, union members focused their fury on the black workers who crossed the picket line. Relations between labor and management had deteriorated severely in the city, and workers in other industries contemplated going on strike as well.[133] East St. Louis appeared to be in a swirl of racial, political, and labor unrest. By May, the city had reached a breaking point.

On May 10, several union members met with Mayor Mollman to demand that he put a halt to the steady stream of incoming African Americans taking jobs and creating labor strife in East St. Louis. Unless he did so, they advised, an eruption in the city would cause the Springfield, Illinois, race riot nine years earlier to look like "a tame affair."[134] Two incidents in late May suggest the men—and other whites in the city—were serious. On May 23, union officials publicized another meeting with the mayor and other city leaders to be held the next week. They insisted that "drastic action must be taken if we intend to work and live peaceably in this community."[135] That evening, in what the newspapers described as a race riot, groups of white and black teenagers hurled rocks at each other. Police arrested some of the black youths, but none of the whites. A few hours later, a "mob of blacks" denounced the detainment of a black man who supposedly had spit on the sidewalk. One man was shot during the fracas. Three days later another skirmish broke out between the races. "Threatening negroes are reported to have congregated," the *Journal* asserted, "and made insulting remarks concerning the whites."[136]

The most serious clash that month, however, occurred on May 28, the day the city's labor interests scheduled their meeting with the mayor and city council. That afternoon, the *Daily Journal* led its first edition with "Police Watch Many Threatening Negroes" and detailed the activities of the police making the rounds through several black neighborhoods (where they apparently found numerous firearms).[137] By the time of the meeting that evening, hundreds of white union members (both men and women), sympathizers, and curious onlookers crammed into the city council chambers—so many, in fact, that the meeting had to be moved to a larger room. Although the gathering started calmly and the mayor assured the crowd that he had a grip on the influx of blacks, a white lawyer and former city treasurer (who had bilked the city during his tenure in office) addressed the audience and warned of colored people moving into white neighborhoods. He then insinuated that something could be done to stop them, and, he continued, "As far as I know, there is no law against mob violence."[138] Much of the crowd erupted in applause, and a number of them then stampeded out the door toward one of the main thoroughfares in the city.

Unfortunately, they met another throng of whites outside who had just heard the news that a black man had shot a white man during a robbery (the wound was slight, but as the news circulated, rumors flew that the white man had died). The police brought in a suspect to shouts of "Get a rope!" and "Lynch him!" from the gathering mob.[139] The mayor and other city officials—as well as some of the union leaders, who did not want organized labor linked to a race riot—tried to quell the tension. Just at that time, however, the police escorted another handcuffed black man into downtown. "That nigger shot somebody," a person yelled out, and the crowd sprang into action targeting any black person who had the misfortune of being in its path.[140] For several hours, whites attacked any black person in sight, wounding dozens of them. Mayor Mollman sent for the National Guard, and troops entered the city the next evening, which was fortunate since the rioters were back in action by that time.[141] Again the white mob targeted blacks in the city, setting fire to their neighborhoods and attacking them as they got off of work. Although it seemed clear that the city's whites intended to inflict pain and worse on their black neighbors, East St. Louis police appeared to be more concerned about blacks' possession of firearms as they continued to focus on disarming blacks rather than reining in whites.[142] Just before midnight on May 29, the National Guard had the city under control.

No one was killed during the two-day rampage. One of the city's white ministers suggested that the rioters had probably just planned to drive African Americans out of the city, not kill them.[143] And, indeed, perhaps some 6,000 blacks did leave to escape the violence, but only for a few days.[144] Most of the troops left the city in the next several weeks, however, and white-on-black attacks continued almost daily (just not on the same scale).[145] At the beginning of July, the city would erupt again; this time a full-fledged race riot would occur and people would die. Rumors had been circulating for weeks throughout both the black and white communities that each planned an attack on the other on July 4.[146] By the evening of July 1, several accounts of white-on-black attacks spread through the city's African American community. Then, between 10:30 P.M. and midnight, whites driving a Ford shot into black homes along Market Street. During the car's second pass through, black inhabitants shot back and hit the car, which quickly left the scene. The police did not pursue the whites but decided to look into accounts of blacks shooting at whites. A Ford squad car full of police and a *St. Louis Republic* reporter quickly headed to the black neighborhood.[147]

The reporter's article the next morning stated that as they went out, "more than 200 rioting negroes . . . without a word of warning opened fire."[148] One detective died immediately and another died later from his wounds. Another policeman had been shot in the arm.[149] Although the reporter later told a congressional committee investigating the riot that the assailants might have confused the patrol car for the earlier white attackers, he failed to mention this fact in his news story.[150] Indeed, much of his account contained inaccuracies (it also made no reference to the white attacks). Mayor Mollman soon got on the line to Springfield requesting national guardsmen back to the city. But, of course, it would take time for them to arrive. Very early on the morning of July 2, residents woke up to front-page headlines, "Policeman Killed, 5 Shot in E. St. Louis Riot; Negroes, Called Out by Ringing of Church Bell, Fire When Police Appear."[151] That day, the city white residents could plainly see near the police station a squad car with blood stains on its seats and looking "like a flour sieve, all punctured full of holes."[152] This evidence confirmed to many whites that blacks stood ready to attack.

After a hastily called meeting downtown, white mobs fanned out, and the first black victim was shot in plain view near one of the busiest streetcar stops in the city just before 10:00 A.M.[153] For well over the next 12 hours, white residents of East St. Louis sought out and tormented, tortured, and killed any black person they could find. Press reports the next day and eyewitness accounts told of unimaginable scenes of carnage carried out by white men, women, and even children. Those rare whites who did condemn the violence ran the threat of becoming targets of violence themselves.[154] Descriptions of lynchings or attempting lynchings, attacks on black children, and base brutality spoke to the depths to which the rioters would sink.[155] Many blacks had to make agonizing choices during the reign of terror. If they tried to escape from their houses that a white throng had set on fire, they faced a hail of bullets as the fled.[156] In one of the most graphic and disturbing accounts of a lynching, *St. Louis Post-Dispatch* reporter Carlos Hurd wrote,

> I saw the most sickening incident of the evening when they got stronger rope. To put the rope around the negro's neck, one of the lynchers stuck his fingers inside the gaping scalp and lifted the negro's head by it, literally bathing his hand in the man's blood. "Get hold, and pull for East St. Louis," called the man as he seized the other end of the rope. The negro was lifted to a height of about seven feet and the body left hanging there for hours.[157]

Onlookers described the white rioters that day as "in good humor" and possessing "a visible coolness," and "not the hectic and raving demonstration of men suddenly gone mad."[158]

Adding to the death toll, police and national guardsmen did little to stem the attacks, and some even joined in with the rioters. Moreover, the man sent to command the guardsmen in East St. Louis, Colonel Stephen Orville Tripp, proved to be a "hopeless incompetent."[159] Had stronger leadership and less complicit authorities stepped in, the East St. Louis riot would neither have lasted as long nor been as severe as it was. Indeed, when Adjutant General Frank S. Dickson, commander of the Illinois National Guard, did arrive in East St. Louis just past midnight on July 3, he quickly took command of the city and ended the riot.[160] By then, however, more than 200 black-owned homes and other buildings had gone up in flames, and most of the black vice district—called the Black Valley—was destroyed. Although some blacks no doubt fought back during the hours of violence, many had been unarmed by the police during the previous weeks leading up to the riot.[161] During the chaos, thousands of the city's African Americans fled to St. Louis across the Free Bridge, many of them never returning.[162] According to official reports, 39 blacks and 9 whites died; unofficial reports, however, put the death toll and injuries of blacks well into the hundreds.[163]

In the days following the riot, the city's whites exhibited little regret. Many toured downtown, which buzzed with a mardi-gras environment, showing off mementos that they had gathered during the unrest (mainly pieces of clothing from dead bodies).[164] They also blamed their black neighbors for the July 2 disturbance. One New York columnist quoted some city elites as saying, "Well, you see too many niggers have been coming in here. When niggers come up North, they get insolent. You see they vote here and one doesn't like that. And one doesn't like their riding in street cars next to white women—and, well what are you going to do when a buck nigger pushes you off the sidewalk?"[165] The national press gave wide coverage to the events in East St. Louis. Northern newspapers primarily denounced what had happened, and editors in Chicago, Boston, and St. Louis gave partial blame to national and local politics, and particularly to the deterioration of race relations since Southern Democrats took over the nation's capital.[166] Southern outlets pointed to the hypocrisy of a supposedly more tolerant northern state engaging in violence. "Never again can one section of the country," the Augusta, Georgia, *Chronicle* averred, "select and set apart any other section as barbarians to a greater extent than other places."[167]

Black and white national leaders also stepped into the fray of the East St. Louis riot. Ida Wells-Barnett arrived in East St. Louis on July 5 to see the destruction firsthand. "Every which way we turned," she asserted, "there were women and children and men, dazed over the thing that had come to them and unable to tell what it was all about."[168] W.E.B. Du Bois visited the city shortly after the riot as well. At first he met with Mayor Mollman and other city leaders, but soon turned to regular citizens when officials blamed the black community for the outburst of violence. In a September issue of the *Crisis,* Du Bois lay most of the onus on the labor unions, business interests, and city politicians. He also detailed in vivid descriptions the horrors that black East St. Louisans endured.[169] Other national leaders debated the causes of the riot as well. Former president Theodore Roosevelt and American Federation of Labor leader Samuel Gompers had a heated exchange at a Carnegie Hall forum on July 6. Roosevelt suggested that the "appalling outbreak of savagery" came with "no real provocation." Gompers, on the other hand, blamed companies and their "luring of these colored men to East St. Louis."[170]

Wells and other black leaders urged President Woodrow Wilson to take federal action in the riot's aftermath. On July 28, leaders of the NAACP organized a "Silent Parade" down Fifth Avenue in New York City. Thousands of blacks congregated to march against the violence being inflicted upon them in the form of the East St. Louis riot and recent lynchings in Waco, Texas, and Memphis, Tennessee.[171] Although Wilson refused to take action, Congress—led by Missouri representative L. C. Dyer—formed the Committee to Investigate Conditions in Illinois and Missouri Interfering with Interstate Commerce between Said States, also called the Special Committee Authorized by Congress to Investigate the East St. Louis race

Silent protest parade in New York City against the East St. Louis riots, 1917. (Library of Congress)

riots.[172] In its final report, the committee placed the blame for the riot predominantly on the city's white politicians, police, and entrepreneurs, as well as East St. Louis's delinquents—both white and black.[173] A grand jury eventually handed down indictments to 134 people, about one-third of them black. Most of the whites paid a small fine or spent a few days in jail. Six substantial trials stemmed from the riot—four involving whites and two blacks. Nine whites and twelve blacks served time in prison.[174] Unfortunately, the East St. Louis riot served as a harbinger for more racial violence soon to come.

TULSA—1921

At the turn of the century, Tulsa enjoyed the distinction of being "a boom city in a boom state."[175] The population swelled from almost 1,400 in 1900 to a little more than 72,000 after 20 years.[176] Oil discoveries around Tulsa assured its financial success in these halcyon years, and locals deemed it the "Magic City."[177] Blacks had long inhabited the area—brought in as slaves by Native Americans—and proceeded to participate in Tulsa's political and economic scene following emancipation, but only to a limited degree. While white Tulsans allowed blacks to work in the labor, domestic, and service sectors, they excluded them from frequenting white businesses south of the railroad tracks and other portions of the city. As a result, African Americans built up their own community north of the city, the heart of which centered on Greenwood Avenue and Archer Street. Known widely as the Negro Wall Street, the Greenwood District witnessed great economic strides during these years. As Tulsa grew, so did Greenwood, which had a population of almost 11,000 by 1921. Two schools, a hospital, two theaters, a public library, two newspapers, and 13 churches also shaped its landscape.[178]

While structural changes in the form of a booming economy and a growing population characterized Tulsa during the early 20th century, ideological currents swirled around as well. Like many of their counterparts, black Tulsans went overseas to fight for their country in World War I. Upon their return to the states and at the urgings of African American leaders such as W.E.B. Du Bois and Marcus Garvey to "adopt every means to protect [themselves] against barbarous practices inflicted upon [them] because of [their] color," African Americans gained a new sense of purpose and worth. In the political realm, however, the war discredited two organizations that espoused black rights and included African Americans among their ranks, the Oklahoma Socialist Party and the Industrial Workers of the World (IWW), thereby debilitated important sources of support. Moreover, the Ku Klux Klan had reemerged in 1915 as a source of terror and violence, and Tulsa had a thriving chapter by the time of the riot six years later.[179] Racist ideology permeated Tulsa's popular culture as well. "Tulsa," the Tulsa *Democrat* proclaimed as early as 1912, "appears now to be in danger of losing its prestige as the whitest town in Oklahoma." Similarly, words such as "Little Africa" and "Niggertown" sprinkled the newspaper's pages when it referred to the Greenwood District.[180] Often, as in the case of the Tulsa race riot itself, these words led to action.

Two events in Tulsa—in 1917 and 1919—indicated that mob rule existed there. The first incident occurred on October 29, 1917, when a bomb exploded in the home of an affluent oil man in Tulsa, J. Edgar Pew. The Tulsa *World* declared the bombing an IWW plot, whose "danger cannot be exaggerated."[181] In addition to its stance on black rights, the IWW had been affiliated with the Oil Field Workers' Union in organizing close to 300 oil workers in the Tulsa area—two marks against it in such a racist and oil rich environment. Police raided the IWW headquarters and arrested everyone present. Although they had the semblance of a trial, the judge ordered these 12 individuals, plus the 5 witnesses who supported them in court, carted off to jail. However, between 40 and 50 armed men in black robes and masks met the group in transit, tied their hands and feet, and instructed the police to take them to a remote ravine west of the city. The mob stripped each man to the waist, secured them to a tree, and whipped them. They then poured hot tar and feathers on their open wounds, and ran them out of town. Signs soon appeared around town stating, "Notice to the IWW's. Don't let the sun set on you in Tulsa.—Vigilance Committee."[182] Authorities punished no one for these actions.

The second occurrence happened on March 17, 1919, when two armed men attempted to rob a white ironworker. They ordered him to raise his hands and then shot him when he refused to do so. Before he died, the man told officials that his assailants were black and gave a vague description of them. Soon thereafter, authorities arrested three black men, and rumors began to circulate in Greenwood that lynchings were imminent. A group of 15 armed blacks drove to the Tulsa jail to ensure the safety of the defendants, and eventually around 200 blacks congregated outside the jail. The police allowed the group's spokesman to go inside and "see for himself that none of their race had suffered anything."[183] The crowd then dispersed. Several days later, after a meeting in Greenwood to talk about the recent events, three black policemen were shot at by two whites. The officers returned fire, wounding and capturing the gunmen. No lynchings followed this incident, but the potential for mob rule remained evident.

These two events, along with the influx of people and economic prosperity in Tulsa, the heightened assertions of the African American community of their rights, and the racist tenets that characterized the region, led directly into the race riot that Tulsa endured in 1921. Moreover, Tulsa carried the reputation of a corrupt and lawless city. Gambling, prostitution, bootlegging, robbery, and narcotics became commonplace.[184] The rule of law held no special value there. Therefore, structural change and ideology both played a critical role in the realization of this mob violence.

The precipitating event follows a familiar pattern. Dick Rowland, a 19-year-old African American, worked in downtown Tulsa at a white shoe-shining parlor. Although he earned only five dollars a week, the job paid fairly well. One of Rowland's coworkers declared,

> [T]he tips were just out of sight. At that time, you see, Tulsa was in the oil boom, and everybody would go to bed poor as Lazarus, and wake up rich as country butter. They didn't know what to do with their money, and they'd come down there and get a shine, and they'd give you a dollar as [soon as they'd give you] fifteen cents.[185]

Since the black employees could not use the white restrooms, the store owner arranged for them to go the top floor of the nearby Drexel building

to do so. On the morning of May 30, 1921, Rowland stepped into the elevator, operated by a young white woman named Sarah Page, in order to go to
the top of the building.

Several versions exist as to what transpired, but white Tulsans immediately believed that Rowland had assaulted the young woman, scratched her
hands, and torn her clothes. What probably happened was that Rowland
stepped on Page's foot, and when he tried to grab her to break her fall, she
screamed, and he ran out of the elevator. The initial police report did not
identify Page by name, and officials did not detain Rowland until the next
day. While the police attempted to piece together the story, however, the
Tulsa Tribune ran with its own on the afternoon of May 31. Unfortunately,
all existing copies of the newspaper that day have been lost or partially
destroyed.[186] Later accounts quoted the paper's headline as "Nab Negro for
Attacking Girl in Elevator," with a story following that detailed an attack by
Diamond Dick on Page.[187] Another resident remembered an article titled
"To Lynch Negro Tonight." While still another averred,

> The Daily Tribune, a White newspaper that tries to gain its popularity by re-
> ferring to the Negro settlement as "Little Africa," came out on the evening of
> Tuesday, May 31, with an article claiming that a Negro had had some trouble
> with a White elevator girl at the Drexel Bldg. It also said that a mob of whites
> were forming in order to lynch the Negro.[188]

Adjutant General Charles Barrett, who commanded the National Guard
in Tulsa shortly after the riot broke out, attributed the violence to "the
fantastic write-up of the incident in a sensation-seeking newspaper."[189]
Clearly, the newspaper, in the already tense environment of early 20th-
century Oklahoma, played a large role in precipitating the mob action that
followed.

Shortly after the Tribune appeared, a man notified the police that there
was talk of a lynching in Tulsa. Between 6:00 and 7:00 in the evening, a
crowd of whites began to assemble in front of the courthouse, where officials had Rowland incarcerated. Some accounts held that the mob grew
to 400 people by 9:00 that night. Sheriff Willard McCullough ordered everyone to go home and declared to three white men who walked into the
courthouse around 8:20 P.M. that a lynching would not be occurring. The
crowd remained, and McCullough dispatched his own guards to Rowland's
jail cell to protect him. By this time, tensions had heightened considerably.

News of the developments around the courthouse spread quickly
throughout Greenwood, and groups of African Americans met to weigh
their options. Around 9:15 P.M., inaccurate announcements reached northern Tulsa that the white mob had stormed the courthouse. A few minutes

later, 25 to 30 black men, many of them World War I veterans, carrying rifles and shotguns arrived there to assist Sheriff McCullough in securing Rowland's safety. Convinced that the sheriff and his men maintained control, they left shortly thereafter. However, fueled by accounts that a mob of whites attempted to break into the Tulsa armory for guns and ammunition, and new reports that the crowd in front of the courthouse had grown to almost 2,000, between 50 and 75 armed blacks returned to this site around 10:30 P.M. Again persuaded to leave, they were on their way out when a white man approached one of the African Americans according to one version. "Nigger," he sputtered, "what are you doing with that pistol?" "I'm going to use it if I need to," the black man answered. "No," the white man declared, "you give it to me." "Like hell I will," came the response.[190] A scuffle ensued, and a shot rang out. At this juncture, according to Sheriff McCullough, "all hell broke loose."[191]

Initial casualties numbered 12 in the immediate wake of the scuffle between the two men. One wounded black man "lay writhing on the sidewalk," surrounded by a white crowd that prevented white doctors from assisting him until they ascertained that he had died.[192] Greatly outnumbered by whites, the denizens of Greenwood fled back to their neighborhood. About 500 white volunteers received special commissions to help the Tulsa police. One light-complexioned African American, however, was deputized mistakenly. He later recalled that one of his newly minted cohorts suggested that "now you can go out and shoot any nigger you see and the law'll be behind you."[193] He also learned that they intended to invade the Greenwood District from the west. Clearly, these men offered dubious support. After contacting Tulsa Police Chief John Gustafson, Major James Bell of the Tulsa National Guard, and Governor James Robertson, Adjutant General Barrett mobilized the Tulsa National Guard to offer any assistance necessary to the civil authorities. Sensing that this action fell short, Governor Robertson ordered that the National Guard be sent into the city—an action allowed by state law only after the securement of the signatures of the local police chief, the county sheriff, and a local judge.[194] By 3:00 A.M., this task had finally been completed.

After the black citizens had retreated from the courthouse, the members of the white mob spent the next few hours arming themselves. Store owners later reported more than $42,000 worth of merchandise—much of it guns and ammunition—stolen that night. The white mob arrived at the outskirts of Greenwood around 1:00 A.M. and summarily set the area on fire. Although firefighters approached, more than 500 whites prevented them from doing their job. The African Americans hunkered down to defend their property. They, along with some of the white police force, managed to hold back the white crowd for several hours. Around 6:00 A.M., however, the mob broke through the barrier and charged into the center of Greenwood. Looting, burning, and violence occurred with abandon, as blacks were overwhelmed by the white Tulsans. Moreover, the police focused on interning African Americans primarily, greatly assisting the whites in the quest to destroy the black section of town.

The National Guard finally arrived from Oklahoma City at 9:15 A.M., only to set up camp and eat breakfast. Upon gauging the damage and disorder, Adjutant General Barrett requested permission from Governor Robertson to declare martial law. He did so at 11:29 A.M. and then had announcements posted throughout Tulsa. The guard focused first on the fires and then on imprisoning any remaining black citizens. Whites generally only had to give up their arms and were then sent home. Less than 24 hours after it had begun, the Tulsa race riot had ended. Martial law was terminated on June 3. More than 6,000 African Americans suffered incarceration throughout the night of the riot. Even after their release they had to wear green tags until July 7, identifying their name and employer.[195] Many other black Tulsans left the city during the riot, and some of these did not return. Death estimates range from 27 to more than 250. Red Cross records indicate that they treated 183 blacks within 24 hours of the riot. Overall, they aided 531 individuals and performed 163 operations. The cost of property loss was conservatively estimated at $1.5 million.[196]

In the weeks and months following the riot, Tulsa's city officials formed an Executive Welfare Committee and, following this organization, a Reconstruction Committee. Members, comprised largely of white Chamber of Commerce officials and other civic leaders, purported,

> Tulsa can only redeem herself from the countrywide shame and humiliation in which she is today plunged by complete restitution of the destroyed black belt. The rest of the United States must know that the real citizenship of Tulsa weeps at this unspeakable crime and will make good the damage, so far as can be done, to the last penny.[197]

Of course, these platitudes to the national press fell flat in actual practice, even to the degree of denying any outside aid since it "was strictly a Tulsa affair."[198] Veils of token support to the black community seemed to be Tulsa's official course of action, as the whites really aimed at usurping the land and rebuilding for themselves. However, black Tulsans stood resolute in protecting their property. What aid they did receive came from the NAACP and the Red Cross. In the end, they primarily rebuilt Greenwood by themselves.

Governor Robertson ordered a grand jury investigation of the whole affair on June 2. Not surprisingly, their final report on June 25 declared,

Tulsa race riot of 1921. (Tulsa Race Riot of 1921 archive, Coll. No. 1989.004. Department of Special Collections and University Archives, McFarlin Library, University of Tulsa, Tulsa, Oklahoma.)

We find that the recent race riot was the direct result of an effort on the part of a certain group of colored men who appeared at the courthouse on the night of May 31, 1921, for the purpose of protecting one Dick Rowland. . . . We have not been able to find any evidence either from white or colored citizens that any organized attempt was made or planned to take from the sheriff's custody any prisoner; the crowd assembled about the courthouse being purely spectators and curiosity seekers resulting from rumors circulated about the city. There was no mob spirit among the whites, no talk of lynching and no arms. The assembly was quiet until the arrival of the armed negroes, which precipitated and was the direct cause of the entire affair.[199]

They went on to assert that the black citizens of Tulsa also caused trouble by believing in "equal rights [and] social equality."[200] No white Tulsans were ever sent to prison for the murders, destruction, and looting that took place in the early hours of June 1, 1921. Ironically, Sarah Page would not prosecute Dick Rowland; he received full exoneration.[201]

BEAUMONT—1943

Texas cities, and especially the port city of Beaumont, saw a large influx of blacks and rural whites during World War II. East of Houston near the Gulf of Mexico, Beaumont became heavily populated as workers moved there to support the war effort through shipbuilding, as well as petroleum and chemical production. The city's inhabitants expanded from 59,000 in 1940 to almost 80,000 by 1943.[202] The black population had remained stagnant between 1930 and 1940 at around 18,000. But during the war, it grew to roughly 27,000.[203] Overcrowding created serious tensions in city services, such as housing, health care, and transportation. Housing remained so scarce that workers often slept in cars or rented hot beds, used by two or three people in shifts.[204]

The transportation system especially led to racial conflict. Automobiles remained in short supply, so both white and black workers had to depend on the overcrowded bus system. Bus drivers strictly enforced the Jim Crow line in the busses, with African Americans relegated to the back. However, when the busses overflowed, drivers forced blacks to give up their seats altogether to whites. Several episodes in early 1943 served to foretell the impending riot. A series of violent bus incidents in January between whites and blacks led city officials to set up completely separate busses for blacks and whites.[205] And a push for a recall election of the mayor, the acting mayor, and five other city officials, although not centered on racial concerns but instead Beaumont's proclivity for vice, added to the tension in the city.[206]

Hostility also permeated the Pennsylvania Shipyards, Beaumont's largest defense contractor, after large numbers of black workers arrived, creating competition for the bitter and often rural white workforce. President Franklin Roosevelt's Executive Order 8802 in June 1941 had helped a number of African Americans gain jobs in the defense industries.[207] And with the establishment of the Fair Employment Practices Committee, although small and with little enforcement abilities, some improvement in the hiring of African Americans did take place.[208] Preparations for two upcoming meetings stirred hostilities between the races as well. The local chapter of the Ku Klux Klan arranged for a regional convention to take place in Beaumont at the end of June.[209] And the African American community organized their annual Juneteenth commemoration of emancipation for June 19, when hundreds of area blacks planned to visit the city. Rumors of a Juneteenth armed black revolt began to circulate among Beaumont's whites.[210]

Relations turned particularly dismal on June 5, after information surfaced that a black man purportedly raped, beat, and stabbed an 18-year-old telephone operator, whose father worked at the already tense Pennsylvania Shipyards. The woman escaped, and the police promptly shot and apprehended a 24-year-old black defense worker and ex-convict at the scene of the crime. As the alleged assailant lay dying in the hospital, both of Beaumont's newspapers circulated stories of the incident. A group of around

150 men gathered outside the hospital with the intention of lynching the man. Without any discernable leader, however, they simply hovered. They later dispersed after being persuaded by the police chief who had rushed to the scene that he would soon die of his wounds anyway. Nevertheless, the police feared that another incident would provoke violence.[211]

Another rape accusation less than two weeks later amplified rampant rumors of black aggression and quickly incited the race riot. In the early afternoon of June 15, a young woman, the wife of a shipyard worker, reported to the police that a black man invaded her home and raped her as her three children lay sleeping nearby. News of the alleged rape spread swiftly, especially among workers at the Pennsylvania Shipyards. That evening around 2,000 workers left the shipyards for the downtown jail, where they assumed the police held a suspect. Another 1,000 joined the mob, and they demanded that the suspect be given to them. The police, and even the alleged victim, convinced them they had no suspect incarcerated. But the crowd remained agitated and turned toward Beaumont's two black districts. "Let's go to nigger town," someone in the crowd yelled.[212]

Fifteen hours of brutality followed. Whites wielding guns and other weapons burned and looted black-owned structures and attacked any African American they encountered. One assault occurred at the bus station, where 52 black war draftees sat waiting to return home. "[H]ere they are," someone in the white mob yelled, "a whole bunch of them. Let's get them."[213] Two blacks and one white died as a result of the riot, and at least some 50 people suffered injuries. Although the local police appeared to try to contain the violence, their numbers simply proved too few. Only 50 full-time, 150 auxiliary officers, and a few sheriff's deputies stood in the way of the mob.

A Texas State Guard battalion and other law officials rushed to Beaumont on June 16, and the acting Texas governor declared the city under martial law for four days, sealing it off and setting a curfew. The Texas Rangers ended the riot when they fired tear gas at some 200 shipyard workers headed toward the burning black section of Beaumont on the morning of July 16. The police never found evidence of sexual assault, and the woman left quietly after the riot. Some 2,000 black residents fled Beaumont as well. Although the police arrested more than 200 riot participants, most went free due to insufficient evidence.[214]

The racial pogroms that erupted throughout the country between the Progressive Era and World War II share many important features. Structural conditions, such as black migration to southern and northern cities, political coalitions, Jim Crow measures, and ineffective authorities provided the backdrop against which whites and blacks interacted with each other.

Cultural concerns also came into play. Radicalism permeated white society, with its strident calls for black exclusion and worse. The ideas of white supremacy and the virtuous white woman connected whites in a way that made it critical to hold blacks down. These fire tenders stoked the racial flames. At the same time, African Americans carved out a world of their own. Through organizations, newspapers, and literature, they provided a voice to assert their own rights and to counter the ideals of white society.

Other similarities emerged in these riots as well. The precipitating events centered on something held up as sacred to white America. Alleged or actual African American attacks on white women and authorities signified to whites that they must act. And conversion specialists, such as the Secret Nine in Wilmington, made certain this action would happen. Rumors of supposed African American aggression spread rapidly among the white communities, with white newspapers ensuring that these reports became widespread. Moreover, while blacks fought back against the white aggression in all of these cases, their efforts proved mostly futile. In some instances, whites had actually even confiscated their guns beforehand, and the weapons that blacks had hidden away often proved substandard. Indeed, at the end of these riots, whites remained firmly in control. Afterward, as Brass suggests, the white press and politicians provided the official version of events that placed the culpability directly on blacks. They diffused the blame away from whites so that none or very few of them ever received punishment.

Chapter 4

THE RED SUMMER OF 1919

The Red Summer of 1919 proved brutal to African Americans. Throughout the year, white mobs lynched 78 blacks, 10 of whom had served in the military and 11 of whom were burned alive.[1] Between the tumultuous months of April and October 1919, at least 26 race riots erupted throughout the United States.[2] In response, James Weldon Johnson, the African American literary and political leader, deemed this period the Red Summer, for the racial tension that permeated the land and for the blood that flowed in the streets as a result.[3] As historian Herbert Shapiro explains,

> [W]ithin a span of weeks racial violence spread from one city to another, and every city feared its turn was next. It was clear that these confrontations could not be explained as simply a local phenomenon. As Americans learned the news of racial outbreaks in such diverse cities as Omaha, Washington, Knoxville, and Chicago, it was apparent that these explosions expressed tensions afflicting the national society.[4]

With structural factors of great demographic shifts and labor strife, and cultural conditions fostered by World War I contributing to racial strains in these cities, a precipitating event—in these cases, alleged or actual instances of murder or rape, or a supposed infraction against racial separation—caused white residents to seek out their African American neighbors deliberately with the intention of killing them and destroying their property. After discussing these three aspects leading up to the Red Summer of 1919, I provide six case studies in the next chapter—six of the seven major race riots that year.

STRUCTURAL FACTORS

Beginning in the 1890s, American blacks left the South for the hope of better opportunities in the North and West. This Great Migration saw an outflux of 500,000 African American southerners between 1916 and 1919, and close to one million more the following decade.[5] World War I especially prompted this exodus to the North, as blacks found that more jobs—and therefore more money—existed there as foreign immigration dwindled and the military draft created even more labor shortages.[6] Although the Depression muted the movement out of the South for a while, World War II spurred its momentum once again.[7]

These black migrants found employment and dwellings for themselves, and soon for their family and friends to join them, especially as a wave of infestations and floods destroyed the South's cotton crops. After these calamities, southern planters focused on livestock and food crops, neither of which demanded as many laborers. Therefore, the need in the South for tenant and day workers declined at the same time the North required more unskilled laborers. Adding to this demographic shift, meanwhile, the *Chicago Defender* and other black newspapers urged black southerners to flee the South for the promised land of the North.[8] Furthermore, overt violence and disdain by white southerners caused their black neighbors to try their luck elsewhere. Decades of brutal lynchings likely made them believe they had nothing left to lose.[9] This influx of people in northern cities often resulted in strains on housing and food, contributing to already tense racial relations. Moreover, northern whites accepted the image of blacks concocted by white southerners around the turn of the century. "When blacks appeared in their midst," writes historian Joel Williamson, "especially in large numbers, their response was not vastly different from that of southern whites. In the North, as in the South, white women locked their car doors when they drove through black communities and closed and locked the doors of their houses when they saw a black man walking down the street. Black people, the myth ran, were supersexual creatures, uninhibited and possessed by large, almost insatiable appetites."[10]

This arrival of blacks in the North, and the resulting friction, during the first few decades of the 20th century seems to confirm many of the social science theories regarding racial balance. The power-threat hypothesis, for instance, posits that intolerance in whites proves more prevalent where the nonwhite population size poses a threat to the white social, political, and economic population.[11] This theory coincides with studies done on the social distance whites desire between racial minorities and themselves. Lawrence Bobo and his colleagues conclude that since whites want to secure their own group interests, they disdain significant numbers of minorities moving into their neighborhoods, or at least prefer to maintain racial pre-dominance within their neighborhood.[12] In a more recent study, Green, Strolovitch, and Wong find that "racially motivated crime appears to coin-cide with patterns of demographic change, rising where non-whites move into white strongholds."[13]

As blacks moved into northern cities from the 1890s through World War I, they found a society in transition. Whites who had not made ra-cial segregation a major issue became increasingly averse to having blacks in their neighborhoods. In 1910, for example, less than a third of African Americans lived in predominately black neighborhoods in the North; in 1920, over half lived in black neighborhoods.[14] Many factors contributed to this segregation. The loss of federal protection after Reconstruction, the Republican Party's move to become lily white, and Supreme Court deci-sions such as *Plessy v. Ferguson* (1896) affected northern actions as well as southern.[15] Before the Great Migration, "not a single hotel in Boston dared to refuse colored guests," W.E.B. Du Bois observed in 1934, but "few Bos-ton hotels [now exist] where colored people are received." Du Bois made similar comments about most northern cities, with the exception of New York, "where a Negro can be a guest at a first-class hotel."[16] Moreover, rac-ist anthropological studies, social Darwinism, and the Spanish-American War brought both sectional reconciliation and white agreement on white supremacy. Indeed, the *New York Commercial* stated in 1906 that "North-ern sentiment on the race question is not at bottom a million miles away from Southern sentiment."[17]

Black migration combined with white hostility led to residential seg-regation in the North, especially in midwestern cities such as Chicago, Cleveland, and Detroit. Not surprisingly, this segregation took place as African Americans gained numbers and more political power.[18] Although most northern cities did not adopt de jure segregation, white-dominated market structures and racism allowed residential segregation to flourish in them.[19] Real estate agents and their associations, bankers, white property owners, suburban developers, and city governments pushed for residential separation of the races.[20] The Hyde Park Protective Club, a neighborhood association in Chicago, for example, boycotted any real estate firms that al-lowed blacks to buy or even show blacks property in white neighborhoods. Real estate agents systematically directed blacks away from white enclaves and into the growing black ghetto that had astronomical rents and few services. Newspapers advertised for colored ads in the real estate section of the paper.[21]

The most effective way that whites found to consolidate residential seg-regation, however, became the neighborhood covenant. Neighborhood associations required home owners to sign covenants that prohibited the sale of their property to blacks. "Those who had no black neighbors," writes historian Kevin Boyle, "organized to keep their areas lily-white. They formed legal organizations—protective associations, they called them—to write clauses into their deeds prohibiting the sale of their homes to blacks. They monitored real estate sales to make sure no one broke the color line. And if a black family somehow managed to breech the defenses, they could always drive them out, quietly if possible, violently if necessary."[22]

Indeed, vigilante violence and intimidation always remained an option for whites to keep out blacks. Between 1917 and 1921 in Chicago, for example, some 58 white terrorist bombings occurred against black residents in white neighborhoods.[23] One of the most famous incidents occurred in Detroit in 1925.[24] Authorities charged Dr. Ossian Sweet with murder after he defended his house from a white mob. The Detroit Ku Klux Klan played an important role in fomenting the horde. The National Association for the Advancement of Colored People (NAACP) saw this case as an important challenge to northern segregation, and Dr. Sweet was eventually found not guilty.[25] Unfortunately, those blacks "who followed the North Star looking for the Promised Land," avers historian Harvard Sitkoff, "found hell instead: educational and residential segregation, dilapidated housing milked by white slum lords, discrimination by labor unions and employers, [and] brutality by white policemen."[26]

Economic conditions played a large role in racial violence leading up to and during the Red Summer as well. "Lynchings were more frequent," Tolnay and Beck stress, "in years when the 'constant dollar' price of cotton was declining and inflationary pressure was increasing." Moreover, they discover that "relative size of the black population was also positively related to lynching."[27] These findings confirm earlier work done by Hovland and Sears, who link racial violence to the economy. Their frustration-aggression model reveals that "the economic conditions of an area are intimately related to the amount of mass aggression displayed in that area as measured by lynchings."[28] In other words, as the economy worsens, racial violence increases. More recent scholarship parallels this relationship. Jacobs and Wood assert that data from the 1980s show that cities with more economic competition between the races have a higher percentage of whites killing blacks and blacks killing whites.[29]

Economic fluctuation, at both the local and national level in the early 20th century, commonly left workers unemployed for weeks or months at a time.[30] When jobs became scarce, whites resented competition from black workers. Out of this resentment emerged widespread discrimination against blacks in the workforce, especially against skilled black workers. From 1870 to 1910, for example, the percentage of black skilled workers in Cleveland fell from 32 percent to 11 percent.[31] The labor strife of the late 19th century carried forward well into the 20th as workers tried to organize and businesses resisted, often with violence. Adding fuel to the fire of racial resentment, businesses often used blacks as strikebreakers and sometimes even kept them on after the strike ended.[32] Susan Olzak explores this labor unrest and violence against African Americans in her scholarship. She traces these factors primarily to foreign immigration and black migration, which created competition in labor markets (leading to conflict), and an increase in national labor unions (whose leaders found ways to thwart black workers).[33] Indeed, most unions shunned African Americans or even lashed out violently against them.[34]

When whites went on strike at a southern Illinois coal mine in Carterville in May 1899, the company brought in blacks from Chicago as strikebreakers. The response proved explosive. W. W. Duncan, a leading citizen in nearby Marion, Illinois, begged the governor by telegraph to send in troops before a catastrophe occurred:

> There are 500 or more union and non-union men at war in Carterville. Both sides are determined to fight it out. A Sheriff and posse can do nothing with the situation until the factions are disarmed by the state. The Sheriff's presence only increases the danger. My judgment is that many lives and the Brush mines will be destroyed without state aid to disarm both factions. Firing from ambush with Winchesters still continues. More union men are gathering, and while quiet now reigns the situation is ominous. I advise troops at once.[35]

The governor refused to intervene. Six days later a riot broke out. As 15 black workers made their way to the mine, a white mob met them at the train station, and a white man screamed, "Come out, you damned black scab son-of-bitches; we've got you—come out and take your medicine." The white mob opened fire, and when the shooting stopped, five blacks lay dead. Two more riots erupted over the next few days.[36]

Another 1913 incident in New York's garment district also exemplifies the violence stemming from union organization and businesses' use of strikebreakers:

> More than 100 negro women were at work in the white goods factory of Mitchell Brothers on the ninth floor of 543 Broadway yesterday when three men entered, drew revolvers, and fired at the ceiling. . . . The members of the firm said that the garment workers' union was responsible for the outrage. When their operators walked out in a recent strike they employed negro women as strikebreakers, and, when the strike ended, retained them.[37]

Indeed, blacks suffered the brunt of the violence, particularly as they supplied the main source of new labor during World War I.[38] During the war, when jobs were plentiful, racial hostility still brewed. Many whites did not want to work next to blacks on the shop room floor. At an integrated Chicago ordnance plant, white workers put a sign on the lavatory: "Niggers not allowed to use this toilet."[39] The 1917 race riot in East St. Louis also erupted, in part, from this labor unrest. Following the riot, Samuel Gompers, founder and president of the American Federation of Labor, wrote down what many white East St. Louisans expressed in the weeks leading up to the violence:

> [T]he packing plants and stockyards of Armour, Swift, and Morris, the Aluminum Ore Company, the American Steel Foundry, the Commercial Acid Company and twenty-seven railroad lines . . . employed many foreigners until workers were called home to their colors. They began the policy of negro importation from the south. Negro importation became a regular business—agents were sent throughout the south who collected groups of negroes and paid the railroad fair to East St. Louis. . . . As a result, East St. Louis became a sort of convention center for excited, undisciplined negroes who were intoxicated by higher wages than they had ever known. Some of these as in the case of the Aluminum Ore Company, were used as strike breakers, and the element of racial industrial competition was added to other trouble-breeding influences.[40]

Companies in other cities frequently used black strikebreakers as well. New York, Cleveland, Detroit, Milwaukee, and Chicago, for example, saw this method employed during labor disputes, thereby creating more racial friction.[41] Labor organizations, such as the Knights of Labor and the American Federation of Labor, became so distressed with black strikebreakers, they often devoted their annual convention to this concern.[42] Not until the passage of New Deal legislation, the National Industrial Recovery Act, did it become illegal to use blacks as strikebreakers, eventually creating a coalition between black and white workers.[43]

Ineffective or complicit authorities also allowed race riots to occur. In many riots during the first half of the 20th century, local or state officials had to call in the state militia or National Guard to quell the violence. Unfortunately, their record of protecting victims proved decidedly mixed. Although Illinois guardsmen put down a white mob in East St. Louis in May 1917, for example, two months later, in a brutal attack on the city's African American community, some in their ranks did nothing to protect black lives or even participated in the violence as well. Moreover, during the melee, they apprehended none of the white rioters. Two years later, however, Illinois guardsmen "behaved with discipline and impartiality in ending the violence" of the Chicago race riot, "despite some reports of pro-riot [*sic*] sympathies."[44]

President Woodrow Wilson castigated mob action:

I say plainly that every American who takes part in the action of a mob or gives it any sort of countenance is no true son of this great Democracy, but its betrayer, and does more to discredit her by that single disloyalty to her standards of law and of right than the words of her statesmen or the sacrifices of her heroic boys in the trenches can do to make suffering peoples believe her to be their savior.[45]

Yet his administration and the federal government made no effort to alleviate the plight of black Americans. It shunned requests for the end to military desegregation, discrimination of federal employees, and Jim Crow measures, for example. And the U.S. Supreme Court not only reviewed fewer civil rights cases between 1916 and 1920 but also decided in favor of blacks less often in those cases. Moreover, as tensions flared between the races on the home front as the war wore on, Wilson ignored appeals from African Americans to decry publicly the violence and the subsequent negligence from state and local officials. Not until the Franklin Roosevelt administration did African Americans receive relief in the form of increased and more favorable Supreme Court decisions (many intending to kill Jim Crow), equal wages from the War Labor Board, and more and higher positions in the federal government.[46] Unfortunately, even his administration proved hesitant to intervene in race riots, however.

Structural factors, then, helped set up the circumstances that prompted whites to riot so violently during the Red Summer of 1919. The Great Migration put strains on housing and jobs. In response, the North, much like the South had, began establishing separate spheres for the two races. Economic and labor concerns also plagued the country leading up to and during the war, as blacks strove to find an equal footing in the market, and whites, just as vehemently, worked to shut them out. Finally, authorities did little in the way to ensure African Americans the basic rights and protection they deserved as citizens.

CULTURAL FRAMING

The ideas of southern white radicalism spread throughout the country during the early 20th century. Many whites saw blacks as threats not only to their economic position but also to social order. Overwhelmingly, newspapers served as the vehicle for developing this cultural consensus that allowed white on black race riots to thrive during the Progressive Era through World War II. Newspapers not only provided the fuel before race riots—running stories of alleged black crimes and atrocities while downplaying white infractions—but also generated the official version of events (inevitably the white account) that transpired during the imbroglios. In an examination of 11 riots that erupted between 1917 and 1943, Terry Ann Knopf uncovers "a general pattern of misreporting" by major (white-owned and white-operated) newspapers monitoring racial violence.[47] Rumor-mongering, race-baiting, loaded language, and advancing the white version of events, according to Knopf, all played a role in inflaming and perpetuating racial tensions.

In the days leading up to the July 1919 riot in Washington, D.C., for example, local newspapers featured in prominent font alleged black assaults on white women. Finally, on July 19, a *Washington Post* headline blared NEGROES ATTACK GIRL . . . WHITE MEN VAINLY PURSUE. In the small print of the story, however, the affront turned out to be that two black men tried to wrest an umbrella from the hands of a white woman—the wife of a military man—but fled when she resisted. Within hours of the news report, a mob of marines and sailors searched for black suspects (who the police had let go), and when they could not find them, they turned their attention to any African American in sight.[48] Similarly, police, local leaders, and the press labeled blacks in Omaha, Nebraska, criminals and other slurs leading up to the 1919 riot there. Two years earlier, an NAACP-sponsored gathering ominously fingered Omaha's newspapers as "using in glaring and sensational headlines expressions of special reference to the race."[49] The Chicago Commission on Race Relations, set up after the 1919 riot in the Windy City, placed particular blame on the press for inciting racial tensions both before and during the riot. Again, biased newspaper reports enhanced black criminality and downplayed white aggression, such as the bombing of black dwellings.[50]

And now Hollywood also contributed to white racial hatred. In 1913, Thomas Dixon took his words to still another audience when he sold the movie rights of *The Clansman* for $2,000 and 25 percent of the profits to D. W. Griffith, who turned it into the first American blockbuster, *The Birth of a Nation*.[51] The Los Angeles premier on February 8, 1915, proved a success, and Dixon's old college friend, President Woodrow Wilson, screened the film at the White House 10 days later. Wilson praised the movie, likening it to "writing history with lightening" and concluding "my only regret is that it is all so terribly true". With the president's endorsement behind it, the film opened to packed theaters in New York on March 3, 1915.[52] "The birth of a nation," historian Joel Williamson avers, "was the very heart of what Dixon had been talking about since 1902, and, more, it was his life. . . . He had again just saved a larger than life American white woman from the monstrous black beast. He had saved a whole nation of people from division and racial damnation and given them life."[53] School teachers arranged special outings with their students to attend the show, and ministers praised its merits.[54] Yet others castigated it harshly.

After its New York debut, social reformer Jane Addams lamented its "pernicious caricature of the Negro race."[55] James Weldon Johnson, novelist, lawyer, diplomat, and NAACP official, responded to the film in the *New York Age*:

> "The Clansman" did [African Americans] much injury as a book, but most of its readers were those already prejudiced against us. It did us more injury as a play, but a great deal of what it attempted to tell could not be represented on the stage. Made into a moving picture play it can do us incalculable harm. Every minute detail of the story is vividly portrayed before the eyes of the spectators. A big, degraded-looking Negro is shown chasing a little golden-haired white girl for the purpose of outraging her; she, to escape him, goes to her death by hurling herself over a cliff. Can you imagine the effect of such a scene upon the millions who seldom read a book, who seldom witness a drama, but who constantly go to the "movies"?[56]

W.E.B. Du Bois, in a *Crisis* (the NAACP's official mouthpiece) editorial, weighed in that Dixon only proved capable of "seek[ing] to capitalize [on] burning race antagonisms."[57] For its part, the NAACP did all it could to ban *The Birth of a Nation* and, when that failed, to have it censored.

The organization pushed for an injunction to stop its nationwide premier in Los Angeles, and it appealed to the National Board of Censorship to prevent its showings in New York. Both attempts failed, but the NAACP did not back down. Members picketed New York's Liberty Theatre, and eventually some of the most blatantly racist scenes got dropped from the film in New York, Boston, and other cities. Even after this partial victory, black leaders continued to fight. In Boston, activist and publisher William Monroe Trotter marched with 200 African Americans to the Tremont Theater on April 17, 1915, to buy tickets for the film. Told the show had sold out, Trotter protested, a skirmish broke out, and the police carried him and several other blacks off to jail.[58] After the show that night, another melee broke out between whites and blacks. The NAACP had sporadic success in squelching the racist film—Missouri, Kansas, Ohio, and Maryland banned it completely, for example—but it could not, in the end, smother its incendiary message of hatred, often luring even more viewers to see the film with its protests.[59]

Indeed, Dixon's words—in print and on stage and screen—resonated with millions of whites throughout the nation and played a significant role in stoking racial violence and the second Ku Klux Klan's call to arms.[60] Spurred on by black migration to the North, rising numbers of immigrants, religious intolerance, xenophobia tied to World War I, and the cancerous growth of cities, the Ku Klux Klan grew at an explosive rate during and after the war. Whites saw much to admire in an organization that trumpeted Victorian values, prohibition, morality, fundamentalist religion, and white supremacy.[61] Klan leaders boasted a membership of 350,000 or 10 percent of the population in Indiana alone.[62] The Klan stood against moral decay and for 100 percent Americanism, by which they meant white Anglo-Saxon Protestantism. In Marion, Illinois, the Klan walked into a Protestant church in 1923 and had the preacher read this letter to the congregation:

Rev. Scoville, Dear Sir:

Please accept this token of our appreciation of your efforts and great work you are doing for this community. The Knights of the Ku Klux Klan are behind this kind of work to a man and stand for the highest ideals of the native-born white Gentile American citizenship which are:

The tenets of the Christian religion; protection of pure womanhood; just laws and liberty; absolute upholding of the Constitution of the United States; free public schools; free speech; free press and law and order.

Yours for a better and greater community.

Exalted Cyclops[63]

"Many native-born whites," Boyle argues, "were appalled by the cities' celebration of immigrant and black cultures, with its implicit condemnation of traditional standards and its unmistakable whiff of amalgamation. Political conflict and economic strain made the backlash even more incendiary." In Detroit, Klan membership grew to 35,000 by 1924 and it played a significant role in enforcing residential segregation and fomenting violence against African Americans who crossed the color line.[64] The Klan contributed editorials to newspapers and spread rumors of black crime, especially attacks on white womanhood, threats to white jobs and property values, and predicted and encouraged future race wars that helped create the conditions for race riots.

African Americans responded to this white violence and oppression in many different ways. Black writers and other leaders lent their voices to asserting rights and calls for equality throughout the Progressive Era and beyond. Du Bois and Johnson joined other African American (and white) authors, scholars, activists, and politicians in pursuing their dream of a free and equal society. Through the anti-lynching campaign, the Niagara Movement, the NAACP, the Harlem Renaissance, and both World Wars, black leaders took every opportunity to sound a clarion call to their fellow Americans that African Americans would not assume a subordinate position in the world. The NAACP, for example, focused its efforts on exposing and putting a stop to the lynching that had spread throughout the country. Through its newspaper, the *Crisis,* it provided detailed statistics, and in 1919, it published the book *Thirty Years of Lynching in the United States, 1889–1918* to highlight the causes and atrocities of this type of violence. With this ammunition, the organization backed federal antilynching legislation. It took out an advertisement titled "The Shame of America" in major American newspapers in November 1922, for example, urging citizens to "telegraph your senators today" to exhort them to pass the Dyer anti-lynching bill.[65] The House of Representatives passed anti-lynching bills in 1922, 1937, and 1940, but southern senators successfully killed the measures each time.[66]

In addition to promoting anti-lynching legislation, the NAACP used the courts to advance its causes. From its inception until the mid-1930s, the group especially focused on garnering civil liberties for African Americans, protecting blacks accused of crimes, securing equal pay for black school teachers, and protesting the omission of blacks from juries.[67] In the aftermath of the Phillips County, Arkansas, riot in 1919, for instance, white authorities indiscriminately rounded up those blacks who stayed in the area after the violence subsided. This witch hunt and the sham trial that followed prompted the NAACP to mount a challenge that eventually went all the way to the U.S. Supreme Court.[68] By the 1930s, the group turned its attention to the segregated school system in America. This shift, and increasingly frequent clashes with other NAACP officials over the stances the organization should advocate, caused Du Bois to resign his membership, relinquish the editorship of the *Crisis,* and go back to Atlanta University in 1934.[69] But for the next 20 years, the NAACP, under the leadership of Walter White, the organization's legal department, put all its efforts into fighting school segregation, as well as its continued battle against lynching and Jim Crow.[70] Charles Houston and Thurgood Marshall mounted a legal strategy that exposed the inherent inequality of separate but equal established by the Supreme Court in *Plessy v. Ferguson,* which finally culminated in the reversal of this decision in *Brown v. Board of Education* in 1954.[71]

As the NAACP lobbied Congress and used the court system to integrate blacks into society, other black leaders used various methods to advance their race as well. Marcus Garvey, who initially drew his inspiration from Booker T. Washington, led two million members of his Universal Negro Improvement Association (UNIA) based in Harlem after he arrived in the United States in 1916 from his native Jamaica. Highlighting racial pride and the appeal of harkening back to Africa, Garvey exhorted, "Up you mighty race! You can accomplish what you will!"[72] A self-made man, he gave African Americans hope during a time when they desperately needed it.

"Above all," avers scholar Mark Robert Schneider, "Garvey was a race-proud black nationalist who preached self-reliance. Negroes would free themselves from oppression not by appealing to the dubious better natures of white people, or to the supposedly inclusive principles of the American founding documents, but by doing for the race first."[73]

Garvey, however, ultimately considered the United States "a white man's country," which he declared during a tour through the South in 1922, and he urged blacks to go "Back to Africa" to free the continent from its European oppressors. He even went so far as to meet with the Ku Klux Klan in Atlanta, defending this act by labeling the group pro-white, not anti-black. Although the meeting shocked some, his sentiments had often sounded eerily similar to those of the racist organization itself. "[The UNIA] believes that both races have separate and distinct destinies," he announced in the fall of 1921, "that each and every race should develop on its own social lines, and that any attempt to bring about the amalgamation of any two opposite races is a crime against nature."[74] His rapprochement with the Klan, nonetheless, signaled to many blacks that he had gone too far, particularly in light of the white violence erupting throughout the country.[75]

Moreover, the World War I era proved a rich and powerful time for black inspiration, producing the New Negro Movement and the Harlem Renaissance, which stressed a sense of worth and boldness.[76] African Americans used poems, stage plays, lyrics, and music—ragtime, the blues, gospel, and jazz—to express both the pride and the horror that they faced in the United States. Poet Langston Hughes expressed black pride in 1926 in his poem "I, Too," for example.[77] Other African Americans tapped into American life as well by highlighting their rights and the need to fight back against white violence. Claude McKay captured these sentiments poignantly in his 1919 poem, "If We Must Die" in response to the Harlem race riot that year.[78] Chicago's African Americans appeared to heed this call during the riot there in the Red Summer of 1919.[79] "The colored people do not seem disposed to recede from what they consider a just position in the community," the *Chicago Daily Tribune* acknowledged during the riot. "The colored people insist upon just and equal advantages."[80] Indeed, while 23 blacks died during the violence, blacks fought back with a vengeance and killed 15 whites.

Black newspapers, such as the *Boston Guardian* and especially the *Chicago Defender*, also became outspoken critics of black America's plight. Robert Abbott, creator of the *Defender*, often practiced yellow journalism (just as the white press did) and allowed his staff creative liberties in their reports on violence and crime. During the 1919 Chicago riot, for example, one report falsely declared, "The homes of blacks isolated in white neighborhoods were burned to the ground and the owners and occupants beaten and thrown unconscious into smoldering embers."[81] Another fabricated *Defender* article regarding the Chicago riot disseminated widely among African Americans:

> An unidentified young woman and three-months-old baby were found dead on the street at the intersection of Forty-Seventh and Wentworth. She had attempted to board a car there when the mob seized her, beat her, slashed her body to ribbons, and beat the baby's brains out against a telegraph pole. Not satisfied with this one rioter severed her breasts and a white youngster bore it aloft on a pole triumphantly while the crowd hooted gleefully.[82]

This visceral account intended to stir emotions, and no doubt it did.[83]

But the *Defender* and other black newspapers served an important function of exposing white violence and hypocrisy and played a large role in trying to better the lives of African Americans by luring them north during the Great Migration. Indeed, writer, diplomat, and activist James Weldon Johnson asserted in his *New York Age* column, "Negro weeklies make no pretense at being newspapers in the strict sense of the term. They have a more important mission than the dissemination of mere news. . . . They are race papers. They are organs of propaganda."[84] During the world wars, although black editors tended to favor each war, they highlighted the irony that while black soldiers traveled abroad to support and promote the principles of democracy, they failed to enjoy those same rights at home. Several white mobs purportedly even killed black soldiers still in uniform.[85]

Through poems, songs, and novels, then—in addition to the realms of politics and the media—African Americans fought back against the injustices of white America during the first half of the 20th century. They carved out a world "behind the veil" where black pride and assertion resonated. And as their men marched off to defend democracy in both world wars, they used these words to draw attention to the hypocrisy that white Americans uttered and believed.

Although blacks went into war hopeful of the promises it held for them to progress in society,[86] they grew increasingly frustrated, disillusioned, and bitter when their men in uniform received no respect (or even worse) as they defended the ideals that the United States stood for. "[W]hy should we be loyal to any Government that does not protect our lives and property," William Bridges, editor of the *Challenge,* inquired in 1919, "why should we disclaim all previous respect for Germans and Germany, why were we shipped 3000 miles oversea [*sic*] to wage war on people against whom we had less real grievances than against that lawless element of America that robs us of lives?"[87] He went on to castigate the American government for worrying more about bootleggers than lynchers. Du Bois shared in this disenchantment and lectured African Americans that they would be "cowards and jackasses if now that the war is over, we do not marshal every ounce of our brain and brawn to fight a sterner, longer, and more unbending battle against the forces of hell in our own land. *We return.* / *We return from fighting.* / *We return fighting.* Make way for Democracy! We saved it in France, and by the Great Jehovah, we will save it in the United States of America, or know the reason why."[88] He also warned whites of the "fight for freedom which black and brown and yellow men must and will make unless their oppression and humiliation and insult at the hands of the White World cease. The Dark World is going to submit to its present treatment just as long as it must and not one moment longer."[89]

Tellingly, the United States experienced "an ascending war-borne curve," as white lynchers unleashed their wrath on 38 blacks in 1917, 58 in 1918, and more than 70 in 1919.[90] Race riots erupted all over the country during the war as well.[91] Indeed, World War I and its aftermath created many factors that led to violence in 1919. During the war, anti-immigrant feelings grew and the government contributed to this xenophobia with its anti-German propaganda. As well, the Espionage Act of 1917 and the Sedition Act of 1918 greatly curtailed civil liberties in the name of patriotism and national unity. Grassroots efforts to attack anyone who threatened community standards and the war effort led to vigilante violence. Once the war ended, however, it proved difficult to turn off the spigot of hate. Sociologist Georg Simmel argues that the search for an inner enemy became institutionalized during the war.[92] By 1919, blacks and Bolsheviks appeared to whites as the greatest threats to social order. The 1917 Russian Revolution and the birth of the Communist International led many Americans to believe that the smallest act could be a precursor to revolution in the United States. The pipe-bombs that went off in scattered locations only heightened this paranoia. The so-called Palmer Raids that rounded up thousands of immigrants who held unpopular political views marked the high-tide of the Red Scare. "Moreover," historian William Tuttle argues, "black people, visibly distinct and with behavior patterns ostensibly alien to whites, were convenient scapegoats, especially for whites who feared that their social status had dropped because of the influx of blacks from the South."[93]

Culture, therefore, played a crucial role in stoking the racial flames during the Red Summer of 1919 and its aftermath. Black and white newspapers, literature, film, and music provided powerful sources of inspiration for both races. White leaders sounded the call daily in their race war to suggest why it proved critical for their race to remain dominant and keep blacks in their place. Whites had everything to lose. Black leaders, equally determined, took every chance they could to elicit their people to advance and push for their basic rights as Americans and as people to live in a free society. Blacks had nothing left to lose.

PRECIPITATING EVENTS

Structural factors and cultural framing probably existed in many cities around the country that did not experience race riots. Thus, a precipitating event provided the tipping mechanism that activated this type of violence. These events confirmed the existence of structural and cultural concerns, and they supplied the immediate motivation to act on this anxiety. With one or more of the structural and cultural factors in place, then, a precipitating event prompted a race riot to occur. In 1919, real or alleged attacks on white women still resonated with white Americans. Moreover, as African Americans continued to assert their rights as citizens, whites strove to hold them back. World War I only heightened these tendencies. With fire tenders, such as the Ku Klux Klan, and rumors spreading through the terrain, precipitating events tipped the equilibrium. As the black population rose, and when whites believed that blacks encroached into their spheres of work, neighborhoods, and recreation, violence often resulted. Again, newspapers amplified these issues by spreading rumors. In the case studies in the next chapter, the precipitating events centered on instances of alleged assaults on white women, black infractions against white authorities, or blacks stepping over supposed societal boundaries.

Chapter 5

"LOOK OUT: YOU'RE NEXT FOR HELL": CASE STUDIES OF SIX RACE RIOTS

In the case studies that follow, I demonstrate that structural factors, cultural framing, and precipitating events came together to create race riots. Like other riot locales that year, Longview, Washington, D.C., Chicago, Knoxville, Omaha, and Phillips County (six of the seven places where major riots broke out) displayed all of these components. Although racial pogroms still cropped up, all-out race wars also appeared during the Red Summer of 1919. Chicago's African Americans, for example, fought determinedly and killed numerous whites during the riot there. Demographic changes, political struggles, Jim Crow laws, segregation, economic tumult, labor discord, and useless authorities helped set up the structural scene from which the violence emerged. Moreover, white newspapers, writers, and politicians spread the gospel of white authority and dominance, and contended that blacks continually confronted these principles. Meanwhile, blacks strove to push for equality and a decent chance at being true American citizens with all its benefits. Each race framed these struggles to benefit and advance their own cause—whites in order to keep blacks down and blacks for a chance to move up in society. Finally, a precipitating event, such as an alleged or actual infraction against white society, provided the immediate spark caused "all hell to break loose."

LONGVIEW

Some 5,700 inhabitants resided in Longview, Texas, in 1919, with almost 1,800—or just under one-third of them—comprising the flourishing black community.[1] Gregg County, of which Longview stands as the county seat, was home to almost an equal number of blacks and whites that year—some 8,200 and 8,500 respectively. An industrial and lumber center, Longview attracted area commerce and a bustling manufacturing sector. African Americans united closely to build their own neighborhoods, schools, churches, and a thriving chapter of the Negro Business League promoted independence from Longview's white businesses. Moreover, influential local African Americans urged black cotton growers to circumvent white middlemen and do business with buyers themselves. The city's blacks also read the national publication, the *Chicago Defender,* which sold on the streets as well as in local black businesses.[2] Many of Longview's white denizens feared this independence clearly evident in their black neighbors, an anxiety that ultimately led a mob of whites to attack the city's back community on July 10.

In the period before the riot, race relations stood on edge in the city. Two local African American leaders had been especially instrumental in pushing for black power in Longview. Samuel L. Jones came to the city in 1913 to work as an instructor for the Longview School District. In addition, he became the area agent for the *Chicago Defender* and several other black newspapers. Dr. Calvin P. Davis moved to Longview in 1909 to establish his medical practice. He also founded the local chapter of the Negro Business League, the medium used in pushing for black competition to white-owned establishments.[3] Not surprisingly, whites focused much of their ire on these two men during the lead-up to the riot and during the riot itself. The men served as a threat to the supposed white supremacist thought still gripping the country. On June 17, just a few weeks before the riot, some of Longview's white community also took care of another black man who purportedly posed a threat to them. His naked, bullet-laden body was found just outside the city.

Authorities arrested and jailed Lemuel Walters for allegedly being found in a white woman's bedroom in the nearby town of Kilgore.[4] Two versions exist as to whether the relationship was consensual, as well as the sheriff's involvement in allowing a group of white men to remove Walters from jail and lynch him.[5] Walter's arrest came after the woman's two brothers attacked him because they claimed he had made unwanted sexual gestures toward their sister. Many decades later, the sheriff's son suggested that his father did all he could to protect Walters after his arrest, even to the point of hiding him in their home and putting him on an outbound train.[6] However, the *Chicago Defender* offered different, probably more feasible, accounts in a July 5, 1919, article titled "Police Work to Keep Lynching a Secret." It was this article that served as the precipitating event for Longview's riot five days later.

With a dateline of "Longview, Tex., July 4," the article begins, "Despite the fact that every effort has been made by officials here to keep the outside world from learning of the lynching of Lemmel [*sic*] Walters at this place June 17, the news has leaked out."[7] The article continues:

> Walters was taken from the Longview jail by a crowd of white men when a prominent white woman declared she loved him, and if she were in the North would obtain a divorce and marry him. . . . The sheriff of the jail gladly welcomed the mob, and acknowledged recognitions from the men as they passed in the gate to seize the prisoner. Walters was taken to the outskirts of the town and shot to pieces. His nude form was thrown near the roadside. . . . White people here are angered because our people have been leaving this part of Texas in droves, and since this lynching all the farm hands have left.[8]

Samuel Jones, the black instructor and local *Defender* agent, had also probed into the events surrounding the lynching just after they occurred and discovered a similar account of what transpired. After talking with one white and three black prisoners jailed at the same time as Walters, Jones asked a county judge to step in since the sheriff appeared to collaborate with the lynchers. A few days later, the other prisoners "had been taken away."[9]

Some in the white community then focused on Jones himself. Five days after the *Defender* article, he found himself under attack while walking on a city sidewalk near the courthouse. Three white men, two of them the brothers of the woman from Kilgore, accused Jones of actually penning the article and then began to hit him with a wrench. He denied writing the article and escaped to Dr. Calvin Davis's office to have his wounds bandaged. Throughout the day, tensions escalated. African Americans began to congregate at Dr. Davis's office when the word got out about Jones's beating. At the same time, local white officials met and urged both Jones and Davis to leave Longview. Instead, when he learned the mayor called a town meeting at city hall, Davis went there to convince the white leaders that Jones did not write the article and to ask what protection officials would offer the city's African American community that night (rumors of a lynching had begun circulating by then). Once there, he learned that the white community also suspected him of being the author, a claim he also denied. When he inquired into safeguards for the black community, the mayor retorted, "You will have to take your chances."[10]

Davis left the meeting and headed to Jones's house, where 25 African Americans stood guard to protect their comrade. In the meantime, some 15 white youths gathered near the courthouse intent on showing Jones who ruled supreme in Longview. Close to midnight they got into cars and made the short drive to Jones's house, where they were met with a hail of shots as they tried to enter the back door. Four of the whites suffered injuries, and most ran away. A short time later, a fire alarm sounded downtown, signaling whites to gather for another attack, and Jones's black defenders quickly left his house. More than 100 whites responded to the call, some of them armed with material by plundering a downtown hardware store. Loaded with kerosene and firearms, the white mob made their way back to Jones's house. Now close to morning, the group set the house on fire and then headed down the street to look for other targets. They set fire to a black-owned business and then Dr. Davis's house, with his wife and children still huddled inside (they did permit a black man to go inside and save them). The white mob then proceeded to burn down two more nearby houses and horsewhipped the occupants—including an 80-year-old woman—when they objected.[11]

Local officials began contacting the governor in the early morning of July 11. At first sending only eight Texas Rangers who would arrive the next morning, Governor William P. Hobby ordered almost 100 National Guardsmen to Longview when a county judge requested more immediate assistance. They arrived in the city on the evening of July 11 and made their presence known by setting up their command center by the courthouse. In the meantime, a group of whites searched intently for Davis and Jones to no avail. Davis hid out in his in-laws' house and then fled Longview by train disguised as a soldier. Jones left a few hours later. Both men escaped the city safely and eventually made their way to Chicago. Unfortunately, Davis's father-in-law, Marion Bush, became the riot's one casualty. On the night of July 12, the local sheriff tried to convince Bush—as Davis's father-in-law—to seek protection in the jail from any vindictive whites. Instead, Bush fired a .45-caliber revolver at the sheriff, who then returned fire. Both missed, and Bush fled. The sheriff called a friend and asked him to hunt down Bush. The friend did, ordered him to stop, and shot him dead when he did not.[12]

Upon hearing this news around midnight on July 12, the mayor called the governor asking for reinforcements. The governor complied, and 150 more National Guardsmen arrived shortly thereafter. Their commander, Brigadier General R. H. McDill, began actions to declare the county under martial law starting at noon on July 13. He also established a curfew from 10:30 P.M. to 6:00 A.M., banned groups of three or more people from congregating in the street, ordered all residents of Longview and Kilgore to hand over their guns by the evening of July 13, and barred long-distance telephone calls.[13] McDill then requested that a citizens' committee form to assist him in bringing Longview back to normalcy. The

all-white committee met the next morning and issued a series of resolutions about the riot. They denounced the *Defender* article, as well as Jones
for distributing it, and the assault on the whites who initially tried to enter
Jones's house. "We will not permit the negroes of this community and
county to in any way," they declared, "interfere with our social affairs or to
write or circulate articles about the white people of our city or county."[14]
They also, however, castigated the white rioters: "We do not believe in ap-
plying the torch, even to the homes of Negroes."[15]

In the end, officials arrested 26 white men, all of whom went free on
bond, for attempted murder and/or arson. All charges against them were
soon dropped. Twenty-one black men were also taken into custody for assault with attempt to murder. Officials placed them in the county jail and
shortly moved them to Austin, where they were eventually freed but urged
not to go back to Longview.[16] McDill informed Governor Hobby that the
situation appeared to be stable in the city, and the governor ended martial
law on July 18, at noon. By then, most of the National Guard had left, and
only three Texas Rangers remained in the city. On July 19, McDill allowed
residents to reclaim their firearms.[17] Although relatively little blood was
shed during the Longview riot, the incident fit a pattern of terror during
the Red Summer. Washington, D.C., and Chicago (ironically where Jones
and Davis eventually chose to settle after they fled Longview) would experience the next major riots that bloody summer.

WASHINGTON, D.C.

Washington, D.C., actually experienced the third major riot of 1919 after
Charleston, South Carolina, and Longview, Texas, but, being the country's
center of government, it received the first nationwide attention. That July,
the city suffered one of its hottest summers to date. Adding to the discomfort, World War I had created an influx of people—adding more than
100,000 individuals to the population—when thousands of jobs opened
as American soldiers left for war. Many white newcomers to D.C. hailed
from the South, and they remained determined to "teach any fresh 'nigger' his place."[18] Although the racial composition of the population of the
city did not change significantly as a result of the wartime growth (in fact,
the ratio of blacks to whites had diminished since 1910), blacks generally
enjoyed more economic prospects than in previous years.[19] When new federal jobs opened as a result of the war boom, whites left their private sector
positions, and black workers readily filled these gaps. As some of these
African Americans came to earn more money than the whites who moved
into government positions, many whites became resentful.[20] Moreover, as
hundreds of discharged white servicemen from nearby camps returned in

search of work, jobs for them could no longer be readily found. Amplifying these tensions, with the rapid population expansion during the war, blacks had a more difficult time finding housing in traditionally African American neighborhoods and began to move into the northwestern white sections of town.[21]

Relations worsened between whites and blacks, spurred on by rumors of black rapists prowling the streets in search of white women.[22] In June and July, seven women in the D.C. area reported that they had been assaulted, and the four Washington dailies related their stories in lurid detail. One white accuser provided a detailed description of her alleged black attackers, only to recant two weeks later that she had not been assaulted after all. Of course, this revelation received little notice in the newspapers.[23] Moreover, the Washington newspapers duly noted that each of the seven attackers had been a black man accosting a white woman. Yet in its study three years later, the Chicago Commission on Race Relations reported that four of the seven incidents involved black women, not white. And, even more significant, three of the suspects were white men, two of whom were later prosecuted.[24] The white papers simply skimmed over these facts, fueling rumors that ran through the white community.

Post owner Ned McLean, on a mission to discredit local leaders, especially played up these tensions, real or imagined. Partially embittered by a grudge against D.C.'s crackdown on Prohibition, McLean ran a series of articles in the summer of 1919 disparaging the police force for not responding effectively to the supposed crime wave plaguing the city.[25] The most prominent reports featured the familiar racist theme of black rapists assaulting white women. Roused by these stories, whites organized and began to form posses. The chief of police, Raymond Pullman, called out a posse of 1,000 white members of the wartime police auxiliary on July 6 to search for a suspect in three Northwest city rapes. Authorities took 135 black men into custody, and Pullman himself offered a $2,500 reward for the head of the Negro fiend. On July 9, the NAACP dispatched letters to all four white newspapers stressing that they were "sowing the seeds of a race riot by their inflammatory headlines and sensational news articles."[26]

Unfortunately, this call for calm went unheeded. On July 18, 1919, two black men confronted a young white woman, the wife of a naval officer, returning home from work. The *Post* treated it as another serious affront to white womanhood.[27] The next morning's headline blared, "Negroes Attack Girl . . . White Men Vainly Pursue," but the body of the article revealed that the men had merely tried to steal her umbrella unsuccessfully.[28] In response to this latest alleged black infraction, police chief Pullman directed that any young man "found in isolated or suspicious parts of the city after nightfall" be detained for questions. Instead of letting the law handle the situation, some 200 marines and sailors served as conversion specialists and took it upon themselves to retaliate on behalf of their fellow sailor and his wife. They headed for the black part of the city to look for two African American suspects who the police had let go. Along the way, crowds of white civilians joined them in their mission. A riot call brought out city and military police, who managed to disperse this initial mob. Authorities arrested two white sailors and eight African Americans.[29] When police later confronted three more blacks out in the streets, one shot and wounded a policeman.

In the morning of July 20, NAACP officials urged Secretary of the Navy Josephus Daniels[30] to bring his marines and sailors under control, but he made no serious effort to rein them in. And although some congressmen condemned the violence and called for a stop to it, they took no definite action to do anything toward that end.[31] That night the city blew up. Hundreds of white vigilantes, primarily drunken veterans, worked themselves into a frenzy after a minor dispute on Pennsylvania Avenue and began attacking any African American they could find. A mob of 100 whites beat one man as his wife looked on in horror. Others pulled unsuspecting blacks off of streetcars and out of restaurants, and chased them through alleys.[32] The police did little to stop the white throng, due both to ineffectualness and complicity, and the press continued to feed into the violence.[33] The *Washington Times,* for example, reported that "Armed Posses Near Capitol Heights Talk of Lynching."[34] And although it gave no details as to who authorized it, the *Post* ran an announcement for "a mobilization of every available service man" for a "clean up that will cause the events of the last two evenings to pale into insignificance."[35]

For three days, white mobs—both military and civilian—freely hunted down the African American citizenry of Washington, D.C., once even passing by the White House in their quest. By Monday, July 21, blacks, dismayed at the wanton bloodshed, began to buy guns (or they pulled out the ones they had used in France as soldiers in the U.S. military) to defend themselves or to even strike back. One group of blacks attacked a streetcar, thrashing its workers. Other blacks shot into a group of sailors on the grounds of the Navy Hospital from a passing car. Another black mob formed to charge the Navy Yard, but police dispersed them before they could attack anyone.[36] Monday night saw even more violence in a form far worse than before. Five African Americans and six white police, three white civilians, and one white marine died or suffered serious injuries that night. Numerous others needed medical attention. Authorities arrested 300 men, either for rioting or having concealed weapons.[37]

Although some 700 D.C. police and another 400 military men equipped as an emergency provost guard attempted to quell the situation, the city's whites and blacks continued to attack each other. In addition to shared public spaces (such as the streetcars), whites targeted black residential areas, and blacks fired upon white residences.[38] Finally sensing that the local authorities maintained no control over the violence, President Wilson had Secretary of War Newton Baker call up 2,000 army soldiers, marines, and sailors on July 22 to maintain order. Major General William G. Haan led these new forces, and he quickly placed them in all parts of the city. He also clamped down on Washington's newspapers. "When I got them [the newspapers] to agree to say approximately what I wanted them to say," he noted to a fellow officer, "then soon everything was over."[39] Meanwhile, police officials met with local black leaders to temporarily close down near-beer saloons and poolrooms in the black sections of town. And black ministers exhorted their flocks to stay home.[40]

By the next morning, with federal troops standing guard and rainfall soaking the city, the riot ended.[41] Although newspapers reported that 15 people died during the hostilities, historians calculate it may have been two to three times that many.[42] In the wake of the riot, both the police chief and the general in charge of the federal troops that finally calmed the situation highlighted the necessity for more manpower and better pay to ensure a stronger police force in the future. Black leaders stressed that more African Americans should be on the force to engender trust between the police and the black community. They particularly underscored the fact that no black patrolman had been hired for four years. Moreover, neutral rather than stronger police, according to blacks, proved much more crucial to the maintenance of peaceful race relations.[43] One black New York newspaper even suggested that since the police "failed to protect the Negroes of the capital there is but one course open. Let every Negro arm himself and swear to die fighting in defense of his home, his rights and his person. In every place where the law will not protect their lives, Negroes should buy and hoard arms."[44]

Indeed, some blacks praised the heroic resistance of Washington's African Americans to white violence, "def[ying] the point of bayonets, the sting of blackjacks and the hail of bullets in defending themselves." Only with the end of the "Mobocratic Lyncherized system . . . of Jim Crow," they suggested, would blacks in the nation's capital be contented.[45] Meanwhile, the NAACP urged Attorney General A. Mitchell Palmer to investigate the role of the *Washington Post* in provoking the riot (which he did not do). And after the riot, newspapers, both northern and southern, continued to sound the familiar racist themes that had whipped up antagonisms in the first place. The *Brooklyn Eagle,* for instance, announced, "Race War in Washington Shows Black and White Equality Not Practical." The article suggested that high wages, full employment, and blacks' growing autonomy spurred the riot.[46] The *New York Times* lamented,

The majority of the negroes in Washington, before the great war, were well behaved . . . , even submissive. . . . In the last few months crimes of violence have reached such proportions in Washington that The Herald of that city recently declared it to be the most lawless city in the Union. The are mainly committed by negroes, and the police force, trained as it has been, has been unable to cope with them. The assumption must necessarily be that in the new Washington which has replaced the old, the hurly-burly, crammed, jammed town that has succeeded the placid and easy-going old city, the town where hotels are bursting and lodging houses turning people away, there has been an influx of negroes as well as of white people. It is certainly not the old, law-abiding negro population, the friends of the white man, that has been committing these crimes against women, these daylight holdups, and all the other outrages that have incited white men to a general war against negroes. It must be the new negro population brought in by the war. . . . The thing seems to be a regrettable by-product of the war; and, painful as it is to say, it could not have arisen in any Northern city where the police had been trained to expect riot duty.[47]

Yet less than a week later, Chicago suffered the same fate.

CHICAGO

In the years preceding Chicago's race riot, several clashes flared between the city's white and black populations. Fed in large part by a demographic shift that doubled Chicago's blacks between 1917 and 1918, and an irresponsible and racist press, tensions ran high between the communities.[48] Moreover, "[t]he race riot was in many ways," historian William Tuttle asserts, "the tragic culmination of . . . twenty-five years of conflict between blacks and whites in the labor market."[49] During a series of strikes from the 1890s up until the 1919 riot, white workers came to see blacks as a scab race, while industries relied on African Americans more and more as strikebreakers.[50] Blacks proved willing to step into that role, both because of their distrust of unions and their need for income. By May 1919, in large part boosted by soldiers returning from overseas and troops mustering out in or around Chicago (many of them black southerners who did not wish to move back to the South), more than 10,000 black laborers needed work as the postwar recession began to appear.[51] When a violent strike occurred at the Corn Products Refinery at Argo in early July, rumors flowed that the company had urged black workers to "come back Monday and bring all of your friends."[52] And, indeed, 600 blacks stepped in as strikebreakers there. Only a month earlier, union workers at the stockyards, a perennial source of racial friction, launched a strike, claiming "they could no longer work with nonunion blacks."[53]

The wartime influx of people also forced competition for housing, and blacks eventually began to search for homes in white and immigrant neighborhoods. "Practically no new building had been done in the city during the war," concluded the commission set up by Illinois Governor Frank Lowden to study race relations in the aftermath of the riot, "and it was a physical impossibility for a doubled Negro population to live in the space occupied in 1915."[54] Moreover, the existing black housing was abysmal. "On the South Side, where most of the Negro population lives," the commission reported "the low quality of housing is widespread. . . . Bathrooms are often missing . . . , and electric lighting is a rarity. Heating is commonly done by wood or coal stoves, and furnaces are rather exceptional. . . . [L]arge rat holes [are] all over."[55] The Black Belt also bordered the quarters of Chicago's Irish and Polish communities, groups who displayed a stern hostility toward blacks who represented their economic and political competition.[56] In response to the black invasion into white neighborhoods, between July 1917 and the riot just two years later, 24 bombs blasted African American homes, and the homes and offices of the black and white realtors who catered to black clients.[57] Flyers warned blacks, "Look out: you're next for hell." Others alerted black occupants, "We are going to BLOW these FLATS TO HELL and if you don't want to go with them you had better move at once."[58] Police made little effort of apprehending those responsible.[59]

Politics also played a critical role in stoking racial animosities in the months leading up to the riot. During World War I, two Chicago mayoral races hinged largely on the black vote, and three African Americans won seats on the city council. "The blacks' voting behavior," historian William Tuttle avers, "aroused and reinforced the hostility and racial hatred of numerous groups."[60] In the 1915 mayoral race, for example, blacks overwhelmingly voted for Republican William Big Bill Hale Thompson. Much to the chagrin of his fellow whites, the new mayor rewarded several African Americans with prominent appointments for their support. "I am glad to take the full responsibility and the honor for making every one of those appointments," he responded to angry whites, "and I want to ask my critics to be as manly and to come out in the open light of day with such unAmerican sentiments."[61] Unlike many other white politicians, Thompson also lambasted *The Birth of a Nation* and barred it from being shown in Chicago as long as he held the mayor's office. " 'Big Bill,' " the *Chicago Daily Tribune* criticized him in response to this action, "listened to a complaint from negro voters."[62]

Adding to whites' discomfort with Thompson's symbiotic relationship with African Americans, migration during the war also doubled his support in the black sections of the city. Even though he had disaffected many of Chicago's other groups and sectors during his first term as mayor, as a result of the arrival of more African Americans (who he readily reached out to), he eked out a reelection victory in April 1919.[63] Indeed, Thompson garnered only 38 percent of the overall vote, while Democrats won more than 60 percent of the city's other significant offices. "The white people of Chicago," one Democrat explained, "greatly resented" the black voters' strength, and "the way in which the colored vote put Mayor Thompson into office again at this last election." Even more damning, "the preference given to the colored people by the Thompsonites" truly served as an affront to many of Chicago's whites. "The colored people freely talk of their power over the whites through their hold over 'Big Bill' Thompson," especially "their equality with the whites."[64] As in other cities around the nation, this push for equality proved deadly.

Several minor clashes, spurred on by the media, preceded the riot. In July 1917, two years before the Red Summer, a white saloonkeeper died of a heart attack. Rumors circulated that the man had been killed by African Americans, prompting some young white men riding in a car to fire into a group of blacks in retaliation.[65] These gangs of white thugs, comprised largely of members of so-called athletic or social clubs, continually attacked African Americans as they walked through their territory on their way to and returning from work. Mary McDowell, head resident of the University of Chicago Social Settlement, testified before the commission after the riot that she could identify at least five of these clubs made up of young men between 17 and 22 years old:

> Especially before the war they were always under obligation to some politi-
> cian. . . . The Ragen Club is mostly Irish-American. The others are from the
> second generation of many nationalities. . . . I think they get into these ways,
> and then they are used and exploited often by politicians. . . . It is about the
> most dangerous thing that we have in the city. [On one day of the riot,] they
> went down Forty-seventh Street with firearms showing in their hands in
> autos . . . and shouting as they went, "We'll get those niggers!"[66]

Throughout the spring of 1919, these gangs grew more boldly active, and on June 21, 1919, one of them murdered two black men crossing through their neighborhood. Even though eyewitnesses pointed out those responsible, authorities took no action.[67]

The white and black press shares a large portion of the blame for igniting this already tenuous racial situation. Before and during the riot, Chicago's newspapers played upon racial stereotypes and fears. In 1918, for example, the *Chicago Tribune,* one of the city's three major white dailies, printed 145 articles that "definitely placed Negroes in an unfavorable light." Of these stories, 23 appeared on the newspaper's front page, and 20 on the first page of section two. During the same period, the *Tribune* published 84 reports more favorable to African Americans. Out of these, two appeared on the front page, and three on page one of the second section.[68] Not surprisingly, the city's blacks "almost without exception point to the Chicago press as the responsible agent for many of their . . . difficulties."[69] During the riot itself, although only 10 women suffered injuries, and 8 of those by accident, white newspapers reported repeated attacks on white women by black men. And the black press inflamed African Americans during the riot with false stories about alleged white atrocities against them.[70] "Reports of numbers of dead and injured tended to produce a feeling that the score must be evened up on the basis of 'an eye for an eye,' a Negro for a white, or vice versa."[71] As in many other riots, newspaper served as one of the driving forces behind the outbreak of and continuation of the violence.

Finally, on a sultry summer day, the precipitating event for the race riot.[72] On the afternoon of July 27, 1919, residents crowded the lakeside beaches looking for relief from the heat and sun. A scuffle broke out when four African Americans walked across the tacitly designated white section of the beach. Told to leave, they instead retrieved some friends and returned, prompting a stone-throwing fight between the two groups. In the lake itself, an imaginary boundary also marked the water, partitioning the African American and white sections of the lake. As 17-year-old Eugene Williams and his friends swam in the cool water, he accidentally drifted across the line. Although the official report concluded that he did not receive a blow to the head from one of the stones, rumors soon flowed through the African American community that a white man had struck him with a stone and he drowned as a result. Whatever the case, as stones flew around him during the melee, Williams sank below the water and drowned. Blacks who witnessed the scene demanded that a nearby policeman arrest one of the white men on the beach. He refused and instead detained one of the African Americans. Several black men then attacked the officer. Surrounding whites responded, and the race riot began.

Blacks injured 10 whites in clashes near the beach, and between 9:00 P.M. and 3:00 A.M., white mobs beat 27 blacks, stabbed 7, and shot 4. The next morning, a Monday, people went back to work as usual. But as people returned home that afternoon, the white gangs flew into action. "But for them," the post-riot commission asserts, "it is doubtful if the riot would have gone beyond the first clash."[73] Moreover, evidence suggests that these gangs often worked in tandem with at least some of the police force before, during, and after the riot. On Monday afternoon, these gangs pulled trolleys from their wires and dragged black passengers out into the streets, and again beat, stabbed, and shot them. Raids into the black residential areas then ensued. The African American citizens retaliated by shooting back at their attackers out of their homes and neighborhoods. Fighting continued on and off for seven days. According to Tuttle, 41 percent of the fighting took place in the principally white stockyards and 34 percent in black neighborhoods.[74] As soon as the hostility would die down, both the white and black press would inflame passions again with exaggerated or bogus reports. And like the authorities in D.C., the police offered little support to Chicago's black community. One black man, wounded and abandoned in the street, felt relieved when he saw a patrolman approaching him. Instead of offering to help, however, the policeman questioned him, "Where's your gun, you black son of a bitch? You damn niggers are raising hell."[75] The policeman then beat him with his nightstick until he lost consciousness. "It is believed that had the Negroes not lost faith in the white police force," the commission report states, "it is hardly likely that" much of the violence "would have occurred."[76]

Although the local police obviously could not (or did not care to) quell the violence themselves, both the police chief and the mayor remained reluctant to call in the state militia.[77] At last, the worst of the fighting slowed down three days after the rioting began, when, convinced by a group of black leaders, Mayor Thompson finally asked for the militia to help on the night of July 30, and rain began to soak the city.[78] Unlike many of the local police, the state militia did their job.[79] According to the commission report, "The troops themselves were clearly of high caliber. . . . The militia discipline was of the best."[80] On August 8, authorities believed the situation under control, and the troops left the city. By the time the conflict ended, 23 blacks and 15 whites had died, more than 500 people suffered injuries, and some 1,000 black families had no home.[81] Although more blacks than whites died during the violence, a grand jury handed down indictments for 81 blacks and 47 whites.[82] The NAACP and other groups stepped in to defend those African Americans accused of crimes during the riot, and at least 58 of them received acquittals.[83]

Unfortunately, the riot did nothing to alleviate Chicago's dreadful race relations. Between February and May 1920, more bombs destroyed black houses, at a rate even higher than before the riot. And in the end, "no measures were taken," historian Arthur Waskow concludes, "to deal with the underlying conflicts that had sparked the great riot of 1919."[84] Although the *Birmingham News* declared of Chicago's riot that "this ugly business could not have occurred in the South," only a few weeks later, Knoxville, Tennessee, experienced the same misfortune.

KNOXVILLE

Knoxville possessed many of the structural and cultural factors that other riot cities did in 1919. Some 11,300 blacks made up its 77,800 inhabitants by 1920, up from 7,600 10years earlier.[85] Moreover, many Knoxville blacks exercised their right to vote, held public office, sat on juries, and served on the police force. Also the existence of Knoxville College, one of the first black schools established after the Civil War, the *East Tennessee News,* the area's biggest black newspaper, and a local chapter of the NAACP showed the growing role of African Americans in the community.[86]

These institutions and organizations reminded white residents of Knoxville that they shared their city with a growing, thriving African American community. And, indeed, severe animosities existed between the two races. For example, in June 1913, a gang of whites almost lynched a black man suspected of murdering a white policeman. Economic hardships and job competition aggravated the problem. Although World War I provided jobs, Knoxville's inability to accommodate new residents strained racial harmony. The postwar recession inflamed these hostilities as the city's industries closed. Some whites formed a local chapter of the Ku Klux Klan.[87]

The situation remained tense in August 1919. The homicide of a white woman allegedly by a black man served as the catalyst that destroyed any remaining civility between the races. On August 30, an intruder shot and killed Bertie Lindsey, a 27-year-old white woman, in her home. Her 21-year-old cousin, Ora Smyth, lay motionless in their bed. After the intruder grabbed a purse and ran away, Smyth fled next door to the house of a city policeman. Only minutes after Smyth sought help from her neighbors, several policemen rushed to the scene of the crime, where some 30 or 40 people had already congregated.[88]

One of the patrolmen, Andy White, immediately thought of Maurice Mays. More than once, others heard White castigate Mays for interacting with white women. Often at the center of controversy, the striking, eloquent, and married 31-year-old Mays attracted numerous women, both black and white. He owned a cafe and dance hall in Knoxville's red light district frequented by both races. Mays also delivered the black vote to John E. McMillan, the white mayor of Knoxville, who many people believed to be Mays's father. In fact, Mays handed out blank poll tax receipts on August 29 for McMillan for his upcoming reelection bid.[89]

White and two other policemen were ordered to arrest Mays. They arrived at his house at 3:30 A.M., discovered him sleeping, and searched the premises for evidence. In his dresser they found a revolver, which the three lawmen claimed had recently been discharged. Both Mays's foster father and the black driver of the patrol wagon denied this claim, however.

Moreover, although muddy tracks led away from the crime scene, Mays's clothes, shoes, and carpet were clean and dry. Nevertheless, White arrested Mays and took him to the crime scene for Ora Smyth to identify. Less than two hours after her cousin's murder, Smyth, "hanging limberly in [two men's] arms hardly able to walk, with hair hanging down over her face and crying," identified Mays as the culprit. "From that moment," Mays later recalled, "I have never had a fair and impartial chance for my life."[90] He soon stood behind bars, charged with the slaying.

By morning, roving bands of white men moved toward downtown, visibly upset with the news of the crime. By 8:00 A.M., a sizable crowd congregated at the city jail, forcing the police chief to transfer Mays to the county jail. In the early afternoon, the Knoxville *Sentinel* circulated lurid front-page articles describing the crime and arrest. "[T]he afternoon paper came out with a full story of the murder," the Chattanooga *Daily Times* asserted, "and the mob started to form at the moment the paper reached the street."[91] Rumors began to circulate that Bertie Lindsey had been raped, pregnant, or even pregnant with Mays's baby. Again, the authorities decided that Mays would be safer elsewhere. They dressed him as a woman to conceal his identity and sent him to Chattanooga. In the meantime, large crowds gathered at various points around Knoxville.[92]

By 6:00 P.M., a mob of more than 500 surrounded the county jail demanding Mays. In vain, officials allowed four different groups to tour the facility to see that Mays was not there. By 8:00 P.M., a barrage of rocks and bullets battered the building, and the angry crowd soon broke down the doors. For the next few hours, hundreds—if not thousands—of people combed the jail looking for Mays. Although they could not find him, they discovered an impounded moonshine still and some liquor. Imbibing freely, the crowd ransacked the building taking weapons and ammunition. The mob freed all the white prisoners, including convicted murderers, but neither liberated nor injured the African Americans.[93]

Called in after the jailhouse assault, the Fourth Tennessee Infantry—scattered on weekend passes—slowly made its way to Knoxville. The first members arrived at the jail around 10:00 P.M. The 16 soldiers and their officer suffered brutal beatings, along with the loss of their uniforms and firearms at the hands of the white mob. The adjutant general, accompanied by three companies, soon arrived and assured the crowd that Mays had been moved, but to no avail.[94]

While the city's whites assaulted the jail, rumors of impending attacks circulated among Knoxville's blacks. Those who did not flee the city gathered weapons to prepare for an invasion. Well-armed men congregated at the corner of Vine and Central, the hub of the black district, waiting for the mob of whites to appear. Shortly after 11:30 P.M., the clash between

Knoxville's white and black citizens began. While several clusters of rioters from the jail headed for Chattanooga in search of Mays, the rest shifted their attention to shots coming from the black district. Members of the National Guard, strengthened but still badly outnumbered, received orders to march double time to the scene of the new fight. The authorities could do very little, however, as the area became a battleground for the next few hours.[95]

The reinforced National Guard finally sealed off the black district around 3:15 A.M., effectively preventing any whites from entering it or any blacks from leaving. The following day, accounts of lawlessness, mostly unfounded, continued to plague the authorities. As a result, some 200 white civilians became special deputies and patrolmen, and they dispersed throughout the city to maintain order. For the next two days, periodic bursts of violence erupted around Knoxville. But by midnight, August 31, most of the hostility had begun to diminish. In the days after the riot, guardsmen searched blacks on the street. Things slowly began to return to normal, though, and most of the guard left by September 2, the day after the black district reopened. Although newspapers recorded only two deaths, one black man and one white, and 14 wounded, the exact number of casualties remains unknown. Observers placed the number killed between twenty-five and several hundreds.[96] White rioters bragged of mowing niggers down like grass, and that dead black bodies piled up like cordwood. Authorities arrested 55 white men and women for their role in the riot, but many went free.[97]

Under tight security, Maurice Mays returned to Knoxville on September 25, and his trial began a few days later. The all-white jury found him guilty of murder after only 18 minutes of deliberation. Two weeks later, the judge imposed the death penalty. However, the sentence was overturned on appeal because of judicial error. In a second trial, Mays received the same sentence. On March 15, 1922, as he continued to proclaim his innocence, Mays died in the state's electric chair.[98] Although several racial incidents flared up again during the next few years, local authorities met them with stiff resistance and no riot erupted again in Knoxville.[99]

OMAHA

Like other places around the United States, Omaha, Nebraska, was a city in turmoil in the summer of 1919. Omaha's tailors, telegraphers, bricklayers, boilermakers, truck drivers, and teamsters went on strike in the early summer months. By June 21, the Central Labor Union warned of a sympathy general strike by the city's 30,000 union members if the teamsters' requests of higher wages and other demands were not met.[100] In response, the city's reform Mayor Edward Smith (elected the previous year over incumbent James Dahlman, an ally of longtime Omaha Democratic political boss Tom Dennison) inflamed matters when he avowed in a speech at an American Legion meeting on June 25, "If these troubles arise [a general strike], I am going to ask the American Legion, the men who went overseas to fight this same thing and defend it again and fight if necessary. I'm going to ask them to drive the ice wagons and milk wagons that carry the ice and milk to the sick and to the babies of Omaha in spite of opposition."[101] To show its support for the mayor, the convention voted in favor of a decidedly antiunion resolution. Other strikes continued throughout the summer, however, and labor strife intensified; police even suggested that the Industrial Workers of the World had a hand in the call for a general strike in the city.[102]

Rumors also spread that employers would soon bring in black strikebreakers from the riot cities of Chicago and East St. Louis eager for employment.[103] In early August, the Omaha *Bee,* a sensationalist newspaper and the mouthpiece of Tom Dennison, submitted that some 500 black workers had arrived in the city looking for work.[104] Indeed, exacerbating the labor turmoil, Omaha's demographics had been changing dramatically over the last decade. The overall population in the 1920 census revealed an increase by a third from the 1910 census and almost double the residents counted in the 1900 census. Of the 191,000 people living in Omaha by 1920, more than 10,300 were black (a 133 percent increase over the last decade) and just under one-third of the population was foreign born. The city's black community had a flourishing branch of the NAACP, and in 1919 blacks established the Theodore Roosevelt Post of the American Legion (some 800 black Nebraskans served in World War I) and a YWCA for Negro girls in Omaha.[105] Housing was at a premium in 1919, and residents complained that apartment rent had gone up 50 percent from the previous year and that renters faced extensive waiting periods because no accommodations were available.[106] Other controversies such as food prices, prohibition, and women's suffrage rankled residents, adding to the tense summer scene.[107]

Moreover, residents' confidence in city reform officials, and particularly in the police, waned during the summer of 1919. Crimes plagued Omaha: between June 7 and September 27, police documented 21 assaults on women. Some in the local press fed this discontent by condemning government officials and also by stoking up racial fears.[108] While the *World-Herald* presented somewhat even accounts of events over the summer, the *Bee* especially played up the reformers' supposed ineptness (not surprising given the paper's alliance with political boss Dennison) and area racial discord.[109] The *Bee* made a point of highlighting other cities in racial turmoil during the Red Summer. In inflammatory details, the paper featured the riots in Longview, Washington, D.C., Chicago, and Knoxville.[110] The

Monitor, a black publication managed by local NAACP leader Reverend John Albert Williams, also accused the *Daily News* of whipping up racial hatred in its accounts of blacks' alleged activities in Omaha during the summer months.[111] By late September, city residents were entrenched in social, economic, political, and racial acrimony, fueled largely by yellow journalism. This combination provided the perfect kindling for a spark to ignite.

That spark came in the form of an alleged attack by a black man on a white woman. According to Omaha residents Agnes Loeback and Milton Hoffman, late on the night of September 25, as they walked home from a movie, a black man took money and jewelry from them by gunpoint. He then proceeded to pull Loeback into a ravine and rape her.[112] The next morning, the city woke up to the following headline in the *Bee*: "Black Beast First Sticks-up Couple." "The most daring attack on a white woman ever perpetrated in Omaha," the article reads, "occurred . . . last night."[113] Police and hundreds of white vigilantes began searching the area and soon heard of a suspicious negro in a home near the reported attack. Will Brown huddled under a bed as police surrounded him with their guns out. Back at Loeback's house, she and Hoffman recognized Brown as the man who attacked them (although Loeback later expressed doubt), and police escorted him to jail (first to the police station jail cell and then to the county courthouse jail for safekeeping) even as a gathering crowd started calling for his lynching and twice threw a rope around Brown's neck. The chief of police suggested that Brown's guilt had not yet been established and he would need to explore the matter more thoroughly.[114]

Indeed, a physical exam revealed that Brown was "too twisted by rheumatism to assault anyone," and he maintained his innocence.[115] But by September 28, many of Omaha's white citizens had made up their minds that he was guilty. At around 2:00 that afternoon, Hoffman himself led a group of some 200 people to the courthouse with the intention of lynching Brown. Two hours later, the crowd had grown, and police began to form a ring around the structure (at this point, however, the police captain did not deem the situation dire and sent 50 reserve officers home). Some in the crowd shouted racial slurs and demanded Brown's lynching. By 5:00 P.M., the white mob had grown to between 4,000 and 5,000 people. The rioters penetrated the building several times, but officials managed to drive them out each time. By now, both the mayor and the police chief had arrived to try to reinstate stability. Instead, the mob broke inside the courthouse. When police chief Marshall Eberstein and city commissioner Harry B. Zimman tried to convince them to disperse, they threw rocks and yelled, "Lynch the damn Jew."[116] Zimman was struck and quickly retreated. Soon the rioters attacked the officers surrounding the building. By 7:00 P.M.

most officials took refuge inside the courthouse as a mob—containing some women—beat any black they came across in the downtown area as well as anyone who tried to help those victims. Two black police officers also came under attack.[117] An hour later, the angry horde set fire to the courthouse, and some individuals began plundering nearby businesses for fuel, ammunition, and firearms.[118]

Around 10:30 P.M., Mayor Smith made another attempt to convince the unruly crowd to leave. In no mood to back down, some in the mob hit him over the head, slipped a rope around his neck, and dragged him down the street intent on hanging him. Luckily, someone saved Smith just in time and removed the rope from his neck as it was being thrown over a bar. The unconscious mayor was rushed to the hospital where he stayed for several days recovering from serious head wounds.[119] Will Brown, however, was not so fortunate. After nearly killing the mayor, the crowd returned to the courthouse, added more fuel to the already burning building, and attacked firefighters as they tried to put out the blaze. They then used the firemen's ladders to climb into the building to search for Brown. One of the rioters died from a gunshot wound as he led the stampede. Meanwhile, officials escorted all of the prisoners to the roof but had to retreat when met by a volley of gunfire. Convinced to allow all the female prisoners to leave, the mob continued to search the burning building for Brown. They finally captured him after people trapped inside sent off of the west side of the courthouse three notes, one of which read, "Come to the fourth floor of the building and we will hand the nigger over to you."[120]

After much effort to get to the fourth floor, yells and shots went up indicating that Brown was now in the custody of the crowd. By the time they got him outside, Brown was already beaten severely and covered in blood. Just before 11:00 P.M., the white mob exclaimed, "Here he is, here he is," slipped a rope around his neck, and hung him from a pole while bombarding his body with gunfire. They then dragged him behind a stolen police car and burned his remains in a bonfire. Not quite content yet, the throng again rigged what remained of Brown to a car and paraded him throughout downtown Omaha.[121] As the mob finally began to break up (some estimates placed it as high as 20,000 individuals), federal troops from Fort Omaha— at the request of Omaha's police chief—finally arrived after securing (the slow and bureaucratic) permission from the U.S. War Department to help out in the city's affairs.[122] By 2:00 A.M. troops guarded the city, and the next day residents saw the presence of machine guns and cannons on the streets. The city's black residents also stood ready should more violence arise. "The negroes are well armed," a New York Times article asserted. "Negro leaders today told the City Commissioners that practically every one of the 10,000 negroes in Omaha was armed and is ready to fight for his life and home."[123] Over the next few days, 1,600 more soldiers arrived from Kansas, South Dakota, and Iowa, and some stayed until November 15, when the military's presence was deemed no longer necessary.[124]

In the end, three people, including Brown, died in the violence. The courthouse sustained extensive damages, and the fires caused numerous records to be lost forever. The Omaha *World-Herald* won a Pulitzer Prize in the aftermath of the events of September 28 and 29, for its editorials on weak city leadership and the shame that the city had to endure now because of the riot. The *Bee* focused on city leaders and police as well, but suggested that the riot stemmed—at least partially—from black rapists having free reign in the city.[125] A grand jury handed down 189 riot-related indictments, but only a few individuals were prosecuted. Two men (one of whom had exclaimed, "We have showed the nigger what a northern mob can do," as he stood on top of a scorched police vehicle) were charged for Brown's death, but a jury found them both not guilty after deliberating only briefly. The grand jury's final report blamed the riot on numerous factors, including attacks on women, a culture of lawlessness, economic and labor strife, returning veterans, and certain elements in the city (Bolsheviks and

Burning of Will Brown's body, Omaha, Nebraska, 1919. (Nebraska State Historical Society [#RG2281–69])

anarchists) who capitalized on these circumstances.[126] Over his denials, some Omahans suggested that political boss Dennison orchestrated the violence to cause the ouster of the Smith administration. He had ties to both Hoffman and the editor of the *Bee,* and certainly wanted to regain power through his surrogate former mayor, James Dahlman. Whether complicit in the riot or not, Dennison's man was back in power after the next municipal elections in 1921.[127] In response to the Omaha riot, the *Atlanta Constitution* breathed a sigh of relief: "Again the spirit of mob violence has hurled defiance into the face of decency and law," it announced in an editorial, "and again the south looks on—not as a participant, but as a spectator . . . being softened only by our thankfulness that there is no danger of any such an enormous manifestation of gross barbarity and lawless frenzy occurring in our section."[128] Another race riot, however, *had* started unfolding in the South.

PHILLIPS COUNTY

The October riot that erupted in Phillips County, Arkansas, demonstrates that white-on black violence even reached into the rural regions of the United States during the Red Summer of 1919. In the Arkansas Black Belt bordering the Mississippi River, the majority-black county had 44,530 residents by 1920—11,601 of them white and 32,929 African American.[129] The rich soil there grew corn and cotton, largely worked by sharecroppers, with 90 percent of them being African Americans by 1920.[130] Indeed, the three townships where most of the 1919 violence took place—Tappan, Mooney, and Searcy—saw an increase in black farmers over the previous decade, from 289 in 1900 to 1,132 in 1920. The number of white farmers grew only from 36 to 155 during the same time frame. Moreover, most of these farmers of both races had recently come from other states, "and likely knew very little about one another."[131]

Sharecropping proved an especially arduous way to make a living. Sharecroppers became hopelessly indebted to landowners, many of whom owned the local stores that sold supplies on credit at very high interest rates to the croppers.[132] Indeed, sharecroppers ended up owing more than they could grow. Phillips County, Arkansas, proved no different according to one scholar:

> A typical sharecropper in the county in 1919 raised 14 bales of cotton or 7,000 pounds at 43 cents per pound. Each bale contained a half ton of seed valued at 70 dollars per ton. Therefore, the sharecropper's crop was worth about 3,500 dollars. During the year, the farmer bought or "took up" goods worth about $23.50. But in settling with the plantation owner, the value of goods "taken up" totaled the value of his crop.[133]

The lawyer called on by a number of Phillips County's black sharecroppers to help them with their plight later recalled,

> [T]he fact that I prosecuted such cases became known to the class of people affected to such an extent, that they came by the droves to my office telling their stories as to how they were being robbed by the landlords, who took their crops at their own prices, charged whatever they saw fit for the supplies furnished, and as a final consummation of the whole thing, refused to make any kind of settlement with them whatever, the end being that they received a statement, written upon a blank tablet as a rule, showing "balance due" in a lump sum.[134]

And although blacks outnumbered whites by three to one in Phillips County, whites owned most of the stores, the factories, and the farm-land.[135] The longer blacks toiled under this system, the more they became convinced that they must take some action to improve their situation.

Moreover, although World War I had boosted cotton prices by mid-1918, infestations and an August drought severely hurt the crop's harvest. U.S. Department of Agriculture reports placed Arkansas's yield at 50 percent its usual level. Phillips County suffered huge losses with only 1,947 ginned bales by October, compared with 7,522 bales the previous year. The follow-ing year saw similar trends. At the end of 1919, crops sat at only one-third their typical production. Sharecroppers felt the brunt of this economic tur-moil. Their income declined as their crops diminished, but storeowners continued to charge the trapped patrons exorbitant prices.[136] And since African Americans constituted the vast majority of sharecroppers in Phil-lips County, they suffered immensely when crop prices fell.

Politics also demonstrated the role expected of black Arkansans during the early 20th century. By 1916, although Jim Crow measures had shut African Americans out of the political process and out of office, the Demo-cratic primary (which essentially decided the election) continued to center on the race issue. Earle Hodges, an ally of the outgoing governor, accused his opponent, Charles Hillman Brough, of being a "Negrophile."[137] But as a professor at the University of Arkansas, Brough had suggested that African Americans lived more successfully in a segregated society. "He [the black man] does not look upon the 'Jim Crow' car as a humiliation," Brough concluded in his capacity as chair of the Southern Sociological Congress's University Race Commission in the 1910s, "in fact, he infinitely prefers the freedom of his own car to one where the presence of the white race would be felt as a restraint."[138]

Bent on correcting Hodges's accusation, Brough assured voters in news-paper advertisements leading up to the election that "I am not in favor of social equality. . . . I am not in favor of negroes serving on juries, I am not in favor of negroes holding political office in the South." In a campaign speech, he urged his fellow whites "to make a better citizen of the negro and to cause him to render more efficient service to the white man." Evidently his racial declarations worked. Brough won the election (Hodges came in third) and easily won reelection two years later (Republicans did not even offer a challenger in 1918).[139] And when the 1919 violence erupted in Phillips County, Brough himself made the eight-hour train trip there from Little Rock to help settle the situation.

In addition to these demographic, labor, economic, and political (structural) factors in place in Phillips County by 1919, cultural concerns also came into play leading up to the riot. African Americans constituted some 1,218 of the 1,680 men from the county who entered the military during World War I.[140] Like many of their counterparts, a number of these African Americans enjoyed more food and money than they ever had in their lives. Others, who went through boot camp in northern cities, experienced freedoms like they never had before as well. One black soldier from Helena (the government seat of Phillips County) wrote home from Camp Sherman, Ohio, in 1917, "I can go to Cleveland every Saturday if I want to. We have shows and all kinds of music and games for a good time. We play football and have prize fights here at the camp. We do not have to buy anything but stamps."[141] Like African American veterans around the country, those returning to Phillips County after the war expected to be treated with respect.

"We helped you fight the Germans, and are ready to help you fight the next fellows that get after you," one of the area's black organizers of the Progressive Farmers and Household Union of America stated after the riot, "but we want to be treated fairly."[142] Whites tuned into these assertions. Indeed, a military record that appeared after the riot suggested that the most belligerent of the black leaders in the area had served in the military.[143] In addition, rumors circulated among the county's whites before the riot that black veterans had received "letters from French girls urging them to rise up against the white population and secure their 'rights.'"[144] Although no evidence ever emerged to substantiate these claims, whites obviously felt threatened by the effect that the war had on the region's black veterans.

With worsening economic conditions and a renewed urgency shared by African Americans to assert their rights, area blacks decided they needed to organize to improve their situation in Phillips County. Concerned local whites formed a committee to investigate exactly what sort of uprising African Americans had in mind, and they soon came to the conclusion that the area's blacks had hatched a plan to kill the county's white planters.[145] Tensions came to a head on September 30, 1919. That night, at the behest of local black farmer Robert Hill, a group of black men and women met at a small, rural church in Hoop Spur three miles north of Elaine to organize a sharecroppers' and tenant farmers' union, the Progressive Farmers and Household Union of America. For a number of reasons, they remained unhappy over the local landowners' treatment of them—like other sharecroppers, they could purchase provisions only at specific stores, they paid more than the average retail prices, they were not allowed to see an enumerated list of their debts, and they never knew the dollar value of their portion of the cotton sold. Only a few months earlier, one black farmer in Star City, Arkansas, had also objected to this system and refused to work. Shortly thereafter, a group of white men lynched him and tacked a sign to his head that read, "This is how we treat lazy niggers."[146]

Nonetheless, the group gathered at the church to plan. Two white law enforcement officials arrived there a short time later; they exchanged gunfire, and one of the officers fell dead. Two accounts of events emerged. One story related that one of the white officers fired first into the church, and then the black guards surrounding the church returned fire. Another report asserted that the white men had simply parked by the church to fix a tire and soon came under fire by unidentified persons, almost certainly black.[147] As word got out of the shootings, a local sheriff called on men in neighboring areas to come to the aid of their white brethren. Motivated by suggestions that the Progressive Union promoted social equality and by rumors that the blacks in Phillips County had prepared for a slaughter of the white denizens, hundreds of armed men arrived from surrounding counties and states. White newspapers helped spread the word. "The *Helena World,* the white-owned daily paper in Phillips County," according to scholar Grif Stockley, "was the principal instrument by which the leading white citizens of Phillips County disseminated the view that there was a plot to kill planters."[148]

Other newspapers fed into the heightened racial tensions as well. Shortly after the violence erupted, the Arkansas *Gazette* announced what many of the county's whites had suspected for months in its headline, NEGROES HAVE BEEN AROUSED BY PROPAGANDA. The article went on to state that "[c]onsiderable propaganda had been spread in practically every section of Phillips County during the past four or five months, urging negroes to join the Progressive Farmers' Household Union, whose motto is: 'Torch of Liberty and Rights of Man.'"[149] In addition to this union propaganda, the county's whites also knew that area African Americans read with interest the *Chicago Defender.* The paper stridently condemned the Jim Crow practices of the South and trumpeted the advancements of African Americans around the country. And although the *Defender* originally took a neutral stance toward unions, by 1918, it began to support the efforts of these organizations.[150] Moreover, the newspaper's shipping records show that Phillips County and its surrounding area "had among the highest number of subscribers in the South."[151] Tellingly, Governor Brough, convinced that the paper had stirred black passions regarding the labor situation leading up to and after the Elaine riot, lobbied the postmaster general to keep it out of the state.[152]

But as word spread that white men had inundated Phillips County to put down the supposed black insurrection, the area's African Americans hid in the nearby woods.[153] Throughout the day on October 1, bands of whites searched the county for African Americans and killed many of them. The next day, at the behest of local authorities, some 500 federal troops from Camp Pike arrived along with the governor. They patrolled the region, and, with the area now under martial law, the violence quickly abated.[154] At least 25 blacks and 5 whites died, but many observers believed that as many as 200 blacks perished during the riot. On October 3, Governor Brough made the stunning announcement that "[t]he white citizens of the county . . . deserve unstinted praise for their action in preventing violence."[155] Obviously in the white camp of how events played out during late September and early October 1919 in Phillips County, Arkansas, Brough would later declare that the violence erupted because of a "damnable conspiracy [by blacks] to murder white citizens and take possession of their property."[156]

Shortly after the riot ended, a Committee of Seven appointed by the governor (some of whom belonged to the committee that scrutinized the activities of the area's black leaders during the months before the violence) investigated the incident.[157] Not surprisingly, they blamed the county's African Americans. In a statement that ran in several newspapers, the committee concluded:

> The present trouble with the negroes in Phillips County in not a race riot. It is a deliberately planned insurrection of the negroes against the whites directed by an organization known as the "Progressive Farmers and Household Union of America," established for the purpose of banding negroes together for the killing of white people.[158]

Similar to events that played out in other cities that summer, authorities arrested some 700 blacks and 1 white man (the lawyer who agreed to help the area's blacks organize their union), and 67 received prison time. Twelve black farmers acquired death sentences for allegedly killing whites during the riot. During their trial, a crowd of whites rushed the courthouse and warned that it would lynch these men if they were not sentenced to death. Not surprisingly, the judge acquiesced, and all 12 men received the death penalty. The NAACP fought the ruling, taking it all the way to the Supreme

African American men taken prisoner by U.S. Army troops sent from Camp Pike during the riot in Phillips County, Arkansas, 1919. (From the Collections of the Arkansas History Commission)

Court. On February 19, 1923, the court agreed that the trial had been a sham in *Moore v. Dempsey*. All 12 men eventually gained their freedom.[159]

Out of this unstable situation emerged the horrors of the Red Summer. The race riots that erupted throughout the nation in 1919 shared important commonalities with each other. Structural conditions, such as the postwar economic letdown and black urban and northern migration, played a critical role. As many as a third of a million blacks left the Deep South, creating fierce competition for scarce jobs and housing.[160] But even in the South, as evidenced in Phillips County, labor tensions flourished. Adding to this strain, the Red Scare created a general atmosphere of aggression and a warped sense of patriotism.[161] Any appearance of otherness from the norm of white Anglo-Saxon Protestantism caused reason to lash out. Organizations, such as the Ku Klux Klan, served as fire tenders, ensuring that racial animosity remained salient.

Other similarities emerged as well. In almost all of the cases, whites struck out against blacks. Even in Phillips County, where accounts differ of what transpired, the African Americans had assembled peacefully and were approached by the whites. Moreover, in all cases, the African Americans fought back (or stood ready to in the case of Omaha). The old Jim Crow mentality had run up against the New Negro movement. Involvement in World War I and an awareness of their own heritage created a strong sense of importance and self-worth within the black community. Adding to these dynamics, inept or complicit police forces and an irresponsible press added fuel to the fire. In many of the riots, authorities arrested more blacks than whites and oftentimes did not come to the assistance of black victims at all. Moreover, rumors of African American aggression or misdeeds spread rapidly among the white communities, and newspapers only made these reports more widespread. Groups serving as conversion specialists, such as white sailors and marines and white athletic clubs, cued other whites when the time had come to act.

Chapter 6

TRANSITIONS: THE CHANGING NATURE OF RACE RIOTS

Some 50 major white-on-black riots marred the American landscape from the Progressive Era through World War II. With 26 riots during the Red Summer of 1919 alone, these months served as the pinnacle of white riots against African Americans in the U.S. history. While major race riots ignited Tulsa in 1921, and Rosewood, Florida, in 1923, the 1920s and 1930s saw fewer and fewer white-on-black disturbances as the Great Depression gripped the country.[1] Federal assistance for both blacks and whites, less migration, and fewer prospects for interracial competition likely contributed to this relative calm. Like the Great War a generation earlier, however, World War II and its resultant turmoil unleashed more racial violence in the United States in the 1940s.[2] Some of the riots during World War II remained instances of white-on-black violence similar to those of the preceding decades (the main focus of this study), such as in Beaumont and Mobile, Alabama, in 1943.[3] Others, however, like the one in Harlem in 1943, foreshadowed the black ghetto riots (initiated in the black communities against property and businesses) that marked the decade of the 1960s.[4] World War II, therefore, serves as a transition to a new era in the U.S. race riots.[5] The 1943 riot in Detroit provides insights into this shifting nature of race riots in American history, as it held the characteristics of both the white-on-black riots of the preceding era and the black ghetto riots prevalent two decades later.

World War II profoundly affected conditions in Detroit. Bolstered by the powerful car industry, the Motor City became the principal and most prolific defense center in the country during the war, prompting

President Franklin Roosevelt to dub it the "arsenal of democracy."[6] Federal defense contracts worth billions of dollars poured into the region, enticing some 500,000 workers, primarily from the South and Midwest. Blacks comprised a large portion of this migrant labor, and firms that had largely excluded them in the past began to hire them.[7] The 1940 census places approximately 160,000 African Americans in Detroit, but only three years later, an estimated 220,000 blacks resided there.[8] Moreover, a number of cultural and ethnic groups—Lithuanians, Jews, Poles, Hungarians, Scottish, Irish, Italians, and others—called Detroit home, but most of these communities had begun to scatter throughout the city (not living in separate, isolated clusters anymore) by the 1920s. Detroit in the 1920s also saw the ascendance of the Ku Klux Klan, and the group's write-in candidate almost won the mayor's race in 1924.[9] The Klan still had strong ties to the city two decades later. Indeed, by the 1940s, race had become the defining factor in Detroit's geographical makeup.[10]

The wartime influx of people particularly put a great burden on the city's employment, housing, and transportation services, causing most of Detroit's blacks to cramp into a 30-block ghetto called Paradise Valley and amplifying animosity between the races.[11] Racial tensions flared intermittently between 1941 and 1943, most notably at Northwestern High School, the Sojourner Truth housing project, and the automobile plants. Moreover, the Klan and other white supremacist groups frequently organized hate strikes at various factories around the city to protest any advancements made by black employees.[12] One of the biggest of the strikes occurred three weeks before the riot, when 25,000 white workers walked out during the first week of June when the Packard plant upgraded three blacks.[13] "I'd rather see Hitler and Hirohito win," someone yelled over a loudspeaker, "than work next to a nigger."[14]

Finally, tensions came to a head on the hot Sunday evening of June 20, 1943. Various fights broke out between the city's whites and blacks on Belle Isle, a public park surrounded by the Detroit River. After 10:00 that night, another scuffle exploded between white and black youths on the bridge leading back to the city.[15] By 11:20 P.M., estimates placed some 5,000 people, primarily white, near the end of the bridge toward the mainland. "[H]ad the disturbance ended with the incidents at Belle Isle and the bridge approach," a commission subsequently created by the governor concluded, "none of the deaths occurring in the riot would have resulted."[16] Unfortunately, the violence did not end there. Rumors began to flow through both the black and white communities of atrocities committed on their members by the other race. As scholar Marilynn Johnson explains,

In the white neighbourhood along Woodward Avenue, rumours circulated that "a negro had raped a white woman on Belle Island." Army intelligence also reported heavy telephone traffic among whites passing rumours that blacks had slit a white sailor's throat and raped his girlfriend. . . . The social identity of the victims—a sailor and his girlfriend—suggested an attack on both noble white manhood and innocent white womanhood.

In the nearby black district of Paradise Valley, a somewhat different version of the rumour emerged. At approximately 12:30 a.m., a young man seized the microphone at the Forest Club, a popular black nightspot, and urged the 500 patrons to take up arms against whites who had "thrown a colored lady and her baby" off the Belle Isle Bridge. His remarks echoed rumours already circulating in the area that white sailors had "thrown a Negro woman and her baby into the lake." In many ways, the black rumours paralleled the white ones with a simple inversion of villains and victims. But there were important differences as well. In the white versions, the female victim was a young white woman defiled by black rapists; in the black versions, a white mob drowned and/or killed a black mother and child.[17]

Again, rumors, framed similarly to those in past riots, played an important part in ratcheting up the violence between the races.

Indeed, for both blacks and whites, these rumors served as the rallying cry for them to act.[18] Each side assembled in their respective neighborhoods to prepare for the impending race war. And throughout the next day, whites attacked blacks in streetcars and automobiles, and blacks looted and destroyed white-owned businesses and targeted whites passing by in their cars.[19] State and local police had little command over the situation, with less than 900 of them trying to contain the violence. Tellingly, reports also emerged that the police focused primarily on the black rioters. And, in fact, although whites as well as blacks participated in the melee, all 17 people killed by the police during the riot were black.[20] Finally, at 9:25 P.M. on June 21, the governor requested that federal troops be sent to Detroit to stop the riot.[21] Within hours, the federal troops restored order, too late for the 34 people—25 black and 9 white—who died, and the (at least) 775 people who suffered injuries. Some $2 million worth of property damage also occurred.[22]

Detroit's 1943 riot epitomizes the shift in race riots in the middle of the 20th century. The white-on-black riots that erupted with viciousness from the Progressive Era through World War II gave way to the black ghetto riots of the 1960s. The 1943 Detroit riot highlights features of both eras. Detroit's whites still targeted any African American they could find during the riot, pulling them out of streetcars and automobiles, and beating them to bloody pulps. However, like the riots to come in the 1960s, the city's blacks looted and destroyed white-owned businesses, too. Tense economic conditions, police ineffectiveness and complicity, racial segregation, and African Americans serving in uniform abroad all occurred in 1943 Detroit, just as in the earlier riots and the riots that would come in the 1960s.

This study forwards a general approach to explain how structural factors, cultural framing, and precipitating events triggered the race riots in the United States from the Progressive Era through World War II. My research carefully examines the national conditions and local circumstances that constructed an environment that allowed these race riots to erupt. Some scholars argue that race riots can be understood only within their local context and that no distinctive pattern arises across place and time. My work, however, disputes this claim. Although unique in some respects, riots do share common characteristics that can be highlighted within the broader context in which they occur. My work links the national concerns to local circumstances. It also represents an effort to bring a theoretical framework to the understanding of riots in general by focusing on the American riots of the late 19th century and the first half of the 20th. Specifically, my research focuses on two groups of riots—the racial pogroms in Wilmington (1898), New Orleans (1900), Atlanta (1906), East St. Louis (1917), Tulsa (1921), and Beaumont (1943), and the 1919 Red Summer riots in Longview, Washington, D.C., Chicago, Knoxville, Omaha, and Phillips County.

In the racial pogroms, demographic change, economic turmoil, labor strife, political competition, southern whites' codification of disfranchisement and segregation, and the ineffectiveness and complicity of both police and governmental authorities provided the structural factors that produced an atmosphere ripe for conflict. Cultural framing offers an understanding into why white southerners decided they had to act with violence against African Americans. White supremacy created a radical mind-set by the 1890s that would not accept any black social, political, or economic advancement. This notion of racial superiority put virtuous white women on a pedestal and used racial amalgamation and the imagined black beast rapist to produce white anxiety and paranoia. Whites feared that a younger generation of African Americans did not know their place and turned to violence to restore a white view of social order. Newspapers spread this toxic message to great effect. At the same time, blacks used a variety of methods to fight back, survive, and expose the hypocrisy of white Americans. Whites met black assertions of equality with violence and intimidation. Spurred on by rumors, precipitating events in these racial pogroms centered on alleged or real violations against white womanhood or white authority and power.

The 1919 Red Summer riots marked the apex of both white riots against African Americans and a heightened black response to this type of violence. National and international events, especially World War I, profoundly affected race relations throughout the United States. During the Great Migration, hundreds of thousands of African Americans left the rural South for the economic opportunities provided by the war effort. This movement created tensions over housing, transportation, and resources. As a result, whites used violence to enforce separation of the races. Moreover, whites resented labor and political competition from African Americans. Authorities only sometimes provided the needed muscle or inclination to prevent these white attacks on blacks. World War I also produced new visions of equality as Americans fought a war to make the world safe for democracy. African Americans embraced this idea and pushed for social change. At the same time, as blacks moved into their midst, northern whites increasingly adopted southern racial attitudes. These structural factors and cultural frameworks, therefore, created a volatile situation that exploded when a precipitating event appeared. In these cases, alleged black infractions against white women or the color line led to riots.

Political considerations played a significant role in both the racial pogroms and the Red Summer race riots during the late 19th and the first half of the 20th centuries. In Wilmington, for example, white rioters sought to disfranchise African Americans and push them completely out of the political arena. Fusion efforts between Republicans and third parties led the Democratic Party to use violence—including riots—to ensure their own political dominance. As African Americans moved to cities and to the North, they demonstrated growing political strength with their votes. In Chicago in 1919, African Americans' support of the white mayor infuriated many of the city's whites, who wanted to maintain political hegemony and prevent black political participation. Thus, electoral politics provides an important link among the riots that erupted throughout the Progressive Era to World War II. This study uncovers the significance of these political passions.

Although whites had used violence against African Americans since colonial times, the race riots that exploded from the Progressive Era through World War II provide an ideal opportunity to explore what conditions come together to provoke latent racial hostility to boil to the surface and into outright violence. Past scholars examining the riots of the late 19th and first half of the 20th centuries tended to focus on one riot or a narrower time span. Other studies included these riots within a larger framework. The existing literature, therefore, lacked a thorough assessment of this whole period—the Progressive Era through World War II—on its own.

My work fills in this gap, offering an overarching framework that can be applied across cases and over time. By analyzing structural factors, cultural framing, and precipitating events, better insights can be gained into why riots occur. More research can enhance this study, exploring other riots in different eras and even in various places around the world. By looking at structural factors, cultural framing, and precipitating events, we can gain a better understanding of why "all hell breaks loose."

EPILOGUE

American race riots have elicited a variety of official responses in their immediate aftermath, and sometimes even many decades later. Since the 1917 East St. Louis race riot, one way that government officials have reacted in the wake of racial violence in particular cities has been to set up riot commissions or committees directly after the disturbances occurred. These temporary, authoritative bodies undertake the responsibility "to *investigate* and *explain* [these] specific outbursts of illegal collective violence by private citizens."[1] Significantly, they also offer recommendations to government authorities to prevent future bloodshed and destruction. Sometimes the city experiencing the riot itself has created such a commission—the 1935 Mayor's Commission on Conditions in Harlem, and the 1968 Chicago Riot Study Committee, for example. In other instances, commissions have been generated from state-level authorities—the 1919 Chicago Commission on Race Relations, the 1943 Governor's Committee to Investigate Riot Occurring in Detroit, and the 1965 Governor's Commission on the Los Angeles Riots, for instance. Still other commissions have stemmed from the auspices of national officials—such as the 1917 Special Committee Authorized by Congress to Investigate the East St. Louis Riots, and the 1968 National Advisory Commission on Civil Disorders.[2]

These organizations have been vital to pinpointing some of the factors and conditions leading to the riots in the first place and in supplying specific proposals to alleviate these troubles. Unfortunately, several problems have also plagued these commissions. Members of these bodies have invariably included only those individuals from established groups (i.e., Republicans and Democrats, but not independents; organized labor and big business owners, but not nonunion workers). "In this way," scholar Anthony Platt suggests, "riot commissions are inherently conservative, protective of existing institutions and not disposed to propose radical changes which will diminish the power of established groups."[3] Moreover, these groups have predominantly included older white males. Of the four commissions set up following riots that occurred from the Progressive Era through World War II (East St. Louis, Chicago, Harlem 1935, and Detroit), for example, only 1 woman (on the Harlem commission), 13 African Americans (6 on the Chicago commission and 7 on the Harlem commission), and 11 people under the age of 50 (2 in Chicago, 6 in Harlem, and 3 in Detroit) served out of a total of 34 commissioners.[4] Most damning, however, has been the lack of response to the recommendations put forth by these organizations. As one expert testified before the 1968 National Advisory Commission on Civil Disorders:

> I read that report . . . of the 1919 riot in Chicago, and it is as if I were reading the report of the investigating committee on the Harlem riot of '35, the report of the investigating committee on the Harlem riot of '43, the report of the McCone Commission on the Watts riot.
>
> I must again in candor say to you members of this Commission—it is a kind of Alice in Wonderland—with the same moving picture re-shown over and over again, the same analysis, the same recommendations, and the same inaction.[5]

Thus, while these commissions have offered steps in the right direction, governmental authorities have done little in the way of acting on their ideas. African Americans, in other words, have gained few concrete benefits through the efforts of these reports.

In recent years, government officials have adopted another approach to deal with some of the race riots that have erupted throughout American history. Based largely on the truth commissions that emerged around the world in the last few decades, these organizations in the United States have been established to study long-ago riots in order to remedy lingering problems stemming from these incidents. Increasingly popular in the 1990s in a number of countries around the world as a way to heal their populaces in the wake of heinous atrocities committed on them by their own government officials, truth commissions have served similar (but often broader) functions to the riot commissions of earlier eras. While the Truth and Reconciliation Commission of South Africa stands out as one of the most recognized of these bodies on the world scene, numerous places—primarily in Latin America, Africa, and Asia—have used them.[6] As scholar Priscilla Hayner explains,

> Struggling with the limited options for confronting past atrocities, and with an eye towards the challenge of building a human rights culture for the future, many new governments have turned to mechanisms outside the judicial system to both confront and learn from the horrific crimes of the past. There has been increasing interest, especially, in mechanisms of official truth-seeking, through the creation of temporary commissions to dig up, investigate and analyse the pattern of politically motivated rights crimes. . . . A truth commission is not a court of law; it does not determine individual criminal liability or order criminal sanctions. On the other hand, a truth commission can do many things that courts can't or generally don't do. Trials focus on the actions of specific individuals; truth commissions focus on the large pattern of overall events. . . . Also, courts do not typically investigate the various social or political factors which led to the violence. . . . Courts do not submit policy recommendations or suggestions for political, military or judicial reforms. And finally, while court records may be public, court opinions are generally not widely distributed and widely read, as is typical of truth commission reports.[7]

In the United States, although the violence and destruction occurred decades or even a hundred years earlier, several riot cities felt compelled to set up truth commissions as a way to establish the truth of what happened and to make recommendations of how to redress enduring grievances between the races.

To date, the state legislatures in Florida, Oklahoma, and North Carolina have established these commissions for the riots in Rosewood (1923), Tulsa (1921), and Wilmington (1898) respectively. In 2006, 100 years after the Atlanta race riot, that city formed the Coalition to Remember the 1906 Atlanta Race Riot with the Atlanta-based group Southern Truth and Reconciliation. Much like the various truth commissions around the world, the four U.S. organizations not only share similar goals but also differ in their scope and recommendations.

The Florida state legislature appointed the Rosewood group in 1993 to research exactly what occurred in January 1923 and report back to them after a state legislator introduced a bill to grant compensation to the victims. After the investigative team (comprised five scholars from Florida State University, Florida A&M University, and University of Florida) submitted their findings to the legislature, both the House and the Senate approved the bill, and the governor signed it in May 1994. One hundred and seventy-two people received payments between $220 and $450,000 for the emotional trauma and property loss stemming from the riot. The bill also established a scholarship fund for families and descendants of the residents of Rosewood to use at state universities.[8]

The Oklahoma state legislature set up a commission in 1997 to provide the history of the Tulsa riot, gather testimony of survivors, and give advice about reparations.[9] The commission's (consisting of a chairman, nine commissioners, two sponsors, and two advisors) 2001 final report reconciled the events that transpired in 1921 in Tulsa and offered four recommendations: "direct payments to riot survivors and descendants; a scholarship fund available to students affected by the riot; establishment of an economic development enterprise zone in the historic Greenwood district; a memorial for the riot victims."[10] The state legislature, however, proved reluctant to grant reparations, and after a lawsuit made its way through the court system, no one received any (the courts ruled that the two-year statute of limitations on claims had expired).[11] The state legislature did pass a bill to denounce the riot, set up a corporation (therefore using no public money) to award scholarships to descendants of survivors, and create a riot memorial commission (using $750,000 of state money). In a perverse gesture, the legislature "also approved of the use of the state seal on medals, to be minted with private funds, and awarded to riot survivors."[12] In 2008, Tulsans established the John Hope Franklin Center for Reconciliation "to transform the bitterness and mistrust caused by years of racial division, even violence, into a hopeful future of reconciliation and cooperation for Tulsa and the nation."[13]

The North Carolina state legislature set up the Wilmington Race Riot Commission in 2000 to establish what took place before and during the 1898 riot there. The 13-member group also analyzed the economic and demographic devastation the city's African American population suffered as a result of the violence.[14] Its final report, released in May 2006, laid out 15 recommendations—including reparations—under the broad headings of empowerment, economic redevelopment, education, and commemoration.[15] Alternatively, Atlanta's commission for the 1906 race riot, spurred on by efforts of the Southern Truth and Reconciliation organization (and not the state legislature), had broader goals simply "to create public awareness of the riot and its legacy, facilitate open and ongoing dialogue amongst diverse communities, and inspire positive systemic change in Atlanta's racial relations."[16] It held a series of public meetings, showed documentaries about the riot, and led several walking tours for these purposes.

These organizations, like their predecessors created in the immediate aftermath of the riots, grappled with the forces that came together to spur whites into horrific action against their black neighbors. They also strove to deal with the repercussions that continued to plague these communities so many years later. They sometimes met hostility. The Tulsa commission, for example, incited much controversy.[17] But community leaders realized their restorative power as well. By acknowledging the ghastly events of years past, and by establishing an official record of what occurred, these commissions provided a common discourse so that the communities could move forward and work to bring blacks and whites together.

NOTES

INTRODUCTION

1. Scott Ellsworth, *Death in a Promised Land: The Tulsa Race Riot of 1921* (Baton Rouge: Louisiana State University Press, 1982), 48.

2. Lee E. Williams and Lee E. Williams II, *Anatomy of Four Race Riots: Racial Conflicts in Knoxville, Elaine (Arkansas), Tulsa and Chicago, 1919–1921* (Hattiesburg: University and College Press of Mississippi, 1972), 59.

3. W.E.B. Du Bois, *Dusk of Dawn* (Millwood: Kraus-Thomson Organization, 1975), 264.

4. Stephen W. Grable, "Racial Violence within the Context of Community History," *Phylon* 42 (1981): 275, emphasis mine.

5. In fact, most Americans probably think of the 1960s black "ghetto" riots or the 1992 Los Angeles riot that stemmed from the acquittal of the police officers who beat Rodney King when they hear the term "race riot." Numerous studies have examined these riots and their causes. See especially Allen D. Grimshaw, ed., *Racial Violence in the United States* (Chicago: Aldine Publishing Company, 1969) and Mark Baldassare, ed., *The Los Angeles Riots: Lessons for the Urban Future* (Boulder: Westview Press, 1994).

6. See, for example, Ellsworth, *Death in a Promised Land*; William Ivy Hair, *Carnival of Fury: Robert Charles and the New Orleans Race Riot of 1900* (Baton Rouge: Louisiana State University Press, 1976); Mark Bauerlein, *Negrophobia: A Race Riot in Atlanta, 1906* (San Francisco: Encounter Books, 2001); Elliot M. Rudwick, *Race Riot at East St. Louis July 2, 1917* (Carbondale: Southern Illinois University Press, 1964); William M. Tuttle Jr., *Race Riot: Chicago in the Red Summer of 1919* (Champaign: University of Illinois Press, 1996); Harper Barnes, *Never Been a Time: The*

1917 Race Riot That Sparked the Civil Rights Movement (New York: Walker & Company, 2008); and Dominic J. Capeci Jr. and Martha Wilkerson, *Layered Violence: The Detroit Rioters of 1943* (Jackson: University Press of Mississippi, 1991).

7. See Williams and Williams, *Anatomy of Four Race Riots* and Arthur I. Waskow, *From Race Riot to Sit-In, 1919 and the 1960s: A Study in the Connections between Conflict and Violence* (Garden City: Doubleday, 1966).

8. See Joel Williamson, *The Crucible of Race: Black-White Relations in the American South Since Emancipation* (New York: Oxford University Press, 1984); Paul A. Gilje, *Rioting in America* (Bloomington: Indiana University Press, 1996); and Hugh Davis Graham and Ted Robert Gurr, eds., *Violence in America: Historical & Comparative Perspectives* (Beverly Hills: Sage Publications, 1979).

9. See, for example, Steven E. Barkan and Lynne L. Snowden, *Collective Violence* Boston: Allyn and Bacon, 2001), 5, 7, and 29, and James W. Button, *Black Violence: Political Impact of the 1960s Riots* (Princeton: Princeton University Press, 1978), 7. Although other scholars pinpoint a specific number of participants in their surveys of riots, I purposely eschew doing so in this study. See Gilje, *Rioting in America,* 4, for example, who defines a riot as involving 12 or more people; See also William A. Heaps, *Riots, U.S.A. 1765–1970* (New York: Seabury Press, 1970), 5, who identifies Judge Charles P. Daly in the New York City Court of General Sessions as having deemed on September 12, 1849, that "whenever three or more persons, in a tumultuous manner, use force or violence in the execution of any design wherein the law does not allow the use of force, they are guilty of riot." Robert Menschel, *Markets, Mobs & Mayhem: A Modern Look at the Madness of Crowds* (Hoboken: John Wiley & Sons, Inc., 2002), 140, places the origins of "riot" in English law, defining it as "a tumultuous disturbance of the peace by three or more persons." In most riots during the time period under study in this volume, though, tens, hundreds, or often thousands of individuals joined the action.

10. Paul R. Brass, *Theft of an Idol: Text and Context in the Representation of Collective Violence* (Princeton: Princeton University Press, 1997), 8, 14.

11. Richard Maxwell Brown, *Strain of Violence: Historical Studies of American Violence and Vigilantism* (New York: Oxford University Press, 1975), 5.

12. H. Jon Rosenbaum and Peter C. Sederberg, "Vigilantism: An Analysis of Establishment Violence," *Comparative Politics* 6 (1974): 17.

13. David Holthouse, "The Year in Hate, 2008: Number of Hate Groups Tops 900," *Southern Poverty Law Intelligence Report* 133 (2009).

CHAPTER 1

1. Hugh Davis Graham and Ted Robert Gurr, eds., *Violence in America: Historical & Comparative Perspectives* (Beverly Hills: Sage Publications, 1979); Herbert Shapiro, *White Violence and Black Response: From Reconstruction to Montgomery* (Amherst: University of Massachusetts Press, 1988).

2. Paul A. Gilje, *Rioting in America* (Bloomington: Indiana University Press, 1996), 89.

3. Gilje, *Rioting in America,* 92–94.

4. Allen D. Grimshaw, "Lawlessness and Violence in America and Their Special Manifestations in Changing Negro-White Relationships," *Journal of Negro History* 44 (1959): 60.

5. Gilje, *Rioting in America,* 91–92.

6. George C. Rable, *But There Was No Peace: The Role of Violence in the Politics of Reconstruction* (Athens: University of Georgia Press, 1984), 15; David W. Blight, *Race and Reunion: The Civil War in American Memory* (Cambridge: Belknap Press of Harvard University, 2001), 110.

7. Although the Klan became the most recognized terror organization within the United States, other state and local white supremacist groups formed after the Civil War as well. According to one source, 326 "vigilante groups" eventually formed during the postbellum era. See Arnold P. Goldstein, *The Psychology of Group Aggression* (Chichester: John Wiley & Sons, 2002), 107. Their membership often became "ku kluxed," as the Klan eventually embodied "any vigilante band operating in disguise." Steven Hahn, *A Nation under Our Feet: Black Political Struggles in the Rural South from Slavery to the Great Migration* (Cambridge: Belknap Press of Harvard University Press, 2003), 267. Other cabals included the White Brotherhood, the Invisible Empire, and the Constitutional Union Guard in North Carolina; the Hancock Guards, the Seymour Knights, the Innocents, the Swamp Fox Rangers, and the Knights of the White Camelia in Louisiana; and the Knights of the Black Cross, Heggie's Scouts, the Washington Brothers, and the Robinsons Clubs in Mississippi. Hahn, *A Nation under Our Feet,* 267. In some states, in addition to or in place of the Klan itself, the Democratic Party relied on rifle clubs, the Red Shirts (see the Wilmington, North Carolina, riot in this study, for example), and the White Leagues as its "paramilitary wings." Hahn, *A Nation under Our Feet,* 288; James M. McPherson, *Ordeal by Fire: The Civil War and Reconstruction* (New York: Knopf, 1982), 557.

8. Gilje, *Rioting in America,* 87–100; McPherson, *Ordeal by Fire,* 557.

9. Edward L. Ayers, *Vengeance and Justice: Crime and Punishment in the 19th Century American South* (New York: Oxford University Press, 1984): 161.

10. Ayers, *Vengeance and Justice,* 161; Shapiro, *White Violence and Black Response,* 11.

11. Shapiro, *White Violence and Black Response,* 16–19.

12. Melinda Meek Hennessey, "Racial Violence during Reconstruction: The 1876 Riots in Charleston and Cainhoy," *South Carolina Historical Magazine* 86 (1985): 100; see also Gilje, *Rioting in America,* 100.

13. Gilje, *Rioting in America,* 101.

14. Historian Joel Williamson contends this brand of radical mentality emerged around 1889 and lasted until 1915. From 1897 through 1907, he asserts, "it possessed terrific power." Joel Williamson, *The Crucible of Race: Black-White Relations in the American South since Emancipation* (New York: Oxford University Press, 1984), 6.

15. Williamson, *Crucible of Race,* 6, 184.

16. Jacquelyn Dowd Hall, *Revolt against Chivalry: Jessie Daniel Ames and the Women's Campaign against Lynching* (New York: Columbia University, 1993), xxxiv.

17. Williamson, *Crucible of Race*, 306–310.

18. Gilje, *Rioting in America*, 101–102.

19. Donald L. Horowitz, *The Deadly Ethnic Riot* (Berkeley: University of California Press, 2001), 124.

20. I adhere to the term "race riot" in this work not only because previous scholars employ its usage but also because the involved actors and their contemporaries (newspaper editors, reporters, and politicians) did so as well.

21. Horowitz, *Deadly Ethnic Riot*, 1, 14. For distinctions between groups, crowds, mobs, and riots, see Goldstein, *Psychology of Group Aggression*, 105–106; Robert S. Baron, Norbert L. Kerr, and Norman Miller, *Group Process, Group Decision, Group Action* (Pacific Grove: Brooks/Cole Publishing Company, 1992), 2; Clark McPhail and Ronald T. Wohlstein, "Individual and Collective Behaviors within Gatherings, Demonstrations, and Riots," *Annual Review of Sociology* 9 (1983): 581; Eugene E. Leach, "The Literature of Riot Duty: Managing Class Conflict in the Streets, 1877–1927," *Radical History Review* 56 (1993): 42–43; John Bohstedt, "The Dynamics of Riots: Escalation and Diffusion/Contagion," in *The Dynamics of Aggression: Biological and Social Processes in Dyads and Groups*, ed. Michael Potegal and John F. Knutson (Hillsdale: Lawrence Erlbaum Associates, 1994), 257; Ervin Staub and Lori H. Rosenthal, "Mob Violence: Cultural-Societal Sources, Instigators, Group Processes, and Participants," in *The Psychology of Good and Evil: Why Children, Adults, and Groups Help and Harm Others*, ed. Ervin Staub (New York: Cambridge University Press, 2003), 377–378; and William A. Heaps, *Riots, U.S.A. 1765–1970* (New York: Seabury Press, 1970), 5.

22. Douglas S. Massey and Nancy A. Denton, *American Apartheid: Segregation and the Making of the Underclass* (Cambridge: Harvard University Press, 1993), 30.

23. Raymond M. Momboisse, *Riots, Revolts, and Insurrections* (Springfield: Thomas, 1967), 14–20. See also Goldstein, *Psychology of Group Aggression*, 108.

24. Thomas C. Schelling, "The Process of Residential Segregation: Neighborhood Tipping," in *Racial Discrimination in Economic Life*, ed. A. Pascal (Lexington: Lexington Books, 1972); Thomas C. Schelling, *Micromotives and Macrobehavior* (New York: Norton, 1978).

25. Malcolm Gladwell, *The Tipping Point: How Little Things Can Make a Big Difference* (Boston: Little, Brown and Company, 2000); David D. Laitin, *Identity in Formation: The Russian-Speaking Populations in the Near Abroad* (Ithaca: Cornell University Press, 1998).

26. Schelling, *Micromotives and Macrobehavior*.

27. See, for example, Laitin, *Identity in Formation*; Sun-Ki Chai, "Rational Choice and Culture: Clashing Perspectives or Complementary Modes of Analysis?," in *Culture Matters: Essays in Honor of Aaron Wildavsky*, ed. Richard J. Ellis and Michael Thompson (Boulder: HarperCollins Publishers, 1997); Roger Dale Petersen, *Resistance and Rebellion: Lessons from Eastern Europe* (New York:

Cambridge University Press, 2001); and Lisa Baldez, *Why Women Protest: Women's Movements in Chile* (New York: Cambridge University Press, 2002).

28. Baldez, *Why Women Protest*, 6.

29. See Dennis Chong, *Collective Action and the Civil Rights Movement* (Chicago: University of Chicago Press, 1991); Susanne Lohmann, "The Dynamics of Informational Cascades: The Monday Demonstrations in Leipzig, East Germany, 1989–91," *World Politics* 47 (1994); and Charles Cameron and Sunita Parikh, "Riot Games: A Theory of Mass Political Violence" (paper presented at the Wallace Institute Conference on Political Economy, Rochester, New York, October 19–20, 2000).

30. James R. Grossman, *Land of Hope: Chicago, Black Southerners, and the Great Migration* (Chicago: University of Chicago Press, 1989), 3–4.

31. See Eric Rauchway, *Murdering McKinley: The Making of Theodore Roosevelt's America* (New York: Hill and Wang, 2003).

32. See C. Vann Woodward, *Tom Watson: Agrarian Rebel* (New York: Oxford University Press, 1963).

33. See Stanley Lieberson and Arnold K. Silverman, "The Precipitants and Underlying Conditions of Race Riots," *American Sociological Review* 30 (1965): 887–898.

34. Sun-Ki Chai and Brendon Swedlow, eds., *Culture and Social Theory* (New Brunswick: Transaction Publishers, 1998), 2.

35. David A. Snow and Robert D. Benford, "Master Frames and Cycles of Protest," in *Frontiers in Social Movement Theory*, ed. Aldon D. Morris and Carol McClurg Mueller (New Haven: Yale University Press, 1992), 137.

36. Marc W. Steinberg, "Tilting the Frame: Considerations on Collective Action Framing from a Discursive Turn," *Theory and Society* 27 (1998): 846.

37. Williamson, *Crucible of Race*. See also C. Vann Woodward, *The Strange Career of Jim Crow* (New York: Oxford University Press, 1996) and Howard N. Rabinowitz, *The First New South: 1865–1920* (Arlington Heights: Harlan Davidson, 1992).

38. Quoted in Grif Stockley, *Blood in Their Eyes: The Elaine Race Massacres of 1919* (Fayetteville: University of Arkansas Press, 2001), 6.

39. Stockley, *Blood in Their Eyes*, 7.

40. Neil J. Smelser, *Theory of Collective Behavior* (New York: Free Press, 1963), 16–17.

41. Smelser, *Theory of Collective Behavior*, 249.

42. Smelser, *Theory of Collective Behavior*, 352.

43. Horowitz, *Deadly Ethnic Riot*, 317, 319.

44. Thomas C. Schelling, *The Strategy of Conflict* (Cambridge: Harvard University Press, 1960), 90. See also David D. Haddock and Daniel D. Polsby, "Understanding Riots," *Cato Journal* 14 (1994): 149.

45. See Terry Ann Knopf, *Rumors, Race and Riots* (New Brunswick: Transaction Publishers, 2006) and Marilynn S. Johnson, "Gender, Race, and Rumours: Re-examining the 1943 Race Riots," *Gender & History* 10 (1998): 252–277.

46. Horowitz, *Deadly Ethnic Riot*, 74–75.

47. Paul R. Brass, *The Production of Hindu-Muslim Violence in Contemporary India* (Seattle: University of Washington Press, 2003), 361.

48. As Terry Ann Knopf avers, race rumors had existed for centuries and cropped up even as early as colonial times. Rumors of slave revolts circulated from the peculiar institution's inception in the Americas. During the American Revolution, moreover, after Virginia's royal governor proclaimed on November 7, 1775, that all slaves would be free if they allied with the British, rumors floated that he met clandestinely with blacks "for the glorious purpose of enticing them to cut their masters' throats while they are asleep." Knopf, *Rumors, Race and Riots*, 17. Just before the Civil War, southerners feared that Abraham Lincoln's election would embolden slaves and abolitionists. "When [the Republican] party is enthroned in Washington," the *Charleston Mercury* predicted, "the *under*-ground railroad will become an *over*-ground railroad. . . . With the control of the Government of the United States, and an organized and triumphant North to sustain them, the Abolitionists will renew their operations upon the South with increased courage." Quoted in Knopf, *Rumors, Race and Riots*, 18.

49. See the Chicago Commission on Race Relations, *The Negro in Chicago: A Study of Race Relations and a Race Riot* (Chicago: University of Chicago Press), 59–67. The commission describes two incidents that occurred in 1920 that could have easily erupted into race riots had the police not remained "vigilant" and had there not been "the careful handling of the matter by the press." Chicago Commission, *Negro in Chicago*, 60. In the second incident, the police chief also "made prompt use of prearranged plans to check all such disorders in their incipiency. He immediately closed [certain] saloons and 'clubs.' . . . [And he] issued a statement which was published conspicuously in the morning newspapers, and was most effectively worded to prevent misunderstanding of the incident and avert use of it to inflame racial hostility." Chicago Commission, *Negro in Chicago*, 66, 67. Historian William Tuttle, moreover, writes of an incident in Chicago in 1921 in which religious tensions trumped racial concerns. Ragen's Colts, a predominantly Irish American gang that played a large role in Chicago's 1919 riot, targeted the Ku Klux Klan for its anti-Catholicism. "In September," Tuttle describes, "3,000 people from the stockyards district watched as the Colts hanged in effigy 'a white-sheeted Klansman.'" William M. Tuttle Jr., *Race Riot: Chicago in the Red Summer of 1919* (Champaign: University of Illinois Press, 1996), 257.

50. See Mona Lena Krook, "Comparing Methods for Studying Women in Politics: Statistical, Case Study, and Qualitative-Comparative Techniques" (paper presented at the annual meeting of the American Political Science Association, Washington, D.C., September 1–4, 2005), 6–9.

CHAPTER 2

1. See especially Leon F. Litwack, *Trouble in Mind: Black Southerners in the Age of Jim Crow* (New York: Alfred A. Knopf, 1998).

2. David W. Southern, *The Progressive Era and Race: Reaction and Reform, 1900–1917* (Wheeling: Harlan Davidson, 2005), 73.

3. Steven Hahn, *A Nation under Our Feet: Black Political Struggles in the Rural South from Slavery to the Great Migration* (Cambridge: Belknap Press of Harvard University Press, 2003), 455–456.

4. Hahn, *Nation under Our Feet,* 456.

5. Hahn, *Nation under Our Feet,* 457.

6. Litwack, *Trouble in Mind,* 198.

7. Litwack, *Trouble in Mind,* 335.

8. Donald L. Horowitz, *The Deadly Ethnic Riot* (Berkeley: University of California Press, 2001), 165–166.

9. See C. Vann Woodward, *Tom Watson: Agrarian Rebel* (New York: Oxford University Press, 1963).

10. David S. Cecelski and Timothy B. Tyson, eds., *Democracy Betrayed: The Wilmington Race Riot of 1898 and Its Legacy* (Chapel Hill: University of North Carolina Press, 1998), 4.

11. Andrea Meryl Kirshenbaum, "'The Vampire That Hovers over North Carolina': Gender, White Supremacy, and the Wilmington Race Riot of 1898," *Southern Cultures* 4 (1998): 25.

12. Ronald L. F. Davis, "Resisting Jim Crow: In-Depth Essay," *The History of Jim Crow,* http://www.jimcrowhistory.org/history/resisting2.htm. See C. Vann Woodward's The Strange Career of Jim Crow in its various versions for an early and influential perspective on the topic. See also Howard N. Rabinowitz, "More Than the Woodward Thesis: Assessing the Strange Career of Jim Crow," *Journal of Southern History* 75 (1988): 842–856. For a good overview of Jim Crow historiography, see Alfred L. Brophy, "Norms, Laws, and Reparations: The Case of the Ku Klux Klan in 1920s Oklahoma," *Harvard BlackLetter Law Journal* 20 (2004): 17–48.

13. Davis, "Resisting Jim Crow."

14. Nancy Bentley and Sandra Gunning, eds., *Charles W. Chesnutt: The Marrow of Tradition* (New York: Bedford/St. Martin's, 2002), 412–413.

15. Susan Falck, "Jim Crow Legislation Overview," *The History of Jim Crow,* http://www.jimcrowhistory.org/resources/lessonplans/hs_es_jim_crow_laws. htm. Although blacks bore the brunt of Jim Crow measures, other groups suffered as well. Western states passed 51, or 12 percent, of these laws, aimed primarily at Asians and Native Americans.

16. Susan S. Kuo, "Bringing in the State: Toward a Constitutional Duty to Protect from Mob Violence," *Indiana Law Journal* 79 (2004): 192–193.

17. *New York Times,* August 17, 1900, 6.

18. Brophy, "Norms, Laws, and Reparations," 30–31.

19. LeRae Umfleet, *1898 Wilmington Race Riot Report* (Raleigh: North Carolina Department of Cultural Resources, 2006), 195, http://www.history.ncdcr.gov/ 1898wrrc/report/report.htm. North Carolina newspapers declared it a "crime" that the federal government even considered sending troops, likening this action to the military's presence in the South during Reconstruction. One Wilmington resident vowed that if troops entered the city, "caskets should be included in their equipment" as residents "would not brook any outside interference." Umfleet, *Wilmington*

Race Riot Report, 198. Moreover, some Americans believed the Spanish-American War had forged a renewed bond between the North and the South that should not be disturbed. Umfleet, *Wilmington Race Riot Report,* 195–198.

20. Umfleet, *Wilmington Race Riot Report,* 370.

21. Umfleet, *Wilmington Race Riot Report,* 371.

22. Umfleet, *Wilmington Race Riot Report,* 375.

23. See Joel Williamson, *The Crucible of Race: Black-White Relations in the American South since Emancipation* (New York: Oxford University Press, 1984).

24. George M. Frederickson, *The Black Image in the White Mind: The Debate on Afro-American Character and Destiny, 1817–1914* (New York: Harper & Row 1971), 252.

25. Frederickson, *Black Image in the White Mind,* 256–257.

26. Frederickson, *Black Image in the White Mind,* 264.

27. Quoted in Williamson, *Crucible of Race,* 379.

28. Quoted in Williamson, *Crucible of Race,* 256–257.

29. Williamson, *Crucible of Race,* 116.

30. See Joel Williamson, "Wounds Not Scars: Lynching, the National Conscience, and the American Historian," *Journal of American History* 83 (1997): 1221–1253.

31. See, for example, Steven Hahn, *The Roots of Southern Populism: Yeoman Farmers and the Transformation of the Georgia Upcountry, 1850–1890* (New York: Oxford University Press, 1983); Olivier Zunz, *Making American Corporate, 1870–1920* (Chicago: University of Chicago Press, 1990); and Bess Beatty, *Alamance: The Holt Family and Industrialization in a North Carolina County, 1837–1900* (Baton Rouge: Louisiana State University, 1999).

32. Jacquelyn Dowd Hall, *Revolt against Chivalry: Jessie Daniel Ames and the Women's Campaign against Lynching* (New York: Columbia University Press, 1993): 146. Unabashed in their remedies, these men evidently thought no idea too extreme. "Whenever the Constitution comes between me and the virtue of the white women of the South," Blease observed in 1930, "I say to hell with the Constitution!" Quoted in William I. Hair, "Lynching," in *Encyclopedia of Southern Culture,* ed. Charles Reagan Wilson and William Ferris (Chapel Hill: University of North Carolina Press, 1989), 174–175.

33. Quoted in Williamson, *Crucible of Race,* 116–117.

34. "Speech of Senator Benjamin Tillman, March 23, 1900," *Congressional Record,* 56th Congress, 1st Session, 3223–3224.

35. Williamson, *Crucible of Race,* 117. According to historian Jacquelyn Dowd Hall, between 1882 and 1946, lynch mobs targeted only 23 percent of their victims because of allegations of rape or attempted rape. Hall, *Revolt against Chivalry,* 149. Two other facts stand out as well: in addition to white women, black women also suffered sexual assaults, often at the hands of white men (Wilmington *Daily Record* editor Alexander Manly highlighted this truth in the article that prompted whites to burn his newspaper office to the ground in 1898: "You set yourselves down as a lot of carping hypocrites; in fact, you cry aloud for the virtue of your women, while you seek to destroy the morality of ours. Don't think ever that your

women will remain pure while you are debauching ours. You sow the seed—the harvest will come in due time."); and lynch mobs did not exclusively focus their wrath on black men—black women and children also came under attack. Bentley and Gunning, eds., *Charles W. Chesnutt*, 12, 408. In other words, although white leaders stoked the racist embers by sounding forth on the black rapist, mobs would take any opportunity to kill African Americans. "The rape scare," asserts historian Glenda Gilmore, "was a politically driven wedge powered by the sledgehammer of white supremacy." Glenda E. Gilmore, *Gender and Jim Crow: Women and the Politics of White Supremacy in North Carolina, 1896–1920* (Chapel Hill: University of North Carolina Press, 1996), 75.

36. *The Atlanta Constitution*, August 1, 1897, A24. See also LeeAnn Whites, "Love, Hate, Rape, Lynching: Rebecca Latimer Felton and the Gender Politics of Racial Violence," in *Democracy Betrayed: The Wilmington Race Riot of 1898 and Its Legacy*, ed. David S. Cecelski and Timothy B. Tyson (Chapel Hill: University of North Carolina Press, 1998), 147.

37. *The Atlanta Constitution*, August 20, 1897, 4. See also Bentley and Gunning, eds., *Charles W. Chesnutt*, 409–410.

38. David W. Blight, *Race and Reunion: The Civil War in American Memory* (Cambridge: Belknap Press of Harvard University, 2001), 345.

39. Hall, *Revolt against Chivalry*, 112.

40. Hall, *Revolt against Chivalry*, 145.

41. Gilmore, *Gender and Jim Crow*, 110.

42. Marilynn S. Johnson, "Gender, Race, and Rumours: Re-Examining the 1943 Race Riots," *Gender & History* 10 (1998): 262–263.

43. Johnson, "Gender, Race, and Rumours," 286.

44. Johnson, "Gender, Race, and Rumours," 287.

45. Davis, "Resisting Jim Crow."

46. Quoted in Hall, *Revolt against Chivalry*, 61–62.

47. Quoted in Grace Elizabeth Hale, *Making Whiteness: The Culture of Segregation in the South, 1890–1940* (New York: Pantheon Books, 1998), 95.

48. Quoted in Hale, *Making Whiteness*, 94.

49. Eric Niderost, "The Birth of a Nation," *American History* 40 (2005).

50. J. Vincent Lowery, "Remembering 1898: Literary Responses and Public Memory of the Wilmington Race Riot," Appendix M in *1898 Wilmington Race Riot Report*, LeRae Umfleet, et al. 1898 Wilmington Race Riot Commission, North Carolina Office of Archives and History, 2006, 423–426.

51. Richard Yarborough, "Violence, Manhood, and Black Heroism: The Wilmington riot in Two Turn-of-the-Century African American Novels," in *Democracy Betrayed: The Wilmington Race Riot of 1898 and Its Legacy*, ed. David S. Cecelski and Timothy B. Tyson (Chapel Hill: University of North Carolina Press, 1998), 238.

52. Quoted in Hale, *Making Whiteness*, 78–79. Dixon had firsthand knowledge of this form of racial violence. His father joined the Ku Klux Klan, and his uncle rose to prominence as a member of North Carolina's branch. Dixon himself attended the lynching of a black man for the alleged rape of a white woman.

53. Thomas Dixon, *The Leopard's Spots: A Romance of the White Man's Burden, 1865–1900* (New York: Doubleday, Page, and Co., 1902), 242.

54. See Hale, *Making Whiteness,* Chapter 2 and Williamson, *Crucible of Race,* Chapter 5.

55. Gilmore, *Gender and Jim Crow,* 64.

56. Williamson, *Crucible of Race,* 141.

57. Williamson, *Crucible of Race,* 174.

58. *The Atlanta Constitution,* October 22, 1905, 2.

59. *The Atlanta Constitution,* October 29, 1905, B2.

60. *The Atlanta Constitution,* October 29, 1905, B2.

61. *Chicago Daily Tribune,* October 20, 1905, 4.

62. Walter White, *A Man Called White* (New York: Arno Press, 1969), 5–12; *New York Times,* October 23, 1906, 3. The "race riot" that broke out at Philadelphia's showing of *The Clansman* is different from those under study in this work. The "riot" erupted after an African American threw an egg at the stage. The mayor most likely prevented a true race riot when he cancelled Philadelphia's remaining performances after African American leaders persuaded him to do so (see *Boston Daily Globe,* October 24, 1906, 11).

63. Kelly Miller, "As to the Leopard's Spots: An Open Letter to Thomas W. Dixon, Jr.," in *Defining Southern Literature: Perspectives and Assessments,* ed. John E. Bassett (Madison: Fairleigh Dickinson University Press, 1997), 262, 266.

64. *The Atlanta Constitution,* November 6, 1905, 7.

65. *The Atlanta Constitution,* November 6, 1905, 7.

66. Tony Seybert, "The Historic Black Press—Essay Overview," *The History of Jim Crow,* http://jimcrowhistory.org/resources/lessonplans/hs_es_black_press.htm.

67. Bentley and Gunning, eds., *Charles W. Chesnutt,* 407–408. Felton's stint in the Senate consisted of a one-day appointment after the death of incumbent Tom Watson in 1922. See Williamson, *Crucible of Race,* 124, and Bentley and Gunning, eds., *Charles W. Chesnutt,* 409.

68. Quoted in Hall, *Revolt against Chivalry,* 143.

69. W.E.B. Du Bois coined this phrase to describe the full and elaborate lives that African Americans created for themselves under Jim Crow. See W.E.B. Du Bois, *The Souls of Black Folk* (Chicago: A. C. McClurg, 1903), xxxi. See also Litwack, *Trouble in Mind* and Leslie Brown and Anne Valk, "Black Durham behind the Veil: A Case Study," *OAH Magazine of History* (2004), for example.

70. Ida B. Wells-Barnett, *Crusade for Justice: The Autobiography of Ida B. Wells,* ed. Alfreda M. Duster (Chicago: University of Chicago Press, 1970), 18–19.

71. Wells-Barnett, *Crusade for Justice,* 19. Although the Civil Rights Act of 1875 gave "all persons within the jurisdiction of the United States . . . the full and equal and enjoyment of the accommodations, advantages, facilities, and privileges of inns, public conveyances on land or water, theaters, and other places of public amusement . . . and applicable alike to citizens of every race and color, regardless of any previous condition of servitude," the United States Supreme Court deemed it unconstitutional in 1883. Statutes at Large, 43rd Congress, 2nd Session, Volume 18,

Part 3; Williamson, *Crucible of Race*, 97. "I can see to this day the headlines in the *Memphis Appeal*," Wells recalls her initial victory in her autobiography, "announcing DARKY DAMSEL GETS DAMAGES." Wells-Barnett, *Crusade for Justice*, 19.

72. Paula Giddings, "Ida Wells-Barnett (1862–1931)," in *Portraits of American Women. Vol. II From the Civil War to the Present*, ed. G. J. Barker-Benfield and Catherine Clinton (New York: St. Martin's Press, 1991), 376.

73. Giddings, "Ida Wells-Barnett," 375–376; Litwack, *Trouble in Mind*, 429–430.

74. Wells-Barnett, *Crusade for Justice*, 47–52, 64.

75. Quoted in Giddings, "Ida Wells-Barnett," 377–378.

76. Wells-Barnett, *Crusade for Justice*, 62.

77. Wells followed Moss's advice in this respect. "Tell my people to go West," he purportedly uttered as he lay dying, "there is no justice for them here." Within two months, some 6,000 of Memphis's blacks moved to the Oklahoma territory. Giddings, "Ida Wells-Barnett," 377.

78. Hall, *Revolt against Chivalry*, 78–79.

79. Giddings, "Ida Wells-Barnett," 377.

80. Hall, *Revolt against Chivalry*, 66.

81. Hall, *Revolt against Chivalry*, 79.

82. Booker T. Washington, "The Atlanta Compromise," in *Ripples of Hope: Great American Civil Rights Speeches*, ed. Josh Gottheimer (New York: Basic Civitas Books, 2004), 131.

83. *Chicago Daily Tribune*, September 25, 1895, 13; Jacqueline M. Moore, *Booker T. Washington, W. E. B. Du Bois, and the Struggle for Racial Uplift* (Wilmington, Scholarly Resources Inc., 2003), xvi. Of course, even this posture did not appeal to radicals, who wanted African Americans to have no part in American society. "I am just as opposed to Booker Washington as a voter, with all his Anglo-Saxon reenforcements [*sic*]" declared Vardaman of Mississippi, "as I am to the coconut-headed, chocolate-colored, typical little coon, Andy Dotson, who blacks my shoes every evening. Quoted in David Levering Lewis, *W. E. B. Du Bois: Biography of a Race, 1868–1919* (New York: Henry Holt and Company, 1993), 261.

84. Quoted in Mark Bauerlein, "Washington, Du Bois, and the Black Future," *Wilson Quarterly* 28 (2004).

85. Quoted in Bauerlein, "Washington, Du Bois, and the Black Future."

86. Du Bois even sent Washington a congratulatory note after his Atlanta speech—"it was a word fitly spoken." Lewis, *W. E. B. Du Bois*, 175.

87. Moore, *Booker T. Washington, W. E. B. Du Bois, and the Struggle for Racial Uplift*, 62.

88. W.E.B. Du Bois, *Dusk of Dawn* (Millwood: Kraus-Thomson Organization, 1975), 72.

89. Bauerlein, "Washington, Du Bois, and the Black Future" and Lewis, *W. E. B. Du Bois*, 226. A group of some 2,000 white men, women, and children scrambled for pieces of Hose's flesh as a mob burned him alive after he killed a white farmer in an argument over money. The farmer's wife claimed Hose also raped her, a detail which Atlanta's five dailies played up. Lewis, *W. E. B. Du Bois*, 226. In its coverage leading up to the lynching, the *Atlanta Constitution* detailed Hose's description,

offered a monetary reward for his capture, and provided rationalization for racial violence. Working at Atlanta University at the time, Du Bois drafted a response to the *Atlanta Constitution,* made his way toward the newspaper's office, but never got there when he discovered that Hose's "blackened knuckles" had been displayed in a white proprietor's front window. This event prompted Du Bois to come to the realization that "one could not be a calm, cool, and detached scientist while Negroes were lynched, murdered and starved." "Something died in me [that day]," he later revealed. Dominic J. Capeci, Jr. and Jack C. Knight, "Reckoning with Violence: W. E. B. Du Bois and the 1906 Atlanta Race Riot," *Journal of Southern History* 62 (1996): 732.

According to historian David Levering Lewis, Burghardt Du Bois contracted diphtheria and died on May 24, 1899, in part due to the fact that white doctors in Atlanta rebuffed even critically ill black patients. Moreover, as Du Bois and his wife escorted their son's coffin to the Atlanta train station for burial back North, white bystanders called them "niggers" as they passed by. "Well sped, my boy" Du Bois later mused on the death of his son, "before their world had dubbed your ambition insolence, had held your ideals unattainable, and taught you to cringe and bow." Lewis, *W. E. B. Du Bois,* 227–228.

90. Elliot M. Rudwick, "The Niagara Movement," *Journal of Negro History* 42 (1957): 179. The group originally planned to meet in New York for their first conference in July 1905, but since hotels in Buffalo refused them, they convened on the Canadian side of Niagara Falls instead. Lewis, *W. E. B. Du Bois,* 316–317.

91. David Levering Lewis, ed., *W. E. B. Du Bois: A Reader* (New York: Henry Holt and Company, 1995), 369.

92. W.E.B. Du Bois, *The Autobiography of W. E. B. Du Bois: A Soliloquy on Viewing My Life from the Last Decade of Its First Century* (New York: International Publishers, 1968), 249–250.

93. In the summer of 1906, the army stationed three all-black companies from the 25th Infantry to Fort Brown, much to the chagrin of the white residents of nearby Brownsville, who either generally ignored them or assailed them with racial epithets. On August 12, a white woman declared that one of the black servicemen assaulted her. The next night, violence came to a head, and witnesses claimed that black gunmen—presumably soldiers—attacked and killed a bartender and wounded, among others, a policeman. At the base, officials rounded up the black soldiers and inspected their guns. Although evidence revealed that none of the weapons had been fired recently and the soldiers (and even their white commanders initially) signed sworn statements denying any involvement in the incident, President Theodore Roosevelt, with the backing of his Secretary of War William H. Taft, dishonorably discharged (with the benefit of no trial—even a Texas grand jury dismissed the case due to lack of evidence) all of the 167 black soldiers in the 25th Infantry three months later. Some of these men had fought in Cuba and the Philippines and only had a few months until their retirement (and therefore access to their pensions, which then became null and void). See John Downing Weaver, *The Brownsville Raid* (New York: W. W. Norton, 1970) and Ann J. Lane, *The Brownsville Affair: National Crisis and Black Reaction* (Port Washington:

Kennikat Press, 1971). In response to Roosevelt's draconian measures, during the Niagara Movement's annual meeting in Oberlin, Ohio, in 1908, its officers urged, "We say to voters: Register and vote whenever and wherever you have a right. Vote not in the past, but in the present. Remember that the conduct of the Republican party toward Negroes has been a disgraceful failure to keep just promises. The dominant Roosevelt faction has sinned in this respect beyond forgiveness. We therefore trust that every black voter will . . . leave no stone unturned to defeat William H. Taft. Remember Brownsville." Quoted in Angela Jones, *African American Civil Rights: Early Activism and the Niagara Movement* (Santa Barbara: Praeger, 2011), 206.

The black press also had harsh words for Roosevelt. "The hand of Ben Tillman nor Vardaman never struck humanity as savagely as did the iron hand of Theodore Roosevelt," Benjamin J. Davis, editor of the *Atlanta Independent*, asserted after Roosevelt issued the dishonorable discharges. "His new dictum is lynch-law, bold and heartless." Quoted in Lewis N. Wynne, "Brownsville: The Reaction of the Negro Press," *Phylon* 33 (1972): 155.

94. Rudwick, "The Niagara Movement," 198–199.

95. Mary White Ovington, *How the National Association for the Advancement of Colored People Began* (New York: National Association for the Advancement of Colored People, 1914). Springfield's riot parallels that of many others during this period. After weeks of sensationalist articles featured in local newspapers, on August 14, 1908, a white mob gathered in front of the city jail and demanded that two black men—one accused of raping a white woman and the other of killing a white mining inspector—be released into their custody. When they discovered that the men had been ushered away to safety, they first vented their rage on the white man who helped police escort the suspects out of town (by demolishing his restaurant and car), then on the black business district (which they destroyed), a black neighborhood (where they lynched Scott Burton, a black barber who stayed behind to defend his property), and a white neighborhood (where they lynched an elderly black man married to a white woman). When the mayor confronted the mob to stem the violence, the crowd met him with shouts of "Throw him into the fire!" *New York Times*, August 15, 1908, 1. "Lincoln freed you," the mob purportedly shouted to Springfield's black denizens, "we'll show you where you belong." *Christian Science Monitor*, May 15, 1969, 13. The state militia stopped the initial violence, but indiscriminate killings continued for several months, and Springfield, home of Lincoln, became synonymous with racial violence. For a full account, see Roberta Senechal de la Roche, *In Lincoln's Shadow: The 1908 Race Riot in Springfield, Illinois* (Carbondale: Southern Illinois University Press, 2008). "The noted statue of Abraham Lincoln, the great emancipator," wrote the *Los Angeles Times*, "stands within a stone's throw of the spot where black men's blood was shed." *Los Angeles Times*, August 16, 1908, I1.

96. Books published near the turn of the century exploring racial issues include *Iola Leroy: Or, Shadows Uplifted* by Frances Ellen Watkins Harper (1892); *Contending Forces: A Romance Illustrative of Negro Life North and South* by Pauline E. Hopkins (1900); *The Sport of the Gods* by Paul Laurence Dunbar (1903); and

The Autobiography of an Ex-Colored Man by James Weldon Johnson (1912). Bentley and Gunning, eds., *Charles W. Chesnutt*, 15.

97. Born in Ohio in 1858 to "free mulatto parents," Chesnutt and his family moved during his youth to Fayetteville, North Carolina, where he witnessed racial violence firsthand. There, he one day stumbled upon the body of a black man accused of rape and who had been killed in broad view by a white man. Bentley and Gunning, eds., *Charles W. Chesnutt*, 6. The 1900 riot in New Orleans also played an important role in his fiction. See Lowery, "Remembering 1898," 418.

Born during the Civil War in Fayetteville, North Carolina, Fulton moved to Wilmington during Reconstruction, and later to New York City, where he worked as a porter and journalist. He "respectfully dedicated" *Hanover* to "the eminent heroine Ida B. Wells-Barnett." David Bryant Fulton [Jack Thorne], *Hanover* (New York: Arno Press, 1969).

98. Bentley and Gunning, eds., *Charles W. Chesnutt*, 6, 8.

99. See Yarborough, "Violence, Manhood, and Black Heroism" and Lowery, "Remembering 1898," 416–418.

100. Racial violence erupted all over the country following the fight. See "Race Riots over Fight," *Boston Daily Globe*, July 5, 1910, 1; "Eleven Killed in Many Race Riots," *Chicago Daily Tribune*, July 5, 1910, 1; "Racial Clashes Follow Victory of Jack Johnson," *Atlanta Constitution*, July 5, 1910, 1; and "Race Clashes in Many Cities," *Washington Post*, July 5, 1910, 1, for example. "All over the country," a white paper in Richmond admonished its black readers, "a simple-minded race is getting into its head a false pride, a foolish impression, a disastrous ambition." Litwack, *Trouble in Mind*, 442. Two years earlier, when Johnson defeated Canadian Tommy Burns in the World Boxing Championship, a judge in Birmingham, Alabama, scolded the friends of a black man killed by a white Baptist deacon (whom the judge released): "You Niggers are getting beside yourselves since Jack Johnson won the fight from a white man. I want you to mind what you do in this town. Remember, you are in the South, and remember further that when you speak to white gentlemen you should speak in a way that is best becoming a Nigger. This act will be repeated daily by the white gentlemen of this city if you Niggers don't find your places." Litwack, *Trouble in Mind*, 442.

Johnson raised white ire for many reasons. "Johnson was no ordinary black man," historian Leon Litwack explains. "He did not know his place, he refused to acknowledge racial barriers. Violating nearly every racial code and custom, making no effort to mask his feelings, he flaunted his lifestyle, his fashionable clothes, his expensive jewelry, his shaved head, his fast automobiles, and the white women he escorted and, in three instances, married. Litwack, *Trouble in Mind*, 442.

101. Davis, "Resisting Jim Crow." "Louis would be the antithesis of everything Jack Johnson had been," scholar David Margolick asserts. "He would always be soft-spoken, understated, and polite, no matter what he accomplished. He would not preen or gloat or strut in the ring. . . . He would always conduct himself with dignity. . . . When it came to women, he would stick to his own kind. . . . He would never fraternize with white women, let alone be photographed with them. He would not drive fast cars, especially red ones. . . . The press would be saturated with stories of Louis's boyish goodness, his love for his

mother, his mother's love for him, his devotion to scripture." David Margolick, *Beyond Glory: Joe Louis vs. Max Schmeling, and a World on the Brink* (New York: Alfred A Knopf, 2005, 65.

102. Davis, "Resisting Jim Crow."

103. See David Margolick, *Strange Fruit: Billie Holiday, Café Society, and an Early Cry for Civil Rights* (Philadelphia: Running Press, 2000) and David Margolick, *Strange Fruit: Biography of a Song* (New York: Ecco Press, 2001). Abel Meeropol (known as Lewis Allan), a white, Jewish schoolteacher from New York wrote the words and later the music after seeing a photograph of a lynching in a magazine. "It was a shocking photograph," he would recall, "and it haunted me for days." Nancy Kovaleff Baker, "Abel Meeropol (a.k.a. Lewis Allan): Political Commentator and Social Conscience," *American Music* 20 (2002).

104. Quoted in James M. McPherson, *Battle Cry of Freedom: The Civil War Era* (New York: Ballantine Books, 1988), 564.

105. Referring to the Spanish-American War, the U.S. ambassador to England John Hay relayed to Theodore Roosevelt, who had led the American troops into battle, that it has been "a splendid little war." R. Hal Williams, *Years of Decision: American Politics in the 1890s* (New York: Wiley, 1978), 141.

106. Edward L. Ayers, *Promise of the New South: Life after Reconstruction* (New York: Oxford University Press, 1992), 330.

107. Williamson, *Crucible of Race,* 338. See also Ayers, *Promise of the New South,* 330.

108. Ayers, *Promise of the New South,* 333–334.

109. This criticism by black newspapers drew the ire of the Post Office and the FBI, which sent agents to several black presses. Seybert, "The Historic Black Press."

110. Pete Daniel, "Going among Strangers: Southern Reactions to World War II," *Journal of American History* 77 (1990): 893–894, quoting a Bureau of Agricultural Economics report. For an excellent overview of racial violence during World War II, see James Albert Burran III, "Racial Violence in the South during World War II," Ph.D. dissertation, University of Tennessee, Knoxville, 1977.

CHAPTER 3

1. See Paul R. Brass, *The Production of Hindu-Muslim Violence in Contemporary India* (Seattle: University of Washington Press, 2003).

2. United States Bureau of the Census, *Thirteenth Census of the United States,* North Carolina, Table 2 (Washington, D.C.: Government Printing Office, 1910), 312. For an overview of the city before the turn of the century, see H. Leon Prather, *We Have Taken a City: Wilmington Racial Massacre and Coup of 1898* (Rutherford: Fairleigh Dickinson University Press, 1984), 17–31.

3. H. Leon Prather, "We Have Taken a City," in *Democracy Betrayed: The Wilmington Race Riot of 1898 and Its Legacy,* ed. David S. Cecelski and Timothy B. Tyson (Chapel Hill: University of North Carolina Press, 1998), 16–17.

4. LeRae Umfleet, *1898 Wilmington Race Riot Report* (Raleigh: North Carolina Department of Cultural Resources, 2006), 60; Prather, "We Have Taken a City," 21.

5. Umfleet, *1898 Wilmington Race Riot Report*, 77. Whites grumbled, for instance, that an "audacious Negro grudge [was] developing against the streetcar conductors because they did not help black women on and off the conveyance as they did white women." Many whites thought this insolence beyond the pale. And a street fight between a white woman and a black woman in September 1898 alerted whites as to how far blacks would go to assert themselves. When the black woman would not move out of the way of a group of white women walking down the sidewalk, one of the white women used her "frail but lovely form" to grab the black woman and push her out of their path. The black woman then proceeded to use her umbrella in retaliation, as a nearby black man yelled, "That's right; damn it, give it to her." "Such exasperating occurrences," white supremacist editor Josephus Daniels lamented, "would not happen but for the fact that the negro party is in power in North Carolina." Glenda E. Gilmore, "Murder, Memory, and the Flight of the Incubus," in *Democracy Betrayed: The Wilmington Race Riot of 1898 and Its Legacy,* ed. David S. Cecelski and Timothy B. Tyson (Chapel Hill: University of North Carolina Press, 1998), 82–83.

6. Umfleet, *1898 Wilmington Race Riot Report,* 79–80.

7. Umfleet, *1898 Wilmington Race Riot Report,* 97. Felton, a native of Georgia and an advocate of women's rights, spent much of her time assisting and advising her husband, Congressman William Felton. In this capacity, she made numerous speeches. She later became the first woman senator of the United States, albeit a one-day appointment upon the death of incumbent Tom Watson in 1922. See Nancy Bentley and Sandra Gunning, eds., *Charles W. Chesnutt: The Marrow of Tradition* (New York: Bedford/St. Martin's, 2002), 409.

8. Some doubt exists over whether Manly or his assistant, William Jeffries, actually wrote the editorial. Jeffries later maintained that he wrote it to "show that there were two sides to the question and that the outrages were not all on one side." He also averred that although whites would "burn and kill" Manly if he ever returned to Wilmington, they would have the "wrong man." Umfleet, *1898 Wilmington Race Riot Report,* 96–98.

9. Prather, *We Have Taken a City.*

10. Prather, *We Have Taken a City.*

11. Prather, "We Have Taken a City," 24.

12. Prather, "We Have Taken a City," 24.

13. Umfleet, *1898 Wilmington Race Riot Report,* 67. The Red Shirts had largely been a South Carolina organization (under the leadership of white supremacist Senator "Pitchfork" Ben Tillman) up until the 1898 election drew them to North Carolina. Tillman himself traveled to North Carolina to stir up racist sentiment in the weeks leading up to the election. "Why didn't you kill that damn nigger editor [Manly] who wrote that [editorial]?" he demanded at one rally. "Send him to South Carolina and let him publish any such offensive stuff, and he will be killed." Prather, "We Have Taken a City," 25.

14. Prather, "We Have Taken a City," 27.

15. Prather, "We Have Taken a City," 28.

16. *The Atlanta Constitution,* November 1, 1898, 1.

17. Prather, "We Have Taken a City," 28.

18. Prather, "We Have Taken a City," 28–29. As two black election officials began counting ballots for the predominantly Republican Fifth Division of the First Ward, for example, a group of some 200 white "strangers" crowded around them. Suddenly, someone knocked the lamps off the table, the room went dark, and when the lights came back on, one of the black officials had fled out of fear for his safety. The other official finished counting the ballots, but he left quickly and failed to sign the election returns. Although about 300 Republicans had registered in the precinct, and only 20–30 whites had registered there, the Democratic candidate "got more votes by nearly two hundred than there were people registered in the precinct." Quote by white election official George Bates; Umfleet, *1898 Race Riot Report*, 109–110. Clearly someone had stuffed the boxes when the lights went out.

19. *The Atlanta Constitution*, November 9, 1898, 1.

20. See Umfleet, *1898 Race Riot Report*, 115, for the full report.

21. Prather, "We Have Taken a City," 31.

22. Umfleet, *1898 Race Riot Report*, 129.

23. Prather, "We Have Taken a City," 34.

24. Prather, "We Have Taken a City," 35.

25. Prather, "We Have Taken a City," 36.

26. Some newspapers reported that over 1,000 African Americans left Wilmington in the next few months. Umfleet, *1898 Race Riot Report*, 205.

27. Alfred M. Waddell, "The Story of the Wilmington, North Carolina, Race Riots," *Collier's Weekly* November 26, 1898.

28. Prather, "We Have Taken a City," 37.

29. United States Bureau of the Census, *Thirteenth Census of the United States,* Louisiana, Table II (Washington D.C.: Government Printing Office, 1910), 790.

30. William Ivy Hair, *Carnival of Fury: Robert Charles and the New Orleans Race Riot of 1900* (Baton Rouge: Louisiana State University, 1976), 69–77.

31. Melvin Johnson White, "Populism in New Orleans during the Nineties," *Mississippi Valley Historical Review* 5 (1918): 10.

32. White, "Populism in New Orleans," 12–14.

33. Hair, *Carnival of Fury*, 104–105.

34. August Meier and Elliot Rudwick, "The Boycott Movement against Jim Crow Streetcars in the South, 1900–1906," *Journal of American History* 55 (1969): 756–775.

35. Hair, *Carnival of Fury*, 72.

36. Hair, *Carnival of Fury*, 139.

37. Hair, *Carnival of Fury*, 91–92.

38. Hair, *Carnival of Fury*, 141.

39. For details of Charles's life and the best analysis of the riot itself, see Hair, *Carnival of Fury*.

40. Hair, *Carnival of Fury*, 118–120.

41. Hair, *Carnival of Fury*, 121–152.

42. Hair, *Carnival of Fury*, 2.

43. Quoted in Hair, *Carnival of Fury*, 148–149.

44. Hair, *Carnival of Fury*, 147.

45. Hair, *Carnival of Fury*, 152–153.

46. *New York Times*, July 27, 1900, 1.

47. Hair, *Carnival of Fury*, 154.

48. Hair, *Carnival of Fury*, 156–172.

49. Hair, *Carnival of Fury*, 172–200.

50. Hair, *Carnival of Fury*, 172–200.

51. *Boston Daily Globe*, July 29, 1900, 17.

52. Mark Bauerlein, "Atlanta (Georgia) Riot of 1906," in *Encyclopedia of American Race Riots*, ed. Walter Rucker and James Nathaniel Upton (Westport: Greenwood Press, 2006), 15.

53. Bauerlein, "Atlanta Riot," 15; Gregory Mixon, *The Atlanta Riot: Race, Class, and Violence in a New South City* (Gainesville: University Press of Florida, 2005), 28.

54. Bauerlein, "Atlanta Riot," 15.

55. Rebecca Burns, *Rage in the Gate City: The Story of the 1906 Atlanta Race Riot* (Cincinnati: Emmis Books, 2006), 17.

56. Burns, *Rage in the Gate City*, 13.

57. Bauerlein, "Atlanta Riot," 15.

58. Burns, *Rage in the Gate City*, 17.

59. Charles Crowe, "Racial Massacre in Atlanta September 22, 1906," *Journal of Negro History* 54 (1969): 153. Whites also frequented these establishments as vice was integrated in most American cities at the time.

60. Crowe, "Racial Massacre in Atlanta," 154.

61. Bauerlein, "Atlanta Riot," 16.

62. Burns, *Rage in the Gate City*, 17.

63. David Fort Godshalk, *Veiled Visions: The 1906 Atlanta Race Riot and the Reshaping of American Race Relations* (Chapel Hill: University of North Carolina Press, 2005), 49–50.

64. Quoted in Godshalk, *Veiled Visions*, 50–51.

65. Burns, *Rage in the Gate City*, 17–18.

66. Gregory Mixon, *The Atlanta Riot: Race, Class, and Violence in a New South City* (Gainesville: University Press of Florida, 2005), 76.

67. Godshalk, *Veiled Visions*, 36.

68. Bauerlein, "Atlanta Riot," 16.

69. Mixon, *The Atlanta Riot*, 80.

70. Godshalk, *Veiled Visions*, 84.

71. His life was spared, but he received a 15-year sentence for his supposed crime. Godshalk, *Veiled Visions*, 149.

72. Burns, *Rage in the Gate City*, 126–128.

73. Bauerlein, "Atlanta Riot," 16.

74. Burns, *Rage in the Gate City*, 128.

75. The headlines read, "Negro Dives and Clubs Are the Cause of Frequent Assaults," and "Negro Clubs the Cause of Assaults?" Burns, *Rage in the Gate City*, 129, 217.

76. Bauerlein, "Atlanta Riot," 20.

77. Godshalk, *Veiled Visions,* 88.

78. Burns, *Rage in the Gate City,* 142.

79. Burns, *Rage in the Gate City,* 152–153. Notably, the riot started at Five Points, the heart of downtown Atlanta, where blacks and whites regularly interacted. Godshalk, *Veiled Visions,* 107.

80. Burns, *Rage in the Gate City,* 137.

81. Godshalk, *Veiled Visions,* 88–90.

82. Burns, *Rage in the Gate City,* 144; Crowe, "Racial Massacre in Atlanta," 161.

83. Mixon, *The Atlanta Riot,* 93.

84. Mixon, *The Atlanta Riot,* 87–89; Burns, *Rage in the Gate City,* 144, 148.

85. Burns, *Rage in the Gate City,* 149, 151–152.

86. Burns, *Rage in the Gate City,* 152.

87. Burns, *Rage in the Gate City,* 153.

88. Bauerlein, "Atlanta Riot," 21.

89. Burns, *Rage in the Gate City,* 158.

90. Bauerlein, "Atlanta Riot," 22.

91. Mixon, *The Atlanta Riot,* 104.

92. Burns, *Rage in the Gate City,* 161–162. Eugene Mitchell, a white lawyer and developer, also guarded his home and family after hearing rumors of plans by the nearby black colleges to organize a revenge attack. His 5-year-old daughter Margaret—who would 30 years later pen *Gone with the Wind*—brought him a heavy Civil War sword from the attic to help him arm himself. Burns, *Rage in the Gate City,* 154; Bauerlein, "Atlanta Riot," 22.

93. Burns, *Rage in the Gate City,* 164–165.

94. Mixon, *The Atlanta Riot,* 107.

95. Burns, *Rage in the Gate City,* 165.

96. Mixon, *The Atlanta Riot,* 110; Bauerlein, "Atlanta Riot," 22.

97. Burns, *Rage in the Gate City,* 167, 169.

98. Burns, *Rage in the Gate City,* 169.

99. Burns, *Rage in the Gate City,* 170.

100. Godshalk, *Veiled Visions,* 137.

101. Burns, *Rage in the Gate City,* 173–174; Mixon, *The Atlanta Riot,* 118; Godshalk, *Veiled Visions,* 139.

102. Bauerlein, "Atlanta Riot," 23.

103. Mixon, *The Atlanta Riot,* 110; Burns, *Rage in the Gate City,* 175.

104. *Washington Post,* September 26, 1906, 6.

105. Gregory Mixon and Clifford Kuhn, "Atlanta Race Riot of 1906," *New Georgia Encyclopedia,* http://www.georgiaencyclopedia.org/nge/Article.jsp?id=h-3033; Burns, *Rage in the Gate City,* 175.

106. Bauerlein, "Atlanta Riot," 23.

107. Godshalk, *Veiled Visions,* 148.

108. Bauerlein, "Atlanta Riot," 23.

109. Mixon, *The Atlanta Riot,* 123.

110. Burns, *Rage in the Gate City,* 192–193.

111. Burns, *Rage in the Gate City,* 190.

112. Burns, *Rage in the Gate City*, 190.

113. Bauerlein, "Atlanta Riot."

114. Bauerlein, "Atlanta Riot," 23.

115. In response to the riot itself, Du Bois penned a poignant poem called "The Litany of Atlanta." Mixon and Kuhn, "Atlanta Race Riot."

116. Mixon, *The Atlanta Riot*, 126.

117. Harper Barnes, *Never Been a Time: The 1917 Race Riot That Sparked the Civil Rights Movement* (New York: Walker & Company, 2008), 61.

118. Elliot M. Rudwick, *Race Riot at East St. Louis July 2, 1917* (Carbondale: Southern Illinois University Press, 1964), 165.

119. Rudwick, *Race Riot at East St. Louis*, 5; Barnes, *Never Been a Time*, 57.

120. Charles L. Lumpkins, *American Pogrom: The East St. Louis Race Riot and Black Politics* (Athens: Ohio University Press, 2008), 74.

121. Barnes, *Never Been a Time*, 72.

122. Barnes, *Never Been a Time*, 76.

123. Barnes, *Never Been a Time*, 73.

124. Lumpkins, *American Pogrom*, 78.

125. Barnes, *Never Been a Time*, 76–77.

126. Barnes, *Never Been a Time*, 78.

127. Rudwick, *Race Riot at East St. Louis*, 7.

128. Barnes, *Never Been a Time*, 80.

129. Barnes, *Never Been a Time*, 80–81.

130. Rudwick, *Race Riot at East St. Louis*, 15.

131. Barnes, *Never Been a Time*, 83–84, 91–92.

132. Lumpkins, *American Pogrom*, 79–83.

133. Rudwick, *Race Riot at East St. Louis*, 18–23.

134. Rudwick, *Race Riot at East St. Louis*, 23.

135. Rudwick, *Race Riot at East St. Louis*, 24; Barnes, *Never Been a Time*, 96.

136. Rudwick, *Race Riot at East St. Louis*, 24–25.

137. Barnes, *Never Been a Time*, 97.

138. Barnes, *Never Been a Time*, 99–100.

139. Barnes, *Never Been a Time*, 100.

140. Barnes, *Never Been a Time*, 101.

141. Even though national guardsmen remained in East St. Louis since the Aluminum Ore strike, their commander stated he could not help the mayor since he said he had not been given the authority. Rudwick, *Race Riot at East St. Louis*, 29.

142. Rudwick, *Race Riot at East St. Louis*, 31.

143. Lumpkins, *American Pogrom*, 101.

144. Rudwick, *Race Riot at East St. Louis*, 34.

145. Barnes, *Never Been a Time*, 103–104; Rudwick, *Race Riot at East St. Louis*, 35.

146. Rudwick, *Race Riot at East St. Louis*, 37.

147. Rudwick, *Race Riot at East St. Louis*, 38.

148. Rudwick, *Race Riot at East St. Louis*, 38.

149. Barnes, *Never Been a Time,* 116–117.

150. Rudwick, *Race Riot at East St. Louis,* 39.

151. Barnes, *Never Been a Time,* 121.

152. Rudwick, *Race Riot at East St. Louis,* 40.

153. Rudwick, *Race Riot at East St. Louis,* 43.

154. Rudwick, *Race Riot at East St. Louis,* 45.

155. Barnes, *Never Been a Time,* 121; Rudwick, *Race Riot at East St. Louis,* 47–48. One man who escaped dying as a group of whites attempted to lynch him was summarily shot and killed as he sat with the rope still dangling around his neck. Barnes, *Never Been a Time,* 155. Rioters also threw a small black boy into a burning building and shot two other small children in their heads. Rudwick, *Race Riot at East St. Louis,* 48; Barnes, *Never Been a Time,* 165.

156. Rudwick, *Race Riot at East St. Louis,* 46.

157. Rudwick, *Race Riot at East St. Louis,* 47.

158. Rudwick, *Race Riot at East St. Louis,* 44, 46.

159. Barnes, *Never Been a Time,* 151–152, 167, 211; Rudwick, *Race Riot at East St. Louis,* 47–48.

160. Barnes, *Never Been a Time,* 169–171.

161. Rudwick, *Race Riot at East St. Louis,* 48, 53–56.

162. Barnes, *Never Been a Time,* 162. The 1920 census recorded 7,437 black residents in East St. Louis, almost 3,200 less than the population estimates of 1917. Rudwick, *Race Riot at East St. Louis,* 165.

163. Rudwick, *Race Riot at East St. Louis,* 48, 50; Barnes, *Never Been a Time,* 175.

164. Rudwick, *Race Riot at East St. Louis,* 67.

165. Rudwick, *Race Riot at East St. Louis,* 69.

166. Rudwick, *Race Riot at East St. Louis,* 58–59.

167. Rudwick, *Race Riot at East St. Louis,* 62.

168. Barnes, *Never Been a Time,* 177.

169. Barnes, *Never Been a Time,* 184–186.

170. Barnes, *Never Been a Time,* 178–179.

171. Barnes, *Never Been a Time,* 187–188.

172. Barnes, *Never Been a Time,* 192, 207. The following year, Dyer also introduced legislation making lynching a federal crime. Barnes, *Never Been a Time,* 191.

173. Barnes, *Never Been a Time,* 212.

174. Barnes, *Never Been a Time,* 201–207; Rudwick, *Race Riot at East St. Louis,* 95–132; John A. Lupton, "East St. Louis (Illinois) Riot of 1917," in *Encyclopedia of American Race Riots,* ed. Walter Rucker and James Nathaniel Upton (Westport: Greenwood Press, 2006), 190.

175. Scott Ellsworth, *Death in a Promised Land: The Tulsa Race Riot of 1921* (Baton Rouge: Louisiana State University Press, 1982), 8.

176. United States Bureau of the Census, *Fourteenth Census of the United States,* Oklahoma, Table 10 (Washington D.C.: Government Printing Office, 1920), 824.

177. Ellsworth, *Death in a Promised Land,* 11.

178. Ellsworth, *Death in a Promised Land,* 14; H. B. Johnson, *Black Wall Street: From Riot to Renaissance in Tulsa's Historic Greenwood District* (Austin: Eakin Press, 1998), 9.

179. Ellsworth, *Death in a Promised Land,* 20.

180. Johnson, *Black Wall Street,* 8.

181. Ellsworth, *Death in a Promised Land,* 25.

182. Ellsworth, *Death in a Promised Land,* 32.

183. Ellsworth, *Death in a Promised Land,* 35.

184. R. Halliburton, Jr., "The Tulsa Race War of 1921," *Journal of Black Studies* 2 (1972): 334.

185. Ellsworth, *Death in a Promised Land,* 45.

186. Oklahoma Commission to Study the Tulsa Race Riot of 1921, "Tulsa Race Riot: A Report by the Oklahoma Commission to Study the Tulsa Race Riot of 1921," February 28, 2001, http://www.okhistory.org/trrc/freport.htm, 58.

187. Ellsworth, *Death in a Promised Land,* 48.

188. Ellsworth, *Death in a Promised Land,* 48.

189. Ellsworth, *Death in a Promised Land,* 48.

190. Ellsworth, *Death in a Promised Land,* 52.

191. Lee E. Williams and Lee E. Williams II, *Anatomy of Four Race Riots: Racial Conflicts in Knoxville, Elaine (Arkansas), Tulsa and Chicago, 1919–1921* (Hattiesburg: University and College Press of Mississippi, 1972), 59.

192. Ellsworth, *Death in a Promised Land,* 53.

193. Halliburton, "Tulsa Race War," 339.

194. Ellsworth, *Death in a Promised Land,* 53–54.

195. Halliburton, "Tulsa Race War," 348.

196. Ellsworth, *Death in a Promised Land,* 67, 70.

197. Ellsworth, *Death in a Promised Land,* 83.

198. Ellsworth, *Death in a Promised Land,* 84.

199. Ellsworth, *Death in a Promised Land,* 95.

200. Ellsworth, *Death in a Promised Land,* 95.

201. Ellsworth, *Death in a Promised Land,* 97.

202. James Albert Burran III, "Racial Violence in the South during World War II," Ph.D. dissertation, University of Tennessee, Knoxville, 1977, 165.

203. United States Bureau of the Census, *Seventeenth Census of the United States,* Vol., Pt. 43, Texas, Table 34 (Washington D.C.: Government Printing Office, 1950), 43–99.

204. Burran, "Racial Violence in the South," 165–167.

205. Burran, "Racial Violence in the South," 167.

206. Burran, "Racial Violence in the South," 169.

207. A. Philip Randolph, the leader of the Brotherhood of Sleeping Car Porters, an all-black railroad workers' union, provided the impetus behind this mandate. A one-time colleague of Marcus Garvey and "the most dangerous Negro in America," according to Attorney General A. Mitchell Palmer during World War I, Randolph threatened to lead a march of 100,000 African Americans through Washington, D.C., if Roosevelt did not desegregate the military and create jobs

for blacks in the defense industries. With Executive Order 8802, he achieved one out of the two goals. David M. Kennedy, *Freedom from Fear: The American People in Depression and War, 1929–1945* (New York: Oxford University Press, 1999), 763–768.

208. Kennedy, *Freedom from Fear,* 767; Michael C. C. Adams, *The Best War Ever: America and World War II* (Baltimore: Johns Hopkins University Press, 1994), 119–120.

209. See James S. Olson and Sharon Phair, "The Anatomy of a Race Riot: Beaumont, Texas, 1943," *Texana* 11 (1973): 64–72.

210. Marilynn S. Johnson, "Gender, Race, and Rumours: Re-examining the 1943 Race Riots," *Gender & History* 10 (1998): 257.

211. Burran, "Racial Violence in the South," 169–171.

212. Burran, "Racial Violence in the South," 171–174.

213. Burran, "Racial Violence in the South," 176.

214. Burran, "Racial Violence in the South," 174–179.

CHAPTER 4

1. William M. Tuttle Jr., *Race Riot: Chicago in the Red Summer of 1919* (Champaign: University of Illinois Press, 1996), 22.

2. W.E.B. Du Bois, *Dusk of Dawn* (Millwood: Kraus-Thomson Organization, 1975), 264.

3. Terry Ann Knopf, *Rumors, Race and Riots* (New Brunswick: Transaction Publishers, 2006), 29.

4. Herbert Shapiro, *White Violence and Black Response: From Reconstruction to Montgomery* (Amherst: University of Massachusetts Press, 1988), 149–150.

5. Eighty percent of blacks lived in the rural South in 1870; a century later, 80 percent lived in urban areas, and almost half of these outside the South. Douglas S. Massey and Nancy A. Denton, *American Apartheid: Segregation and the Making of the Underclass* (Cambridge: Harvard University Press, 1993), 18. For a riveting and masterful portrayal of black southerners' Great Migration, see the prologue in Kevin Boyle, *Arc of Justice: A Saga of Race, Civil Rights, and Murder in the Jazz Age* (New York: H. Holt, 2004).

6. James E. Fickle, "Management Looks at the 'Labor Problem': The Southern Pine Industry during World War I and the Postwar Era," *Journal of Southern History* 40 (1974): 66; David M. Kennedy, *Over Here: The First World War and American Society* (New York: Oxford University Press, 1980), 280.

7. Kerner Commission, *Report of the National Advisory Commission on Civil Disorders* (New York: Bantam Books, 1968), 239.

8. Massey and Denton, *American Apartheid,* 29. Some southern whites grew so concerned about losing their cheap black labor source, though, that they resorted to banning or destroying the black newspapers luring them away. In Meridian, Mississippi, for example, the police chief had the *Chicago Defender* appropriated from dealers. In Franklin, Mississippi, a black minister served five months on the county farm and incurred a $400 fine for selling the NAACP's publication *Crisis*.

Of course, most black newspapers found a way to smuggle copies to their readers anyway. James R. Grossman, *Land of Hope: Chicago, Black Southerners, and the Great Migration* (Chicago: University of Chicago Press, 1989), 44.

Two organizations, the Southern Pine Association and the Southern Lumber Operators' Association, also fought the mass departure by blacks by pushing the *Negro Advocate* on their employees. Run by Milton Hampton, a black Arkansas minister, and partially subsidized by southern lumber operators, the magazine was used by white managers to "keep the colored laborers of the South satisfied with their conditions . . . advise against the exodus of neighbors . . . [and] elevate their morals." Fickle, "Management Looks at the 'Labor Problem,'" 67, 69.

Black newspapers also provided a source of tension by exposing violence around the country. The 1919 Longview, Texas, race riot, for instance, erupted after a scathing article appeared in the *Chicago Defender* detailing a recent Longview lynching. A white mob went after the local newspaper correspondent, and although he escaped town with his life, other blacks and their businesses suffered death and destruction in the wake of the mob. Jan Voogd, "Longview (Texas) Riot of 1919," in *Encyclopedia of American Race Riots*, ed. Walter Rucker and James Nathaniel Upton (Westport: Greenwood Press, 2006), 369–371.

9. See Stewart E. Tolnay and E. M. Beck, *A Festival of Violence: An Analysis of Southern Lynchings, 1882–1930* (Urbana: University of Illinois Press, 1995).

10. Joel Williamson, "Wounds Not Scars: Lynching, the National Conscience, and the American Historian," *Journal of American History* 83 (1997): 1240.

11. Hubert M. Blalock, "Per Cent Non-White and Discrimination in the South," *American Sociological Review* 22 (1957): 677–682; Stewart E. Tolnay, E. M. Beck, and James Massey, "The Power Threat Hypothesis and Black Lynching: 'Wither' the Evidence?" *Social Forces* 67 (1989): 634–641.

12. Lawrence Bobo, "Group Conflict, Prejudice, and the Paradox of Contemporary Racial Attitudes," in Eliminating Racism, ed. P. A. Katz and D. A. Taylor (New York: Plenum Press, 1988); Howard Schuman, Charlotte Steeh, and Lawrence Bobo, *Racial Attitudes in America: Trends and Interpretations* (Cambridge: Harvard University Press, 1985); and Lawrence Bobo, Howard Schuman, and Charlotte Steeh, "Changing Racial Attitudes toward Residential Segregation," in *Housing Desegregation and Federal Policy,* ed. John M. Goering (Chapel Hill: University of North Carolina Press, 1986). See Donald P. Green, Dara Z. Strolovitch, and Janelle S. Wong, "Defended Neighborhoods, Integration, and Racially Motivated Crime," *American Journal of Sociology* 104 (1998): 372–403, for an overview of these and other theories.

13. Green, Strolovitch, and Wong, "Defended Neighborhoods," 397.

14. Davison M. Douglas, *Jim Crow Moves North: The Battle over Northern School Segregation, 1865–1954* (New York: Cambridge University Press, 2005), 124, 137.

15. Douglas, *Jim Crow Moves North,* 125.

16. Douglas, *Jim Crow Moves North,* 134.

17. Douglas, *Jim Crow Moves North,* 124.

18. Douglas, *Jim Crow Moves North,* 125.

19. Boyle, *Arc of Justice,* 9–10.

20. Douglas, *Jim Crow Moves North,* 129; Boyle, *Arc of Justice,* 9, 144.

21. Douglas, *Jim Crow Moves North,* 129, 136.

22. Boyle, *Arc of Justice,* 9–10.

23. Douglas, *Jim Crow Moves North,* 137–138.

24. See Boyle, *Arc of Justice.*

25. Douglas, *Jim Crow Moves North,* 137–138; Boyle, *Arc of Justice.*

26. Harvard Sitkoff, *The Struggle for Black Equality, 1954–1992* (New York: Hill and Wang, 1993), 8.

27. Tolnay and Beck, *Festival of Violence,* 526.

28. Carl I. Hovland and Robert R. Sears, "Minor Studies of Aggression: Correlations of Lynchings with Economic Indices," in *A Social History of Racial Violence,* ed. Allen D. Grimshaw (New Brunswick: Aldine Transaction, 2009), 348.

29. David Jacobs and Katherine Wood, "Interracial Conflict and Interracial Homicide: Do Political and Economic Rivalries Explain White Killings of Blacks or Black Killings of Whites?" *American Journal of Sociology* 105 (1999): 157–190.

30. See Eric Rauchway, *Murdering McKinley: The Making of Theodore Roosevelt's America* (New York: Hill and Wang, 2003).

31. Douglas, *Jim Crow Moves North,* 129.

32. Edna Bonacich, "Advanced Capitalism and Black/White Race Relations in the United States: A Split Labor Market Interpretation," *American Sociological Review* 41 (1976): 40–41.

33. Susan Olzak, *The Dynamics of Ethnic Conflict and Competition* (Stanford: Stanford University Press, 1992), 87.

34. For an interesting account of resistance to biracial unionism in Bogalusa, Louisiana, see Stephen H. Norwood, "Bogalusa Burning: The War against Biracial Unionism in the Deep South, 1919," *Journal of Southern History* 63 (1997).

35. Paul M. Angle, *Bloody Williamson: A Chapter in American Lawlessness* (Urbana: University of Illinois Press, 1992), 101.

36. Angle, *Bloody Williamson,* 103.

37. *New York Times,* April 15, 1913, quoted in Olzak, *Dynamics of Ethnic Conflict,* 88.

38. Interestingly, Olzak finds that "while some conflicts were directed at foreigners, two-thirds of all collective conflicts [from 1880 to 1915] and most of the violence was antiblack. So, even though immigration intensified competition levels among foreigners, native whites, and African-Americans, conflicts were more likely to be directed against African-Americans who had even less power to fight back." Olzak, *Dynamics of Ethnic Conflict,* 108.

In Longview, Texas; Bogalusa, Louisiana; Syracuse, New York; and Phillips County, Arkansas, moreover, "racially inspired labor violence occurred" in 1919. Warren Schaich, "A Relationship between Collective Racial Violence and War," *Journal of Black Studies* 5 (1975): 383.

39. Douglas, *Jim Crow Moves North,* 138.

40. Quoted in Olzak, *Dynamics of Ethnic Conflict,* 92.

41. Massey and Denton, *American Apartheid,* 28.

42. Quoted in Olzak, *Dynamics of Ethnic Conflict,* 98.

43. Bonacich, "Advanced Capitalism," 34, 45. While the U.S. Supreme Court struck down the NIRA in 1935, other laws—the Wagner Act of 1935 and the Fair Labor Standards Act of 1938—allowed its main principles to survive. Bonacich, "Advanced Capitalism," 45.

44. Eugene E. Leach, "The Literature of Riot Duty: Managing Class Conflict in the Streets, 1877–1927," *Radical History Review* 56 (1993): 37.

45. Quoted in Christopher Capozzola, "The Only Badge Needed Is Your Patriotic Fervor: Vigilance, Coercion, and the Law in World War I America," *Journal of American History* 88 (2002). In part, Wilson made this speech in response to civil libertarians and the German press and its propaganda during World War I after a mob lynched a German American coal miner.

46. Karen Rasler, "War, Accommodation, and Violence in the United States, 1890–1970," *American Political Science Review* 80 (1986): 932. The lynching of Cleo Wright in Sikeston, Missouri, in 1942, provides an interesting instance of the federal government's involvement in both stirring up racial hostilities and stepping in to protect the lives and rights of African Americans. Sikeston's whites asserted that their black neighbors had grown "too cocky" and dangerous. Moreover, whites disdained plans by the Farm Security Administration to establish "a Negro settlement" nearby, as well as unions for organizing black sharecroppers. After his brutal death at the hands of an angry white mob (a white woman accused him of attempting to rape her), the Justice Department stepped "directly into that area of civil rights for the first time" in the history of the United States." Dominic J. Capeci Jr., "The Lynching of Cleo Wright: Federal Protection of Constitutional Rights during World War II," *Journal of American History* 72 (1986): 859–861.

47. Terry Ann Knopf, "Race, Riots, and Reporting," *Journal of Black Studies* 4 (1974): 320.

48. *Washington Post,* July 22, 1919, 6.

49. Knopf, "Race, Riots, and Reporting," 312.

50. Knopf, "Race, Riots, and Reporting," 315. In some instances, however, newspapers quelled racial tensions. The *Tampa Morning Tribune* in 1901, for example, urged citizens to allow the legal system to step in after a white woman alleged that a black man attempted to rape her. "Let the courts always be as prompt as they have been in these cases," the newspaper declared, "and the people will leave to them the vindication of outraged law." Robert P. Ingalls, "Lynching and Establishment Violence in Tampa, 1858–1935," *Journal of Southern History* 53 (1987): 624. In this case, peace prevailed.

51. Joel Williamson, *The Crucible of Race: Black-White Relations in the American South Since Emancipation* (New York: Oxford University Press, 1984); Eric Niderost, "The Birth of a Nation," *American History* 40 (2005). Griffith himself, while reaping praise by many for his cinematic masterpiece, also received harsh criticism for the film's racist overtones. A native of Kentucky, he remained mystified at the negative responses, however, explaining that to label him prejudiced "is like saying I am against children, as they were our children, whom we loved and cared for all our lives." Moreover, he lauded the "four old niggers" who stood over his father's

deathbed decades earlier. "I am quite sure," he declared, "they really loved him." Niderost, "Birth of a Nation."

For years after its debut, the film brought in millions of dollars in box office receipts. Oliver and Walker claim $60 million by the end of 1917; Merritt provides the much more modest figure—but still phenomenal for the era—of $18 million by 1931. See Lawrence J. Oliver and Terri L. Walker, "James Weldon Johnson's 'New York Age' Essays on 'The Birth of a Nation' and the 'Southern Oligarchy,'" *South Central Review* 10 (1993): 4; Russell Merritt, "Dixon, Griffith, and the Southern Legend," *Cinema Journal* 12 (1972): 27.

52. Niderost, "Birth of a Nation." This fact is even more remarkable given that movie houses set top ticket prices at $2.00 when most first-run movies cost 25 cents and that the movie ran for almost three hours.

After a public outcry against the film by black and white leaders, Wilson backed off from his praise. The president, his public relations advisor, later asserted, "at no time expressed his approbation of" *The Birth of a Nation,* but simply showed it at the White House as "a courtesy extended to an old acquaintance." Oliver and Walker, "James Weldon Johnson's 'New York Age' Essays," 17, n42.

53. Williamson, *Crucible of Race,* 175.

54. Merritt, "Dixon, Griffith, and the Southern Legend," 28.

55. Niderost, "Birth of a Nation."

56. Quoted in Lawrence J. Oliver, "Writing from the Right during the 'Red Decade': Thomas Dixon's Attack on W. E. B. Du Bois and James Weldon Johnson in the Flaming Sword," *American Literature* 70 (1998): 137; Oliver and Walker, "James Weldon Johnson's 'New York Age' Essays."

57. Quoted in Oliver, "Writing from the Right," 137.

58. Other protesters made their way into the show, however, and barraged the screen with eggs and set off stink bombs. Niderost, "Birth of a Nation."

59. See Thomas Cripps, *Slow Fade to Black: The Negro in American Film, 1900–1942* (New York: Oxford University Press, 1977); Merritt, "Dixon, Griffith, and the Southern Legend."; and Niderost, "Birth of a Nation."

60. Nancy MacLean, *Behind the Mask of Chivalry: The Making of the Second Ku Klux Klan* (New York: Oxford University Press, 1994), 12–13; Jacquelyn Dowd Hall, *Revolt against Chivalry: Jessie Daniel Ames and the Women's Campaign against Lynching* (New York: Columbia University, 1993), 54; and Glenda E. Gilmore, *Gender and Jim Crow: Women and the Politics of White Supremacy in North Carolina, 1896–1920* (Chapel Hill: University of North Carolina Press, 1996), 137. According to historian Nancy MacLean, "nothing in the early years" of the second Ku Klux Klan did more to empower it than *The Birth of a Nation.* MacLean, *Behind the Mask of Chivalry,* 12. Founded by William Joseph Simmons in Georgia, the reincarnated version of the white supremacy organization emerged the same year as the movie, 1915. The Klan even used its showings as a recruiting tool. MacLean, *Behind the Mask of Chivalry,* 12. Dixon also had a profound impact on contemporary and future writers such as *Gone with the Wind* (1936) author Margaret Mitchell, who wrote Dixon that "I was practically raised on your books, and love them very much." Oliver, "Writing from the Right," 132.

61. Stanley Coben, *Rebellion against Victorianism: The Impetus for Cultural Change in 1920s America* (New York: Oxford University Press, 136–141).

62. Wyn Craig Wade, *The Fiery Cross: The Ku Klux Klan in America* (New York: Simon and Schuster, 1987), 218.

63. Angle, *Bloody Williamson,* 135.

64. See Boyle, *Arc of Justice,* 6–8.

65. *The Atlanta Constitution,* November 22, 1922, 6.

66. Ronald L. F. Davis, "Resisting Jim Crow: In-Depth Essay," *The History of Jim Crow,* http://www.jimcrowhistory.org/history/resisting2.htm. Previous attempts died in the House Judiciary Committee. Congressman Leonidas Dyer of St. Louis began introducing anti-lynching legislation in 1918, largely in response to the East St. Louis riot the previous summer. During the 1922 floor debates, southern House members argued against Dyer's bill on the basis of states' rights (even the NAACP initially questioned whether a federal law would withstand constitutional scrutiny since it would introduce federal powers into a realm usually belonging to the states) or because they saw it as unfairly focusing on the South, but others did not bother to hide their racist sentiments. "I would rather the whole black race of the world were lynched," Thomas Sisson of Mississippi declared, "than for one of the fair daughters of the South to be ravished and torn by these brutes." Quoted in Mark Robert Schneider, *"We Return Fighting": The Civil Rights Movement in the Jazz Age* (Boston: Northeastern University Press, 2002), 177. One congressman labeled Dyer's legislation "a bill to encourage rape," while another castigated northerners to "quit howling about lynchings and begin preaching against rape." Schneider, *"We Return Fighting,"* 177. On the day of the vote, local African Americans packed the House galleries. When they broke out in applause in response to a speech, someone from the floor yelled, "Sit down, you niggers!" A shout from the galleries shot back, "You're a liar! We're not niggers" Schneider, *"We Return Fighting,"* 178. The bill passed 230–119. Not until decades later would the Senate acknowledge the travesty of lynching and even then only symbolically. In a nonbinding resolution on June 13, 2005, the Senate, led by two southern senators, formally apologized to lynching victims and their descendants for that body's century-long inaction to stop the grisly practice. *Chicago Tribune,* June 14, 2005.

67. Davis, "Resisting Jim Crow."

68. In the wake of the riot, local white authorities arrested 79 black sharecroppers for the death of one white man (but no whites for the murders of over 200 African Americans). For the black men's trial, prosecutors had witnesses whipped so they would provide supportive testimony, and the defense proved inept at (or unwilling to) representing the defendants. Meanwhile, an enraged white crowd surrounded the courthouse and promised to lynch the men unless the all-white jury found them guilty. Not surprisingly, 12 of the men received the death penalty, and the others got long prison sentences. Largely due to the efforts of the NAACP, in *Moore v. Dempsey* in 1923, the Supreme Court overturned these convictions. Richard C. Cortner, *A Mob Intent on Death: The NAACP and the Arkansas Riot Cases* (Middletown: Wesleyan University Press, 1988); Davis, "Resisting Jim Crow."

69. Now more in alignment with Booker T. Washington's philosophies regarding economic self-improvement, Du Bois believed segregation did not pose a problem in and of itself for African Americans. He became attracted to socialist ideology and wanted to forge an alliance with the working class, eventually joining the Communist Party. Frustrated with political conditions in the United States, Du Bois gave up his citizenship and moved to Ghana, where he died in 1963 at the age of 95. Davis, "Resisting Jim Crow"; Jacqueline M. Moore, *Booker T. Washington, W. E. B. Du Bois, and the Struggle for Racial Uplift* (Wilmington, Scholarly Resources Inc., 2003), 117.

70. Although fair-skinned, White identified himself as an African American. Again, violence played a profound role in his life. A native of Atlanta, he had a firsthand view of the 1906 riot there as a boy. He later recalled:

> Late in the afternoon friends of my father's came to warn of more trouble that night. . . . There had never been a firearm in our house before that day. Father was reluctant even in those circumstances to violate the law, but he at last gave in at Mother's insistence. . . . In a very few minutes the vanguard of the mob . . . appeared. A voice which we recognized as that of the son of the grocer with whom we had traded for many years yelled, "That's where that nigger mail carrier lives! Let's burn it down! It's too nice for a nigger to live in!" . . . In a voice as quiet as though he were asking me to pass him the sugar at the breakfast table, [Father] said, "Son, don't shoot until the first man puts his foot on the lawn and then—don't you miss!" . . . The mob moved toward the lawn. I tried to aim my gun, wondering what it would feel like to kill a man. Suddenly there was a volley of shots. . . . Some friends of my father's had barricaded themselves in a two-story brick building just below our house. It was they who had fired. . . . The mob broke and retreated. . . . I was gripped by the knowledge of my identity, and in the depths of my soul I was vaguely aware that I was glad of it. I was sick with loathing for the hatred which had flared before me that night and come so close to making me a killer; but I was glad I was not one of those who hated; I was glad I was not one of those made sick and murderous by pride. Walter White, *A Man Called White* (New York: Arno Press, 1969), 5–12.

71. Davis, "Resisting Jim Crow." For a good overview of the long struggle for desegregation and integration, see Garrett Duncan, "Desegregation," in *Encyclopedia of American Race Riots,* ed. Walter Rucker and James Nathaniel Upton (Westport: Greenwood Press, 2006).

72. Bernard Magubane, *The Ties That Bind: African-American Consciousness of Africa* (Trenton: Africa World Press, 1987), 97.

73. Schneider, *"We Return Fighting,"* 129.

74. Schneider, *"We Return Fighting,"* 137–138.

75. Convicted of mail fraud in 1925 (eight prominent blacks had petitioned the Attorney General to investigate his business practices), Garvey served two years in jail, after which the government deported him permanently from the United States. He died in London in 1940. Wilson J. Moses, *Creative Conflict in African American Thought: Frederick Douglass, Alexander Crummell, Booker T. Washington, W. E. B. Du Bois, and Marcus Garvey* (New York: Cambridge University Press, 2004, 282). The disunity among blacks prompted some to call for a united front. Kelly Miller, a sociology professor at Howard University, for example, suggested

the Negro Sanhedrin Movement in the 1920s "to make for understanding of the problems of Negroes as a whole and to promote harmonization of effort of existing agencies to serve the desired end." C. Alvin Hughes, "The Negro Sanhedrin Movement," *Journal of Negro History* 69 (1984): 8.

76. See David Levering Lewis, *When Harlem Was Vogue* (New York: Penguin Books, 1997), for a good overview of the Harlem Renaissance.

77. Many scholars use the terms "New Negro Movement" and "Harlem Renaissance" interchangeably. For a good analysis of this topic, see Wilson J. Moses, "The Lost World of the Negro, 1895–1919: Black Literary and Intellectual Life before the 'Renaissance.'" *Black American Literature Forum* 21 (1987): 61–84.

78. Houston A. Baker Jr., *Black Literature in America* (New York: McGraw-Hill Book Company, 1971), 8–9.

79. William Jordon, "'The Damnable Dilemma': African-American Accommodation and Protest during World War I," *Journal of American History* 81 (1995): 1583.

80. *Chicago Daily Tribune,* July 29, 1919, 8.

81. William M. Tuttle Jr., *Race Riot: Chicago in the Red Summer of 1919* (Champaign: University of Illinois Press, 1996), 49.

82. Marilynn S. Johnson, "Gender, Race, and Rumours: Re-examining the 1943 Race Riots," *Gender & History* 10 (1998): 265; The Chicago Commission on Race Relations, *The Negro in Chicago: A Study of Race Relations and a Race Riot* (Chicago: University of Chicago Press), 30–31.

83. This false story echoes a true occurrence well known among black Americans at the time and probably caused the *Defender's* fabrication to resonate that much more during the Chicago riot. In 1918, after Mary Turner argued against the lynching of her husband in Georgia, a mob:

> [s]ecurely . . . bound her ankles together and, by them, hanged her to a tree. Gasoline and motor oil were thrown upon her dangling clothes; a match wrapped her in sudden flames. Mocking, ribald laughter from her tormentors answered the helpless woman's screams of pain and terror. . . . The clothes burned from her crisply toasted body, in which, unfortunately, life still lingered, a man stepped towards the woman and, with his knife, ripped open the abdomen in a crude Caesarian operation. Out tumbled the prematurely born child. Two feeble cries it gave—and received for answer the heel of a stalwart man as life was ground out of the tiny form. Walter White quoted in Johnson, "Gender, Race, and Rumours," 266.

84. Quoted in Oliver and Walker, "James Weldon Johnson's 'New York Age' Essays," 1.

85. See Schneider, "*We Return Fighting,*" 177, for example. "The continued ill treatment of Negroes in uniform," declared the NAACP, meeting in Detroit during World War II, "both on military reservations and in many civilian communities is disgraceful. Negroes in the uniform of the nation have been beaten, mobbed, killed, and lynched." Shapiro, *White Violence and Black Response,* 309.

86. Du Bois even went so far in a *Crisis* column to recommend to blacks that they demonstrate their patriotism: "Let us, while this war lasts, forget our special grievances and close our ranks shoulder to shoulder with our white fellow citizens

and the allied nations that are fighting for democracy." Jordon, "'The Damnable Dilemma,'" 1562. Some scholars suggest he "struck a deal" with the military to write the article in exchange for a captaincy in the army. See David Levering Lewis, *W. E. B. Du Bois: Biography of a Race, 1868–1919* (New York: Henry Holt and Company, 1993), 555; Jordon, "'The Damnable Dilemma,'" 1562.

87. Hughes, "The Negro Sanhedrin Movement," 2.

88. Shapiro, *White Violence and Black Response,* 157.

89. David Levering Lewis, *W. E. B. Du Bois: The Fight for Equality and the American Century, 1919–1963* (New York: Henry Holt and Company, 2000), 14–15.

90. Kennedy, *Over Here,* 283.

91. The Houston race riot of 1917 deserves special mention here. Just after the United States declared war on Germany in the spring of 1917, the army sent the Third Battalion of the black Twenty-fourth United States Infantry to guard Camp Logan, a military installation being built on the outskirts of Houston for the war effort. Houstonians greeted the black soldiers with disdain, and some of these men grew increasingly vocal in their resentment of being treated that way. The black soldiers had also been following the recent atrocities of the East St. Louis race riot in the *Chicago Defender.* If something like that could happen in the North, what might they encounter in Texas? Harper Barnes, *Never Been a Time: The 1917 Race Riot That Sparked the Civil Rights Movement* (New York: Walker & Company, 2008), 197. On August 23, after two policemen detained a soldier for interfering in the arrest of a black woman, Charles Baltimore, a black military policeman with the battalion checked on his status. Tempers flared and a policeman hit Baltimore over the head, chased him when he fled, captured him, and hauled him off to police headquarters. They later released him, but rumors circulated around Camp Logan that he had been shot and killed. Over 100 black soldiers decided to mount an attack on the police station in response, and in their march toward the city they killed 15 whites, four of them police. Four blacks also died. On August 25, authorities restored order, and the army escorted the battalion out of the city. Military tribunals eventually found 110 soldiers guilty of taking part in the mutiny and riot. Nineteen died by hanging and sixty-three got life sentences. For a good account of this riot, see Robert V. Haynes, *A Night of Violence: The Houston Riot of 1917* (Baton Rouge: Louisiana State University, 1976).

92. Tuttle, *Race Riot,* 14–22.

93. Tuttle, *Race Riot,* 21.

CHAPTER 5

1. Kenneth R. Durham Jr., "The Longview Race Riot of 1919," *East Texas Historical Journal* 18 (1980): 13–24.

2. William M. Tuttle Jr., "Violence in a 'Heathen' Land: The Longview Race Riot of 1919," *Phylon* 33 (1972): 325–326.

3. Jared Wheeler, "Prelude to Anarchy," *Texas Ranger Dispatch* 54 (1969): 5–6.

4. Tuttle, "Violence in a 'Heathen' Land," 325.

5. Wheeler, "Prelude to Anarchy," 6–7.

6. Durham, "Longview Race Riot," fn 10.

7. *Chicago Defender,* July 5, 1919, 2.

8. *Chicago Defender,* July 5, 1919, 2.

9. Tuttle, "Violence in a 'Heathen' Land," 325–326.

10. Tuttle, "Violence in a 'Heathen' Land," 327–328; Wheeler, "Prelude to Anarchy," 8.

11. Tuttle, "Violence in a 'Heathen' Land," 328–329; Wheeler, "Prelude to Anarchy," 8–10.

12. Tuttle, "Violence in a 'Heathen' Land," 329–330; Wheeler, "Prelude to Anarchy," 10–11.

13. Wheeler, "Prelude to Anarchy," 11.

14. Tuttle, "Violence in a 'Heathen' Land," 330.

15. Wheeler, "Prelude to Anarchy," 11.

16. Tuttle, "Violence in a 'Heathen' Land," 330; Wheeler, "Prelude to Anarchy," 12.

17. Durham, "Longview Race Riot."

18. Arthur I. Waskow, *From Race Riot to Sit-In, 1919 and the 1960s: A Study in the Connections between Conflict and Violence* (Garden City: Doubleday, 1966), 22. Moreover, with the arrival of southern-born President Woodrow Wilson in 1913, new southern supervisors segregated black subordinates from whites in federal jobs, and a "more 'southern' outlook" pervaded the lives of D.C.'s African Americans. Waskow, *From Race Riot to Sit-In,* 21.

19. Constance McLaughlin Green, *The Secret City: A History of Race Relations in the Nation's Capital* (Princeton: Princeton University Press, 1967), 202.

20. Waskow, *From Race Riot to Sit-In,* 21.

21. *Washington Post,* March 1, 1999, A1.

22. Terry Ann Knopf, *Rumors, Race and Riots* (New Brunswick: Transaction Publishers, 2006), 29; William M. Tuttle Jr., *Race Riot: Chicago in the Red Summer of 1919* (Champaign: University of Illinois Press, 1996), 29.

23. Tuttle, *Race Riot,* 29.

24. Knopf, *Rumors, Race and Riots,* 30.

25. Waskow, *From Race Riot to Sit-In,* 22.

26. Michael Schaffer, "Lost Riot," *Washington City Paper* April 3, 1998; Lee E. Williams II, *Post-War Riots in America, 1919 and 1946: How the Pressures of War Exacerbated American Urban Tensions to the Breaking Point* (Lewiston: E. Mellen Press, 1991), 17.

27. Schaffer, "Lost Riot."

28. Knopf, *Rumors, Race and Riots,* 29; Waskow, *From Race Riot to Sit-In,* 23.

29. Waskow, *From Race Riot to Sit-In,* 23.

30. As editor of the Raleigh *News and Observer* two decades earlier, Daniels himself had played a role in stoking the flames of racial hatred during the months leading up to the Wilmington, North Carolina, race riot in 1898.

31. In fact, one southern congressman even called for a congressional investigation into why the police force had not caught the supposed black attackers

of D.C.'s white women in the days leading up to the violence. He pinpointed this failure as the reason for the riot. Waskow, *From Race Riot to Sit-In*, 26.

32. Jacqueline M. Moore, *Leading the Race: The Transformation of the Black Elite in the National's Capital, 1880–1920* (Charlottesville: University Press of Virginia, 1999), 211.

33. Tuttle, *Race Riot*, 30.

34. Williams, *Post-War Riots*, 18.

35. Tuttle, *Race Riot*, 30; Waskow, *From Race Riot to Sit-In*, 25.

36. Waskow, *From Race Riot to Sit-In*, 25–27.

37. Quote in Waskow, *From Race Riot to Sit-In*, 27; *Washington Post*, July 22, 1919, 6. According to newspaper reports, a 17-year-old black female shot and killed one of the white policemen "point blank." *Washington Post*, July 22, 1919, 1; *Boston Daily Globe*, 1, 6.

38. Waskow, *From Race Riot to Sit-In*, 28.

39. Quoted in Waskow, *From Race Riot to Sit-In*, 29.

40. Waskow, *From Race Riot to Sit-In*, 30.

41. Tuttle, *Race Riot*, 30; Waskow, *From Race Riot to Sit-In*, 28–29.

42. Schaffer, "Lost Riot."

43. Waskow, *From Race Riot to Sit-In*, 30, 32, 34.

44. Waskow, *From Race Riot to Sit-In*, 34–35.

45. Waskow, *From Race Riot to Sit-In*, 32.

46. Waskow, *From Race Riot to Sit-In*, 37.

47. *New York Times*, July 23, 1919, 8.

48. The Chicago Commission on Race Relations, *The Negro in Chicago: A Study of Race Relations and a Race Riot* (Chicago: University of Chicago Press), 79, 520. Most of these 50,000 new blacks came from the rural South. Waskow, *From Race Riot to Sit-In*, 38. The city's black population grew 148 percent in 10 years, from 44,103 in 1910 to 109,594 in 1920. Chicago Commission, *Negro in Chicago*, 2.

49. Tuttle, *Race Riot*, 112. While Tuttle attributes labor strife as a significant factor leading to the riot, others have downplayed its importance. "There were plenty of jobs to absorb all the white and Negro workers available," The Chicago Commission on Race Relations concluded after the riot, "[and only] a few strikes . . . had given the Negro the name of 'strike breaker.'" Chicago Commission, *Negro in Chicago*, 2–3; see also Tuttle, *Race Riot*, 109–112.

50. Tuttle, *Race Riot*, 120.

51. Tuttle, *Race Riot*, 131; see William E. Leuchtenburg, *The Perils of Prosperity, 1914–1932* (Chicago: University of Chicago Press, 1993), 70.

52. Tuttle, *Race Riot*, 138.

53. Tuttle, *Race Riot*, 108.

54. Chicago Commission, *Negro in Chicago*, 3.

55. Chicago Commission, *Negro in Chicago*, 152–153.

56. Tuttle, *Race Riot*, 101–102. Poet Langston Hughes unwittingly crossed into an Irish neighborhood as a high school student his first week in Chicago in 1918. He quickly learned his mistake when he "was set upon and beaten by a group of

white boys, who said they didn't allow niggers in that neighborhood." Tuttle, *Race Riot,* 102–103.

57. Chicago Commission, *Negro in Chicago,* 3.

58. Tuttle, *Race Riot,* 175–176.

59. Chicago Commission, *Negro in Chicago,* 3.

60. Tuttle, *Race Riot,* 184.

61. Quoted in Tuttle, *Race Riot,* 190.

62. *Chicago Daily Tribune,* May 15, 1915, 17; see also *Chicago Daily Tribune,* April 26, 1915, 1 and *Chicago Daily Tribune,* June 9, 1915, 8.

63. Tuttle, *Race Riot,* 191, 200. In addition to alienating the city's racists during his first term, he also managed to anger Chicago's Catholics and "both the antisaloon and liquor interests, and both management and labor." Tuttle, *Race Riot,* 198, 200.

64. Tuttle, *Race Riot,* 203.

65. Chicago Commission, *Negro in Chicago,* 53–54.

66. Chicago Commission, *Negro in Chicago,* 55.

67. Chicago Commission, *Negro in Chicago,* 55–56.

68. Chicago Commission, *Negro in Chicago,* 532.

69. Chicago Commission, *Negro in Chicago,* 520.

70. Tuttle, *Race Riot,* 48.

71. Chicago Commission, *Negro in Chicago,* 26.

72. For excellent descriptions of the riot see Chicago Commission, *Negro in Chicago,* 1–52 and Tuttle, *Race Riot,* 3–10, 32–66.

73. Chicago Commission, *Negro in Chicago,* 11.

74. Tuttle, *Race Riot,* 65.

75. Tuttle, *Race Riot,* 43.

76. Chicago Commission, *Negro in Chicago,* 6.

77. Tuttle reveals that the mayor and Governor Lowden, although both Republicans, so despised each other by the summer of 1919 "that cooperation in subduing the rioting that erupted on a South Side beach on June 27 was, while not impossible, simply not forthcoming." See Tuttle, *Race Riot,* 204–205. The police chief, on the other hand, contended that "inexperienced militiamen would add to the deaths and disorders." After the riot, he and other officials admitted that the police force needed much more manpower to be effective. Chicago Commission, *Negro in Chicago,* 40.

78. Waskow, *From Race Riot to Sit-In,* 43.

79. The militia actually worked closely with the police instead of completely replacing them. Waskow, *From Race Riot to Sit-In,* 43. But during the riot itself, the local police did not act impartially. The coroner's jury on November 3, 1919, for example, relayed:

> Our attention was called strikingly to the fact that at the time of race rioting, the arrests made for rioting by the police of colored rioters were far in excess of the arrests made of white rioters. The failure of the police to arrest impartially, at the time of the rioting, whether from insufficient effort or otherwise, was a mistake and had a tendency to further incite and aggravate the colored population. Chicago Commission, *Negro in Chicago,* 36.

80. Chicago Commission, *Negro in Chicago*, 40–41.

81. Chicago Commission, *Negro in Chicago*, 1.

82. Chicago Commission, *Negro in Chicago*, 35.

83. Waskow, *From Race Riot to Sit-In*, 46–50.

84. Waskow, *From Race Riot to Sit-In*, 55.

85. United States Bureau of the Census, *Fifteenth Census of the United States, Population*, Vol. 3, pt. 2 (Washington D.C.: Government Printing Office, 1930), 903.

86. Matthew Lakin, '"A Dark Night': The Knoxville Race Riot of 1919," *Journal of East Tennessee History* 72 (2000): 3.

87. John Egerton, "A Case of Prejudice: Maurice Mays and the Knoxville Race Riot of 1919," *Southern Exposure* 11 (July/August 1983): 57; Lakin, '"A Dark Knight,'" 3.

88. Lakin, '"A Dark Knight,'" 5–6, 8.

89. Lakin, '"A Dark Knight,'" 6–8.

90. Quotes by Mays in Lakin, '"A Dark Knight,'" 9–10.

91. Quoted in Lakin, '"A Dark Knight,'" 11. Unfortunately no copy of the August 30 afternoon edition of the Sentinel now exists. Lakin, '"A Dark Knight,'" 11, fn 32.

92. Lakin, '"A Dark Knight,'" 11.

93. Lakin, '"A Dark Knight,'" 12–15; Egerton, "A Case of Prejudice," 58.

94. Lakin, '"A Dark Knight,'" 15–16.

95. Lakin, '"A Dark Knight,'" 17–19.

96. Lakin, '"A Dark Knight,'" 23–25.

97. Lakin, '"A Dark Knight,'" 24, 28.

98. Egerton, "A Case of Prejudice," 59–65.

99. Lakin, '"A Dark Knight,'" 28.

100. Michael L. Lawson, "Omaha, A City of Ferment: Summer of 1919," *Nebraska History* 58 (1977): 395–396.

101. Quoted in Lawson, "Omaha, A City of Ferment," 396.

102. Orville D. Menard, "Lest We Forget: The Lynching of Will Brown, Omaha's 1919 Race Riot," *Nebraska History* 91 (2010): 156.

103. Menard, "Lest We Forget," 156.

104. Lawson, "Omaha, A City of Ferment," 398.

105. Jan Voogd, *Race Riots & Resistance: The Red Summer of 1919* (New York: Peter Lang Publishing, 2008), 108–109.

106. Lawson, "Omaha, A City of Ferment," 405, 413.

107. Lawson, "Omaha, A City of Ferment," 400–408.

108. Lawson, "Omaha, A City of Ferment," 412.

109. Orville D. Menard, "Tom Dennison, the Omaha Bee, and the 1919 Race Riot," *Nebraska History* 68 (1987): 157–158; Clayton D. Laurie, "The U.S. Army and the Omaha Race Riot of 1919," *Nebraska History* 72 (1991): 137.

110. Menard, "Tom Dennison," 158.

111. Voogd, *Race Riots & Resistance*, 487.

112. Menard, "Lest We Forget," 154.

113. Menard, "Tom Dennison," 158.

114. Menard, "Lest We Forget," 154–155.

115. Menard, "Lest We Forget," 157–158.

116. Menard, "Lest We Forget," 158.

117. Voogd, *Race Riots & Resistance,* 110.

118. Menard, "Tom Dennison," 159.

119. Menard, "Tom Dennison," 160; Menard, "Lest We Forget," 159.

120. Menard, "Lest We Forget," 160.

121. Menard, "Tom Dennison," 160; Menard, "Lest We Forget," 161.

122. Menard, "Lest We Forget," 161.

123. Voogd, *Race Riots & Resistance,* 111; *New York Times,* September 30, 1919, 1.

124. Menard, "Lest We Forget," 161–162.

125. Menard, "Tom Dennison," 160.

126. Menard, "Lest We Forget," 162.

127. Menard, "Lest We Forget," 163–164.

128. *The Atlanta Constitution,* September 30, 1919, 8.

129. United States Bureau of the Census, *Fourteenth Census of the United States,* Arkansas, Table III (Washington D.C.: Government Printing Office, 1920), 96; United States Bureau of the Census, *Fourteenth Census of the United States,* Population (Washington D.C.: Government Printing Office, 1920), 1329.

130. B. Boren McCool, *Union, Reaction, and Riot: A Biography of a Rural Race Riot* (Memphis: Memphis State University, 1970), 2.

131. Jeannie M. Whayne, "Low Villains and Wickedness in High Places: Race and Class in the Elaine Riots," *Arkansas Review* 32 (2001).

132. A great deal of fraud existed as well. See, for example, the opening chapter of Leon F. Litwack, *Trouble in Mind: Black Southerners in the Age of Jim Crow* (New York: Alfred A. Knopf, 1998).

133. Fon Louise Gordon, "From Slavery to Uncertain Freedom: Blacks in the Delta," in *The Arkansas Delta: Land of Paradox,* ed. Jeannie Whayne and Willard B. Gatewood (Fayetteville: University of Arkansas Press, 1993), 113.

134. Whayne, "Low Villains and Wickedness in High Places."

135. Kieran Taylor, "'We Have Just Begun': Black Organization and White Response in the Arkansas Delta, 1919," *Arkansas Historical Quarterly* 58 (1999): 269.

136. McCool, *Union, Reaction, and Riot,* 6.

137. Grif Stockley, *Blood in Their Eyes: The Elaine Race Massacres of 1919* (Fayetteville: University of Arkansas Press, 2001), 8.

138. Stockley, *Blood in Their Eyes,* 9.

139. Stockley, *Blood in Their Eyes,* 9.

140. This figure provides only an estimate since no data exist broken down by race at the county level. McCool, *Union, Reaction, and Riot,* 8–9.

141. Taylor, "'We Have Just Begun,'" 270.

142. Taylor, "'We Have Just Begun,'" 271.

143. McCool, *Union, Reaction, and Riot,* 13; Taylor, "'We Have Just Begun,'" 271.

144. Taylor, "'We Have Just Begun,'" 271.

145. John William Graves, "Protectors or Perpetrators? White Leadership in the Elaine Race Riots," *Arkansas Review* 32 (2001): 138; Grif Stockley, "The Legal Proceedings of the Arkansas Race Massacres of 1919 and the Evidence of the Plot to Kill Planters," *Arkansas Review* 32 (2001): 141. "[I]n a sense they were undoubtedly right," historian Arthur Waskow asserts, "since a union of sharecroppers that gave Negroes in rural Arkansas equal bargaining power with whites would have constituted a revolution of sorts, for Arkansas." Waskow, *From Race Riot to Sit-In,* 121–122.

146. Tuttle, *Race Riot,* 246. Not surprisingly, whites attacked blacks whom they deemed too successful as well. Author Richard Wright lived with relatives in Elaine for a short time in 1916 as an eight-year-old boy. He soon grew close to his Uncle Silas Hoskins. With the earnings he made as a carpenter, Hoskins had become a successful tavern owner there, a status that the town's whites could not tolerate. Just a few months after Wright arrived, a group of whites killed his uncle. "I learned afterwards," Wright later recalled, "that Uncle Hoskins had been killed by whites who had long coveted his flourishing liquor business. He had been threatened with death and warned many times to leave, but he had wanted to hold on a while longer to amass more money." Richard Wright, *Black Boy (American Hunger): A Record of Childhood and Youth* (New York: HarperPerennial, 1993), 63.

147. Tuttle, *Race Riot,* 247.

148. Stockley, "Legal Proceedings of the Arkansas Race Massacres," 141.

149. Ronnie A. Nichols, "Conspirators or Victims? A Survey of Black Leadership in the Riots," *Arkansas Review* 32 (2001): 124.

150. Taylor, " 'We Have Just Begun,' " 274.

151. Taylor, " 'We Have Just Begun,' " 273.

152. Taylor, " 'We Have Just Begun,' " 273–274.

153. Tuttle, *Race Riot,* 247.

154. Colonel Isaac C. Jenks, the commander of the federal troops, immediately ordered both blacks and whites to be disarmed, "but neither Jenks nor his men seem to have doubted the basic outline of the story with which they were met [by local white authorities] or to have questioned that their major task was to smash a threatened Negro insurrection." Waskow, *From Race Riot to Sit-In,* 131. A more recent work goes further in condemning the actions of the federal troops, implicating them in some of the wanton deaths of African American. Stockley, *Blood in Their Eyes,* 63–66.

155. Tuttle, *Race Riot,* 247.

156. Richard C. Cortner, *A Mob Intent on Death: The NAACP and the Arkansas Riot Cases* (Middletown: Wesleyan University Press, 1988), 72. Scholar Grif Stockley suggests that upon going to the scene of the riot, "Brough was acting out his own childhood fantasy." Brough himself described his time there in a letter to a friend, "I have just had a very thrilling experience in Phillips County, in connection with the race riot there." Stockley, *Blood in Their Eyes,* 63.

157. Waskow, *From Race Riot to Sit-In,* 132.

158. Stockley, "Legal Proceedings of the Arkansas Race Massacres," 142.

159. See Cortner, *Mob Intent on Death.*

160. David M. Kennedy, *Over Here: The First World War and American Society* (New York: Oxford University Press, 1980), 280.

161. Kennedy, *Over Here,* 278–279.

CHAPTER 6

1. On January 1, 1923, a white woman ran screaming from her house in Rosewood that a black man had just assaulted her. A group of white men began searching for the alleged black assailant (an escaped prisoner became the target of their search). The mob used violence (they dragged one man behind a car to get him to talk and hung another one from a tree, cut him with knives, and shot him in the face—killing him—to force him to show them where he had supposedly hid the alleged culprit) on several of the city's African Americans to try to smoke out the suspect. A gunfight broke out between members of the white mob and several African Americans whose house they invaded looking for their suspect. Two of the white men died from gunshots as they tried to enter the house. Whites from surrounding communities came to the aid of their white brethren, killing at least eight blacks and burning down every black-owned home in town. Local authorities did little to thwart the violence, and they arrested no one in connection with the riot. Those African Americans who survived the weeklong slaughter eventually moved away, and the town no longer exists. The white woman's black housekeeper suggested that the woman's white paramour had actually been the one who roughed her up. See Michael D'Orso, *Like Judgment Day: The Ruin and Redemption of a Town Called Rosewood* (New York: G. P. Putnam's Sons, 1996).

2. See Dominic J. Capeci Jr., "Forward," in *Encyclopedia of American Race Riots,* ed. Walter Rucker and James Nathaniel Upton (Westport: Greenwood Press, 2006), xxvii. According to the data from the Social Science Institute at Fisk University, 242 "racial battles" broke out in 47 American cities in 1943 alone. Herbert Shapiro, *White Violence and Black Response: From Reconstruction to Montgomery* (Amherst: University of Massachusetts Press, 1988), 337.

3. The Mobile riot broke out on May 25, 1943, in the shipyards of the Alabama Dry Dock and Shipbuilding Company. A few months earlier, the U.S. government—under the auspices of the Fair Employment Practices Commission—ordered the company to end its routine of not hiring blacks, or not upgrading the African Americans who did work there. Without warning to workers, six months after the government's directive, Alabama Dry Dock upgraded 12 black workers to welding jobs. On May 25, when white workers discovered these black welders on the shipways, the news quickly spread. Soon white men and women workers began to target any black in sight, shouting, "Get going, nigger. This is our shipyard." Fifty African Americans suffered injuries before federal troops stepped in to restore order. Quote from James Albert Burran III, "Racial Violence in the South during World War II," Ph.D. dissertation, University of Tennessee, Knoxville, 1977, 114; see also Shapiro, *White Violence and Black Response,* 338–339.

4. The Harlem riot erupted on August 1, 1943, after a white policeman shot an African American army private when the young man intervened as the policeman arrested a black woman for disturbing the peace. As word got out to African

Americans that a white policeman had shot a black soldier, false rumors circulated that the young man had been killed. In retaliation, blacks began to destroy and loot the white-owned businesses around them. After two days, city and military police and New York guardsmen finally quelled the violence. Six died during the riot, and police arrested more than 500 people. Rioters damaged or destroyed almost 1,500 stores. During the melee, Mayor Fiorello LaGuardia went to the site of the violence himself (at one point even yelling at a group of rioters to disperse). The riot, moreover, highlighted "two critical manifestations of racism appear[ing] . . . together, police brutality and unjust treatment of black servicemen" (quote from Shapiro, *White Violence and Black Response,* 333; see Shapiro, *White Violence and Black Response,* 330–335).

The riot might possibly have been avoided had LaGuardia heeded the recommendations of a commission he established in the wake of a similar riot in Harlem eight years earlier. On March 19, 1935, police cornered an African American teenager accused of stealing a knife from a white-owned store (which refused to hire black sales clerks). Although they eventually released him, false rumors spread among the black community that police had beaten and killed the young man. Violent clashes broke out between blacks and whites and between rioters and police. Rioters also looted and destroyed numerous businesses. Three people died. Police finally quieted the violence after two days. In the wake of the riot, Mayor LaGuardia's commission concluded that economic strife, discrimination, and racism by city administrators led to the Harlem riot in 1935. It made specific proposals for improvements to black education, health care, and, especially, for better relations with the police. "[N]othing revealed more strikingly," the commission noted, "the deep-seated resentments of the citizens of Harlem against exploitation and racial discrimination than their attitude toward the police." LaGuardia and his administration, however, took no measures to remedy these problems. See New York, New York, Mayor LaGuardia's Commission on the Harlem Riot of March 19, 1935, *The Complete Report of Mayor LaGuardia's Commission on the Harlem Riot of March 19, 1935* (New York: Arno Press, 1969), 113–116, and Shapiro, *White Violence and Black Response,* 261–272.

5. See Burran, "Racial Violence in the South," 161.

6. Marilynn S. Johnson, "Gender, Race, and Rumours: Re-Examining the 1943 Race Riots," *Gender & History* 10 (1998): 263; Dominic J. Capeci Jr. and Martha Wilkerson, *Layered Violence: The Detroit Rioters of 1943* (Jackson: University Press of Mississippi, 1991), 3. During the war, Ford and the city's other car manufacturers modified their assembly lines to construct tanks, airplanes, and other military hardware to support the war effort, spurring Detroit to become one of the first military-industrial complexes in the country. Thomas J. Sugrue, *The Origins of the Urban Crisis: Race and Inequality in Postwar Detroit* (Princeton: Princeton University Press, 1996), 19.

7. Historian Thomas Sugrue attributes Detroit's blacks' newfound employment opportunities in the 1940s to three factors: high demand for labor to support the war effort; the work of organizations on their behalf, such as unions reaching out to black workers, and the NAACP's campaign to end employment discrimination; and President Franklin Roosevelt's Executive Order 8802, directing

nondiscrimination in the war industries and forming the Fair Employment Practices Commission to push white employers and workers to accept black employees. Sugrue, *Origins of the Urban Crisis,* 26–27.

8. Elliot M. Rudwick, *Race Riot at East St. Louis July 2, 1917* (Carbondale: Southern Illinois University Press, 1964), 218.

9. Although the Klan's candidate went down in defeat, the winner, whom Detroit's African Americans largely helped to elect, did little to advance race relations when he declared,

> I must say that I deprecate most strongly the moving of Negroes or other persons into districts in which they know their presence may cause riot or bloodshed.
>
> I believe that any colored person who endangers life and property, simply to gratify his personal pride, is an enemy of his race as well as an incitant [*sic*] to riot and murder. These men, who have permitted themselves to be tools of the Ku Klux Klan in its effort to fan the flames of racial hatred into murderous fire, have hurt the cause of their race in a degree that can not be measured.

B. J. Widick, *Detroit: City of Race and Class Violence* (Chicago: Quadrangle Books, 1972), 4.

10. Sugrue, *Origins of the Urban Crisis,* 19, 22.

11. Burran, "Racial Violence in the South," 186.

12. Robert Shogun and Tom Craig, *The Detroit Race Riot: A Study in Violence* (Philadelphia: Chilton Books, 1964), 32.

13. Shogun and Craig, *Detroit Race Riot,* 32; Johnson, "Gender, Race, and Rumours," 263.

14. Shogun and Craig, *Detroit Race Riot,* 32.

15. Robert Williams, an early advocate of Black Power and self-defense, got caught in the fracas on the bridge. See Timothy B. Tyson, *Radio Free Dixie: Robert F. Williams & the Roots of Black Power* (Chapel Hill: University of North Carolina Press, 1999), 40–42.

16. Anthony M. Platt, ed., *The Politics of Riot Commissions: A Collection of Official Reports and Critical Essays* (New York: Macmillan Company, 1971), 207.

17. Johnson, "Gender, Race, and Rumours," 264.

18. Johnson, "Gender, Race, and Rumours," 267.

19. Shapiro, *White Violence and Black Response,* 315–319; Shogun and Craig, *Detroit Race Riot,* 49.

20. Shapiro, *White Violence and Black Response,* 319.

21. Shogun and Craig, *Detroit Race Riot,* 80. Apparently the mayor and governor seemed reticent to call in federal troops (who they worried might declare martial law) for fear of losing constituents. See Shogun and Craig, *Detroit Race Riot,* 75–76.

22. Capeci and Wilkerson, *Layered Violence,* 16, 18.

EPILOGUE

1. Anthony M. Platt, ed., *The Politics of Riot Commissions: A Collection of Official Reports and Critical Essays* (New York: Macmillan Company, 1971), 4, emphasis mine.

2. Platt, *Politics of Riot Commissions,* 4.

3. Platt, *Politics of Riot Commissions,* 20.

4. Platt, *Politics of Riot Commissions,* 14.

5. Kerner Commission, *Report of the National Advisory Commission on Civil Disorders* (New York: Bantam Books, 1968), 483.

6. See Priscilla B. Hayner, *Unspeakable Truths: Confronting State Terror and Atrocity* (New York: Routledge, 2001).

7. Priscilla B. Hayner, "The Contribution of Truth Commissions," in *An End to Torture: Strategies for Its Eradication,* ed. Bertil Dunér (New York: Zed Books, 1998), 203, 205.

8. Leonard A. Steverson, "Rosewood (Florida) Riot of 1923," in *Encyclopedia of American Race Riots,* ed. Walter Rucker and James Nathaniel Upton (Westport: Greenwood Press, 2006), 575–576; see also Charles P. Henry, *Long Overdue: The Politics of Racial Reparations* (New York: NYU Press, 2007), chapter 3.

9. Alfred L. Brophy, "The Tulsa Race Riot Commission, Apology, and Reparation: Understanding the Functions and Limitations of a Historical Truth Commission," in *Taking Wrongs Seriously: Apologies and Reparations,* ed. Elazar Barkan and Alexander Karn (Stanford: Stanford University Press, 2006), 234. Years after the riot, many of Tulsa's younger white residents did not even know that it had occurred. A 1946 hire to the University of Tulsa's sociology department recalled to one of the commissioners:

> I mentioned the race riot in class one day [shortly after I arrived in Tulsa] and was surprised at the universal surprise among my students. No one in this all-white classroom of both veterans, who were older, and standard 18-year-old freshmen, had ever heard of it, and some stoutly denied it and questioned my facts. . . . [M]any students asked their parents and were told, no, there was no race riot at all. I was called to the Dean's office and advised to drop the whole subject. (Oklahoma Commission to Study the Tulsa Race Riot of 1921, "Tulsa Race Riot: A Report by the Oklahoma Commission to Study the Tulsa Race Riot of 1921," February 28, 2001, http://www.okhistory.org/trrc/freport.htm.)

Moreover, some Tulsans made efforts to destroy evidence of the events leading up to the riot as well. According to the commission's final report:

> Precisely what the *Tulsa Tribune* printed in its May 31, 1921 editions about the Drexel Building incident is still a matter of some conjecture. The original bound volumes of the now defunct newspaper apparently no longer exist in their entirety. A microfilm version is, however, available, but before the actual microfilming was done some years later, someone had deliberately torn out of the May 31, 1921 city edition both a front-page article and, in addition, nearly all of the editorial page. (Oklahoma Commission, "Tulsa Race Riot," 58.)

10. Oklahoma Commission, "Tulsa Race Riot," ii.

11. See Brophy, "Tulsa Race Riot Commission," 244–245; *Boston Globe,* March 23, 2004; *Washington Post,* May 31, 2005, A03. "Members of the Oklahoma legislature," scholar Alfred Brophy declares, "ran from the issue as if it were radioactive. It would, quite simply, be political suicide for a legislator to support reparations." Brophy, "Tulsa Race Riot Commission," 244.

12. Brophy, "Tulsa Race Riot Commission," 244.

13. See http://www.jhfcenter.org/.

14. LeRae Umfleet, *1898 Wilmington Race Riot Report* (Raleigh: North Carolina Department of Cultural Resources, 2006), ii, http://www.history.ncdcr.gov/1898-wrrc/report/report.htm.

15. Umfleet, *Wilmington Race Riot Report,* 3–4.

16. Southern Truth and Reconciliation organized in 2003 after South African Archbishop Desmond Tutu "challenged the United States to address its history of racial violence with an effort equivalent to that of the South African process."

17. See Brophy, "Tulsa Race Riot Commission."

BIBLIOGRAPHY

BOOKS, ARTICLES, DISSERTATIONS, AND REPORTS

Abrahams, Naomi. "Towards Reconceptualizing Political Action." *Sociological Inquiry* 62 (1992): 327–347.

Abu-Lughod, Janet L. *Race, Space, and Riots in Chicago, New York, and Los Angeles.* New York: Oxford University Press, 2007.

Adams, Michael C. C. *The Best War Ever: America and World War II.* Baltimore: Johns Hopkins University Press, 1994.

Allport, Floyd H. *Social Psychology.* Boston: Houghton Mifflin, 1924.

Angle, Paul M. *Bloody Williamson: A Chapter in American Lawlessness.* Urbana: University of Illinois Press, 1992.

Archer, Jules. *Riot! A History of Mob Action in the United States.* New York: Hawthorne Books, Inc., 1974.

Ayers, Edward L. *Promise of the New South: Life after Reconstruction.* New York: Oxford University Press, 1992.

Ayers, Edward L. *Vengeance and Justice: Crime and Punishment in the 19th Century American South.* New York: Oxford University Press, 1984.

Baker, Nancy Kovaleff. "Abel Meeropol (a.k.a. Lewis Allan): Political Commentator and Social Conscience." *American Music* 20 (2002): 25–79.

Baker, Houston A., Jr. *Black Literature in America.* New York: McGraw-Hill Book Company, 1971.

Baldez, Lisa. *Why Women Protest: Women's Movements in Chile.* New York: Cambridge University Press, 2002.

Barkan, Steven E. and Lynne L. Snowden. *Collective Violence.* Boston: Allyn and Bacon, 2001.

Barnes, Harper. *Never Been a Time: The 1917 Race Riot That Sparked the Civil Rights Movement.* New York: Walker & Company, 2008.

Baron, Robert S., Norbert L. Kerr, and Norman Miller. *Group Process, Group Deci-sion, Group Action*. Pacific Grove: Brooks/Cole Publishing Company, 1992.

Bauerlein, Mark. "Atlanta (Georgia) Riot of 1906." Pp. 15–24 in *Encyclopedia of American Race Riots*. Walter Rucker and James Nathaniel Upton, eds. West-port: Greenwood Press, 2006.

Bauerlein, Mark. *Negrophobia: A Race Riot in Atlanta, 1906*. San Francisco: En-counter Books, 2001.

Bauerlein, Mark. "Washington, Du Bois, and the Black Future." *Wilson Quarterly* 28 (2004): 74–86.

Baumeister, Roy F. Evil: *Inside Human Cruelty and Violence*. New York: W. H. Free-man and Company, 1997.

Beatty, Bess. *Alamance: The Holt Family and Industrialization in a North Carolina County, 1837–1900*. Baton Rouge: Louisiana State University, 1999.

Bederman, Gail. *Manliness and Civilization: A Cultural History of Gender and Race in the United States, 1880–1917*. Chicago: University of Chicago Press, 1995.

Bentley, Nancy and Sandra Gunning, eds. *Charles W. Chesnutt: The Marrow of Tradition*. New York: Bedford/St. Martin's, 2002.

Berk, Richard A. "A Gaming Approach to Crowd Behavior." *American Sociological Review* 39 (June 1974): 355–373.

Bettinger, Christopher Paul. "Strange Interludes? A Sociological History of Ameri-can Race Rioting, 1900 to 1996." Ph.D. dissertation, University of Michigan, Ann Arbor, 1999.

Blalock, Hubert M. "Per Cent Non-white and Discrimination in the South." *Amer-ican Sociological Review* 22 (1957): 677–682.

Blight, David W. *Race and Reunion: The Civil War in American Memory*. Cam-bridge: Belknap Press of Harvard University, 2001.

Bloombaum, Milton. "The Conditions Underlying Race Riots as Portrayed by Multi-Dimensional Scalogram Analysis: A Reanalysis of Lieberson and Sil-verman's Data." *American Sociological Review* 33 (1968): 76–91.

Blum, John Morton. *V Was for Victory: Politics and Culture during World War II*. San Diego: A Harcourt Brace & Company, 1976.

Bobo, Lawrence. "Group Conflict, Prejudice, and the Paradox of Contemporary Racial Attitudes." Pp. 85–114 in *Eliminating Racism*. P. A. Katz and D. A. Taylor, eds. New York: Plenum Press, 1988.

Bobo, Lawrence, Howard Schuman, and Charlotte Steeh. "Changing Racial At-titudes toward Residential Segregation." Pp. 152–169 in *Housing Desegre-gation and Federal Policy*. John M. Goering, ed. Chapel Hill: University of North Carolina Press, 1986.

Bohstedt, John. "The Dynamics of Riots: Escalation and Diffusion/Contagion." Pp. 257–306 in *The Dynamics of Aggression: Biological and Social Processes in Dyads and Groups*. Michael Potegal and John F. Knutson, eds. Hillsdale: Lawrence Erlbaum Associates, Publishers, 1994.

Bonacich, Edna. "Advanced Capitalism and Black/White Race Relations in the United States: A Split Labor Market Interpretation." *American Sociological Review* 41 (1976): 34–51.

Boyle, Kevin. *Arc of Justice: A Saga of Race, Civil Rights, and Murder in the Jazz Age*. New York: H. Holt, 2004.

Brass, Paul R. *The Production of Hindu-Muslim Violence in Contemporary India*. Seattle: University of Washington Press, 2003.

Brass, Paul R., ed. *Riots and Pogroms*. New York: New York University Press, 1996.

Brass, Paul R. *Theft of an Idol: Text and Context in the Representation of Collective Violence*. Princeton: Princeton University Press, 1997.

Brophy, Alfred. L. "Norms, Law, and Reparations: The Case of the Ku Klux Klan in 1920s Oklahoma." *Harvard BlackLetter Law Journal* 20 (2004): 17–48.

Brophy, Alfred. L. *Reconstructing the Dreamland: The Tulsa Riot of 1921: Race, Reparations, and Reconciliation*. New York: Oxford University Press, 2002.

Brophy, Alfred. L. "The Tulsa Race Riot Commission, Apology, and Reparation: Understanding the Functions and Limitations of a Historical Truth Commission." Pp. 234–258 in *Taking Wrongs Seriously: Apologies and Reparations*. Elazar Barkan and Alexander Karn, eds. Stanford: Stanford University Press, 2006.

Brown, Richard Maxwell. *Strain of Violence: Historical Studies of American Violence and Vigilantism*. New York: Oxford University Press, 1975.

Brown, Leslie and Anne Valk. "Black Durham behind the Veil: A Case Study." *OAH Magazine of History* (2004): 23–27.

Burns, Rebecca. *Rage in the Gate City: The Story of the 1906 Atlanta Race Riot*. Cincinnati: Emmis Books, 2006.

Burran, James Albert, III. "Racial Violence in the South during World War II." Ph.D. dissertation, University of Tennessee, Knoxville, 1977.

Button, James W. *Black Violence: Political Impact of the 1960s Riots*. Princeton: Princeton University Press, 1978.

Cameron, Charles and Sunita Parikh. "Riot Games: A Theory of Mass Political Violence." Paper presented at the Wallace Institute Conference on Political Economy, University of Rochester, Rochester, October 19–20, 2000.

Capeci, Dominic J., Jr. "Foreword." Pp. xix–xlii in *Encyclopedia of American Race Riots*. Walter Rucker and James Nathaniel Upton, eds. Westport: Greenwood Press, 2006.

Capeci, Dominic J., Jr. "The Lynching of Cleo Wright: Federal Protection of Constitutional Rights during World War II." *Journal of American History* 72 (1986): 859–887.

Capeci, Dominic J., Jr. *Race Relations in Wartime Detroit: The Sojourner Truth Housing Controversy in 1942*. Philadelphia: Temple University Press, 1984.

Capeci, Dominic J., Jr. "Race Riot Redux: William M. Tuttle, Jr. and the Study of Racial Violence." *Reviews in American History* 29 (2001): 165–181.

Capeci, Dominic J., Jr., and Jack C. Knight. "Reckoning with Violence: W. E. B. Du Bois and the 1906 Atlanta Race Riot." *Journal of Southern History* 62 (1996): 727–766.

Capeci, Dominic J., Jr., and Martha Wilkerson. "The Detroit Rioters of 1943: A Reinterpretation." *Michigan Historical Review* 16 (1990): 49–72.

Capeci, Dominic J., Jr., and Martha Wilkerson. *Layered Violence: The Detroit Rioters of 1943.* Jackson: University Press of Mississippi, 1991.

Caplan, Nathan and J.M. Paige. "A Study of Ghetto Rioters." *Scientific American* 219 (1968): 15–21.

Capozzola, Christopher. "The Only Badge Needed Is Your Patriotic Fervor: Vigilance, Coercion, and the Law in World War I America." *Journal of American History* 88 (2002): 1354–1382.

Cardyn, Lisa. "Sexualized Racism/Gendered Violence: Outraging the Body Politic in the Reconstruction South." *Michigan Law Review* 100 (2002): 675–867.

Cecelski, David S. and Timothy B. Tyson, eds. *Democracy Betrayed: The Wilmington Race Riot of 1898 and Its Legacy.* Chapel Hill: University of North Carolina Press, 1998.

Chai, Sun-Ki. "Rational Choice and Culture: Clashing Perspectives or Complementary Modes of Analysis?" in *Culture Matters: Essays in Honor of Aaron Wildavsky.* Richard J. Ellis and Michael Thompson, eds. Boulder: HarperCollins Publishers, Inc., 1997.

Chai, Sun-Ki and Brendon Swedlow, eds. *Culture and Social Theory.* New Brunswick: Transaction Publishers, 1998.

The Chicago Commission on Race Relations. *The Negro in Chicago: A Study of Race Relations and a Race Riot.* Chicago: University of Chicago Press, 1922.

Chong, Dennis. *Collective Action and the Civil Rights Movement.* Chicago: University of Chicago Press, 1991.

Citizens' Protective League. *Story of the Riot.* New York: Arno Press, 1969. Coalition to Remember the 1906 Atlanta Race Riot.

Coben, Stanley. *Rebellion against Victorianism: The Impetus for Cultural Change in 1920s America.* New York: Oxford University Press, 1991.

Cohen, Jerry and William S. Murphy. *Burn, Baby! The Los Angeles Race Riot: August, 1965.* New York: E.P. Dutton & Co., 1966.

Conant, Ralph W. and Molly Apple Levin, eds. *Problems in Research on Community Violence.* New York: Frederick A. Praeger, Publishers, 1969.

Cortner, Richard C. *A Mob Intent on Death: the NAACP and the Arkansas Riot Cases.* Middletown: Wesleyan University Press, 1988.

Cripps, Thomas. *Slow Fade to Black: The Negro in American Film, 1900–1942.* New York: Oxford University Press, 1977.

Crowe, Charles. "Racial Massacre in Atlanta September 22, 1906." *Journal of Negro History* 54 (1969): 150–173.

Crowe, Charles. "Racial Violence and Social Reform—Origins of the Atlanta Riot of 1906." *Journal of Negro History* 54 (1968): 234–256

Daniel, Pete. "Going Among Strangers: Southern Reactions to World War II." *Journal of American History* 77 (1990): 886–911.

Davies, James Chowning. "Toward a Theory of Revolution." *American Sociological Review* 27 (1962): 5–19.

Davis, Ronald L. F. "Resisting Jim Crow: In-Depth Essay." *The History of Jim Crow.* http://www.jimcrowhistory.org/history/resisting2.htm.

DeNardo, James. *Power in Numbers: The Political Strategy of Protest and Rebellion.* Princeton: Princeton University Press, 1985.

Dinges, Bruce J. "The San Angelo Riot of 1881: The Army, Race Relations, and Settlement on the Texas Frontier." *Journal of the West* 41 (2002): 35–45.

Dixon, Thomas. *The Leopard's Spots: A Romance of the White Man's Burden, 1865–1900.* New York: Doubleday, Page, and Co., 1902.

Dollard, John, Leonard W. Doob, Neal E. Miller, O.H. Mowrer, and Robert R. Sears. *Frustration and Aggression.* New Haven: Yale University Press, 1939.

D'Orso, Michael. *Like Judgment Day: The Ruin and Redemption of a Town Called Rosewood.* New York: G. P. Putnam's Sons, 1996.

Douglas, Davison M. *Jim Crow Moves North: The Battle over Northern School Segregation, 1865–1954.* New York: Cambridge University Press, 2005.

Downes, Bryan T. "The Social Characteristics of Riot Cities: A Comparative Study." *Social Science Quarterly* 49 (1968): 504–520.

Du Bois, W.E.B. *The Autobiography of W. E. B. Du Bois: A Soliloquy on Viewing My Life from the Last Decade of Its First Century.* New York: International Publishers, 1968.

Du Bois, W.E.B. *Dusk of Dawn.* Millwood: Kraus-Thomson Organization, 1975.

Du Bois, W.E.B. *The Souls of Black Folk.* Chicago: A.C. McClurg, 1903.

Duncan, Garrett A. "Desegregation." Pp. 151–160 in *Encyclopedia of American Race Riots.* Walter Rucker and James Nathaniel Upton, eds. Westport: Greenwood Press, 2006.

Durham, Kenneth R., Jr. "The Longview Race Riot of 1919." *East Texas Historical Journal* 18 (1980): 13–24.

Egerton, John. "A Case of Prejudice: Maurice Mays and the Knoxville Race Riot of 1919." *Southern Exposure* 11 (July/August 1983): 56–65.

Ellsworth, Scott. *Death in a Promised Land: The Tulsa Race Riot of 1921.* Baton Rouge: Louisiana State University Press, 1982.

Falck, Susan. "Jim Crow Legislation Overview." *The History of Jim Crow.* http://www.jimcrowhistory.org/resources/pdf/hs_es_jim_crow_laws.pdf.

Fearon, James D. and David D. Laitin. "Explaining Interethnic Cooperation." *American Political Science Review* 90 (1996): 715–735.

Fearon, James D. and David D. Laitin. "Violence and the Social Construction of Ethnic Identity." *International Organization* 54 (2000): 845–877.

Fickle, James E. "Management Looks at the 'Labor Problem': The Southern Pine Industry during World War I and the Postwar Era." *Journal of Southern History* 40 (1974): 61–76.

Francisco, Ronald A. "After the Massacre: Mobilization in the Wake of Harsh Repression." *Mobilization* 9 (2004): 107–126.

Frederickson, George M. *The Black Image in the White Mind: The Debate on Afro-American Character and Destiny, 1817–1914.* New York: Harper & Row, Publishers, 1971.

Fulton, David Bryant [Jack Thorne]. *Hanover.* New York: Arno Press, 1969.

Gamson, Joshua. "The Organizational Shaping of Collective Identity: The Case of Lesbian and Gay Film Festivals in New York." *Sociological Forum* 11 (1996): 231–261.

Gamson, William A. *The Strategy of Social Protest.* Homewood: Dorsey Press, 1975.

George, Alexander L. and Andrew Bennett. *Case Studies and Theory Development in the Social Sciences*. Cambridge: MIT Press, 2005.

Giddings, Paula. "Ida Wells-Barnett (1862–1931)." Pp. 367–385 in *Portraits of American Women. Vol. II From the Civil War to the Present*. G. J. Barker-Benfield and Catherine Clinton, eds. New York: St. Martin's Press, 1991.

Gilje, Paul A. *Rioting in America*. Bloomington: Indiana University Press, 1996.

Gilmore, Glenda E. *Gender and Jim Crow: Women and the Politics of White Supremacy in North Carolina, 1896–1920*. Chapel Hill: University of North Carolina Press, 1996.

Gilmore, Glenda E. "Murder, Memory, and the Flight of the Incubus." Pp. 73–93 in *Democracy Betrayed: The Wilmington Race Riot of 1898 and Its Legacy*. David S. Cecelski and Timothy B. Tyson, eds. Chapel Hill: University of North Carolina Press, 1998.

Giugni, Marco G. "Structure and Culture in Social Movement Theory." *Sociological Forum* 13 (1998): 365–375.

Gladwell, Malcolm. *The Tipping Point: How Little Things Can Make a Big Difference*. Boston: Little, Brown and Company, 2000.

Godshalk, David Fort. *Veiled Visions: The 1906 Atlanta Race Riot and the Reshaping of American Race Relations*. Chapel Hill: University of North Carolina Press, 2005.

Goering, John M., ed. *Housing Desegregation and Federal Policy*. Chapel Hill: University of North Carolina Press, 1986.

Goldstein, Arnold P. *The Psychology of Group Aggression*. Chichester, West Sussex, England: John Wiley & Sons, Ltd, 2002.

Goode, Eric. *Collective Behavior*. Fort Worth: Harcourt Brace Jovanovich, 1992.

Goodwin, Jeff, James M. Jasper, and Francesca Polletta, eds. *Passionate Politics: Emotions and Social Movements*. Chicago: University of Chicago Press, 2001.

Gordon, Fon Louise. "From Slavery to Uncertain Freedom: Blacks in the Delta." Pp. 98–127 in *The Arkansas Delta: Land of Paradox*. Jeannie Whayne and Willard B. Gatewood, eds. Fayetteville: University of Arkansas Press, 1993.

Gorringe, Hugo. "'Banal Violence'? The Everyday Underpinnings of Collective Violence." *Identities: Global Studies in Culture and Power* 13 (2006): 237–260.

Grable, Stephen W. "Racial Violence within the Context of Community History." *Phylon* 42 (1981): 275–283.

Graham, Hugh Davis and Ted Robert Gurr, eds. *Violence in America: Historical & Comparative Perspectives*. Rev. ed. Beverly Hills: Sage Publications, 1979.

Granovetter, Mark. "Threshold Models of Collective Behavior." *American Journal of Sociology* 83 (1978): 1420–1443.

Granovetter, Mark and Roland Soong. "Threshold Models of Diffusion and Collective Behavior." *Journal of Mathematical Sociology* 9 (1983): 165–179.

Graves, John William. "Protectors or Perpetrators? White Leadership in the Elaine Race Riots." *Arkansas Review* 32 (2001): 130–141.

Green, Constance McLaughlin. *The Secret City: A History of Race Relations in the Nation's Capital*. Princeton: Princeton University Press, 1967.

Green, Donald P., Dara Z. Strolovitch, and Janelle S. Wong. "Defended Neighborhoods, Integration, and Racially Motivated Crime." *American Journal of Sociology* 104 (1998): 372–403.

Grimshaw, Allen D. "Lawlessness and Violence in America and Their Special Manifestations in Changing Negro-White Relationships." *Journal of Negro History* 44 (1959): 52–72.

Grimshaw, Allen D, ed. *Racial Violence in the United States.* Chicago: Aldine Publishing Company, 1969.

Grimshaw, Allen D. "Urban Racial Violence in the United States: Changing Ecological Considerations." *American Journal of Sociology* 66 (1960): 109–119.

Grossman, James R. *Land of Hope: Chicago, Black Southerners, and the Great Migration.* Chicago: University of Chicago Press, 1989.

Gurney, Joan Neff and Kathleen J. Tierney. "Relative Deprivation and Social Movements: A Critical Look at Twenty Years of Theory and Research." *Sociological Quarterly* 23 (1982): 33–47.

Gurr, Ted Robert. *Why Men Rebel.* Princeton: Princeton University Press, 1970.

Haddock David D. and Daniel D. Polsby. "Understanding Riots." *Cato Journal* 14 (1994): 147–157.

Hahn, Steven. *A Nation Under Our Feet: Black Political Struggles in the Rural South From Slavery to the Great Migration.* Cambridge: Belknap Press of Harvard University Press, 2003.

Hahn, Steven. *The Roots of Southern Populism: Yeoman Farmers and the Transformation of the Georgia Upcountry, 1850–1890.* New York: Oxford University Press, 1983.

Hair, William Ivy. *Bourbonism and agrarian protest; Louisiana politics, 1877–1900.* Baton Rouge: Louisiana State University, 1969.

Hair, William Ivy. *Carnival of Fury: Robert Charles and the New Orleans Race Riot of 1900.* Baton Rouge: Louisiana State University, 1976.

Hair, William Ivy. "Lynching." Pp. 174–175 in *Encyclopedia of Southern Culture.* Charles Reagan Wilson and William Ferris, eds. Chapel Hill: University of North Carolina Press, 1989.

Hale, Grace Elizabeth. *Making Whiteness: The Culture of Segregation in the South, 1890–1940.* New York: Pantheon Books, 1998.

Hall, Jacquelyn Dowd. *Revolt against Chivalry: Jessie Daniel Ames and the Women's Campaign against Lynching.* Rev. ed. New York: Columbia University Press, 1993.

Halliburton, R., Jr. "The Tulsa Race War of 1921." *Journal of Black Studies* 2 (1972): 333–357.

Hayden, Tom. *Rebellion in Newark: Official Violence and Ghetto Response.* New York: Vintage Books, 1967.

Hayner, Priscilla B. "The Contribution of Truth Commissions." Pp. 203–221 in *An End to Torture: Strategies for Its Eradication.* Bertil Dunér, ed. New York: Zed Books, 1998.

Hayner, Priscilla B. *Unspeakable Truths: Confronting State Terror and Atrocity.* New York: Routledge, 2001.

Haynes, Robert V. *A Night of Violence: The Houston Riot of 1917*. Baton Rouge: Louisiana State University Press, 1976.

Headley, T. J. *Mass Violence in America: Pen and Pencil Sketches of the Great Riots*. New York: Arno Press and the New York Times, 1969.

Heaps, Willard A. *Riots, U.S.A. 1765–1970*. Rev. ed. New York: Seabury Press, 1970.

Hennessey, Melinda Meek. "Political Terrorism in the Black Belt: The Eutaw Riot." *Alabama Review* 33 (1980): 35–48.

Hennessey, Melinda Meek. "Race and Violence in Reconstruction New Orleans: The 1868 Riot." Pp. 171–185 in *Black Freedom/White Violence, 1865–1900*. Donald G. Nieman, ed. New York: Garland, 1994.

Hennessey, Melinda Meek. "Racial Violence during Reconstruction: The 1876 Riots in Charleston and Cainhoy." *South Carolina Historical Magazine* 86 (1985): 100–112.

Henry, Charles P. *Long Overdue: The Politics of Racial Reparations*. New York: NYU Press, 2007.

Hirsch, James S. *Riot and Remembrance: America's Worst Race Riot and Its Legacy*. Boston: Mariner Books, 2003.

History Matters. "'Their Own Hotheadedness': Senator Benjamin R. 'Pitchfork Ben' Tillman Justifies Violence against Southern Blacks." March 23, 1900. http://historymatters.gmu.edu/d/55/.

Holt, Thomas C. "The Political Uses of Alienation: W. E. B. Du Bois on Politics, Race, and Culture, 1903–1940." *American Quarterly* 42 (1990): 301–323.

Horowitz, Donald L. *The Deadly Ethnic Riot*. Berkeley: University of California Press, 2001.

Hovland, Carl I. and Robert R. Sears. "Minor Studies of Aggression: Correlations of Lynchings with Economic Indices." Pp. 344–349 in *A Social History of Violence*. Allen D. Grimshaw, ed. New Brunswick: Aldine Transaction, 2009.

Huck, Karen. "The Arsenal on Fire: The Reader in the Riot, 1943." *Critical Studies in Mass Communication* 10 (1993): 23–48.

Hughes, C. Alvin. "The Negro Sanhedrin Movement." *Journal of Negro History* 69 (1984): 1–13.

Ingalls, Robert P. "Lynching and Establishment Violence in Tampa, 1858–1935." *Journal of Southern History* 53 (1987): 613–644.

Jacobs, David and Katherine Wood. "Interracial Conflict and Interracial Homicide: Do Political and Economic Rivalries Explain White Killings of Blacks or Black Killings of Whites?" *American Journal of Sociology* 105 (1999): 157–190.

Janowitz, Morris. "Social Control of Escalated Violence." Pp. 501–514 in *Racial Violence in the United States*. Allen D. Grimshaw, ed. Chicago: Aldine Publishing Company, 1969.

Jasper, James M. "The Emotions of Protest: Affective and Reactive Emotions In and Around Social Movements." *Sociological Forum* 13 (1998): 397–424.

Jaspin, Elliot. *Buried in the Bitter Waters: The Hidden History of Racial Cleansing in America*. New York: Basic Books, 2007.

Johnson, James Weldon. *Black Manhattan*. Salem: Ayer Company, Publishers, Inc., 1990.

Johnson, H. B. *Black Wall Street: From Riot to Renaissance in Tulsa's Historic Greenwood District*. Austin: Eakin Press, 1998.

Johnson, Marilynn S. "Gender, Race, and Rumours: Re-examining the 1943 Race Riots." *Gender & History* 10 (1998): 252–277.

Johnston, Hank and Bert Klandermans, eds. *Social Movements and Culture*. Minneapolis: University of Minnesota Press, 1995.

Jones, Angela. *African American Civil Rights: Early Activism and the Niagara Movement*. Santa Barbara: Praeger, 2011.

Jordon, William. "'The Damnable Dilemma': African-American Accommodation and Protest during World War I." *Journal of American History* 81 (1995): 1562–1583.

Karklins, Rasma and Roger Petersen. "Decision Calculus of Protesters and Regimes: Eastern Europe 1989." *Journal of Politics* 55 (1993): 588–614.

Katz, P. A. and D. A. Taylor, eds. *Eliminating Racism*. New York: Plenum Press, 1988.

Kennedy, David M. *Freedom from Fear: The American People in Depression and War, 1929–1945*. New York: Oxford University Press, 1999.

Kennedy, David M. *Over Here: The First World War and American Society*. New York: Oxford University Press, 1980.

Kerner Commission. *Report of the National Advisory Commission on Civil Disorders*. New York: Bantam Books, 1968.

Key, V. O. *Southern Politics in State and Nation*. New York: A. A. Knopf, 1949.

Kirshenbaum, Andrea Meryl. "'The Vampire That Hovers over North Carolina': Gender, White Supremacy, and the Wilmington Race Riot of 1898." *Southern Cultures* 4 (1998): 6–29.

Klandermans, Bert and Dirk Oegema. "Potentials, Networks, Motivations, and Barriers: Steps towards Participation in Social Movements." *American Sociological Review* 52 (1987): 519–531.

Knopf, Terry Ann. "Race, Riots, and Reporting." *Journal of Black Studies* 4 (1974): 303–327.

Knopf, Terry Ann. *Rumors, Race and Riots*. New Brunswick: Transaction Publishers, 2006.

Krook, Mona Lena. "Comparing Methods for Studying Women in Politics: Statistical, Case Study, and Qualitative-Comparative Techniques." Paper presented at the Annual Meeting of the American Political Science Association, Washington, D.C., September 1–4, 2005.

Kuo, Susan S. "Bringing in the State: Toward a Constitutional Duty to Protect from Mob Violence." *Indiana Law Journal* 79 (2004): 177–244.

Laitin, David D. *Identity in Formation: The Russian-Speaking Populations in the Near Abroad*. Ithaca: Cornell University Press, 1998.

Lakin, Matthew. "'A Dark Night': The Knoxville Race Riot of 1919." *Journal of East Tennessee History* 72 (2000): 1–29.

Lamon, Lester C. "Tennessee Race Relations and the Knoxville Riot of 1919." *East Tennessee Historical Society's Publications* 41 (1969): 67–85.

Lane, Ann J. *The Brownsville Affair: National Crisis and Black Reaction*. Port Washington: Kennikat Press, 1971.

Laraña, Enrique, Hank Johnston, and Joseph R. Gusfield, eds. *New Social Movements: From Ideology to Identity*. Philadelphia: Temple University Press, 1994.

Larson, Jennifer L. "Early African American Perspectives on the Wilmington Race Riots of 1898." Documenting the American South. University Library, University of North Carolina at Chapel Hill, http://docsouth.unc.edu/highlights/riots_1898.html.

Laurie, Clayton D. "The U.S. Army and the Omaha Race Riot of 1919." *Nebraska History* 72 (1991): 135–143.

Lawson, Michael L. "Omaha, a City of Ferment: Summer of 1919." *Nebraska History* 58 (1977): 395–417.

Le Bon, Gustave. *The Crowd: A Study of the Popular Mind*. London: T. F. Unwin, 1896.

Leach, Eugene E. "The Literature of Riot Duty: Managing Class Conflict in the Streets, 1877–1927. *Radical History Review* 56 (1993): 23–50.

Leiter, Andrew. "Thomas Dixon, Jr.: Conflicts in History in Literature." Documenting the American South. University Library, University of North Carolina at Chapel Hill, http://docsouth.unc.edu/southlit/dixon_intro.html.

Leuchtenburg, William E. *The Perils of Prosperity, 1914–1932*. 2nd ed. Chicago: University of Chicago Press, 1993.

Lewis, David Levering, ed. *W. E. B. Du Bois: A Reader*. New York: Henry Holt and Company, 1995.

Lewis, David Levering. *W. E. B. Du Bois: Biography of a Race, 1868–1919*. New York: Henry Holt and Company, 1993.

Lewis, David Levering. *W. E. B. Du Bois: The Fight for Equality and the American Century, 1919–1963*. New York: Henry Holt and Company, 2000.

Lewis, David Levering. *When Harlem Was in Vogue*. New York: Penguin Books, 1997.

Library of Congress. African American Odyssey. The Booker T. Washington Era. "Breakthroughs in the Sports Arena." http://memory.loc.gov/ammem/aaohtml/exhibit/aopart6.html.

Lieberson, Stanley and Arnold K. Silverman. "The Precipitants and Underlying Conditions of Race Riots." *American Sociological Review* 30 (1965): 887–898.

Litwack, Leon F. *Trouble in Mind: Black Southerners in the Age of Jim Crow*. New York: Alfred A. Knopf, 1998.

Lohmann, Susanne. "The Dynamics of Informational Cascades: The Monday Demonstrations in Leipzig, East Germany, 1989–91." *World Politics* 47 (1994): 42–101.

Lowery, J. Vincent. "Remembering 1898: Literary Responses and Public Memory of the Wilmington Race Riot (Appendix M)." Pp. 413–428 in *1898 Wilmington*

Race Riot Final Report. LeRae Umfleet, et al. 1898 Wilmington Race Riot Commission. North Carolina Office of Archives and History, 2006. http://www.ah.dcr.state.nc.us/1898-wrrc/report/report.htm.

Lumpkins, Charles L. *American Pogrom: The East St. Louis Race Riot and Black Politics*. Athens: Ohio University Press, 2008.

Lupsha, Peter. "On Theories of Urban Racial Violence." *Urban Affairs Quarterly* 4 (1969): 273–296.

Lupton, John A. "East St. Louis (Illinois) Riot of 1917." Pp. 175–191 in *Encyclopedia of American Race Riots*. Walter Rucker and James Nathaniel Upton, eds. Westport: Greenwood Press, 2006.

MacLean, Nancy. *Behind the Mask of Chivalry: The Making of the Second Ku Klux Klan*. New York: Oxford University Press, 1994.

Madigan, Tim. *The Burning: Massacre, Destruction, and the Tulsa Race Riot of 1921*. New York: Thomas Dunne Books, 2001.

Magubane, Bernard. *The Ties That Bind: African-American Consciousness of Africa*. Trenton: Africa World Press, 1987.

Margolick, David. *Beyond Glory: Joe Louis vs. Max Schmeling, and a World on the Brink*. New York: Alfred A. Knopf, 2005.

Margolick, David. *Strange Fruit: Billie Holiday, Café Society, and an Early Cry for Civil Rights*. Philadelphia: Running Press, 2000.

Margolick, David. *Strange Fruit: Biography of a Song*. New York: Ecco Press, 2001.

Mason, T. David. "Individual Participation in Collective Racial Violence: A Rational Choice Synthesis." *American Political Science Review* 78 (1984): 1040–1056.

Masotti, Louis H. and Don R. Bowen, eds. *Riots and Rebellion: Civil Violence in the Urban Community*. Beverly Hills: Sage Publications, 1968.

Massey, Douglas S. and Nancy A. Denton. *American Apartheid: Segregation and the Making of the Underclass*. Cambridge: Harvard University Press, 1993.

Mazón, Mauricio. *The Zoot-Suit Riots: The Psychology of Symbolic Annihilation*. Austin: University of Texas Press, 1984.

McAdam, Doug. "Culture and Social Movements." Pp. 36–57 in *New Social Movements: From Ideology go Identity*. Enrique Laraña, Hank Johnston, and Joseph R. Gusfield, eds. Philadelphia: Temple University Press, 1994.

McAdam, Doug. *Political Process and the Development of Black Insurgency, 1930–1970*. Chicago: University of Chicago Press, 1982.

McAdam, Doug, John D. McCarthy, and Mayer N. Zald, eds. *Comparative Perspectives on Social Movements: Political Opportunities, Mobilizing Structures, and Cultural Framings*. New York: Cambridge University Press, 1996.

McAdam, Doug, John D. McCarthy, and Mayer N. Zald. "Social Movements." Pp. 695–737 in *Handbook of Sociology*. N.J. Smelser, ed. Newbury Park: Sage Publications, 1988.

McCarthy, John D. and Mayer N. Zald. "Resource Mobilization and Social Movements: A Partial Theory." *American Journal of Sociology* 82 (1977): 1212–1241.

McCool, B. Boren. *Union, Reaction, and Riot: A Biography of a Rural Race Riot.* Memphis: Memphis State University, 1970.

McDuffie, Jerome Anthony. "Politics in Wilmington and New Hanover County, North Carolina, 1865–1900: The Genesis of a Race Riot." Ph.D. dissertation, Kent State University, 1979.

McHaney, Sharon E. "Detroit's 1943 Riot." *Michigan History Magazine* 77 (1993): 34–39.

McLaughlin, Malcolm. *Power, Community, and Racial Killing in East St. Louis.* New York: Palgrave, Macmillan, 2005.

McPhail, Clark. "Civil Disorder Participation: A Critical Examination of Recent Research." *American Sociological Review* 36 (1971): 1058–1073.

McPhail, Clark. "The Dark Side of Purpose: Individual and Collective Violence in Riots." *Sociological Quarterly* 35 (1994): 1–32.

McPhail, Clark. *The Myth of the Madding Crowd.* New York: Aldine de Gruyter, 1991.

McPhail, Clark and Ronald T. Wohlstein. "Individual and Collective Behaviors within Gatherings, Demonstrations, and Riots." *Annual Review of Sociology* 9 (1983): 579–600.

McPherson, James M. *Battle Cry of Freedom: The Civil War Era.* New York: Ballantine Books, 1988.

McPherson, James M. *Ordeal by Fire: The Civil War and Reconstruction.* New York: Knopf, 1982.

McWhirter, Cameron. *Red Summer: The Summer of 1919 and the Awakening of Black America.* New York: Henry Holt and Company, 2011.

Meier, August and Elliot Rudwick. "The Boycott Movement against Jim Crow Streetcars in the South, 1900–1906." *Journal of American History* 55 (1969): 756–775.

Menard, Orville D. "Lest We Forget: The Lynching of Will Brown, Omaha's 1919 Race Riot." *Nebraska History* 91 (2010): 152–165.

Menard, Orville D. "Tom Dennison, the Omaha Bee, and the 1919 Race Riot." *Nebraska History* 68 (1987): 152–165.

Menschel, Robert. *Markets, Mobs & Mayhem: A Modern Look at the Madness of Crowds.* Hoboken: John Wiley & Sons, Inc., 2002.

Merritt, Russell. "Dixon, Griffith, and the Southern Legend." *Cinema Journal* 12 (1972): 26–45.

Miller, Kelly. "As to the Leopard's Spots: An Open Letter to Thomas W. Dixon, Jr." Pp. 262–266 in *Defining Southern Literature: Perspectives and Assessments, 1831–1952.* John E. Bassett, ed. Madison: Fairleigh Dickinson University Press, 1997.

Miller, Abraham H., Louis H. Bolce, and Mark Halligan. "The J-Curve Theory and the Black Urban Riots: An Empirical Test of Progressive Relative Deprivation Theory." *American Political Science Review* 71 (1977): 964–982.

Mixon, Gregory. *The Atlanta Riot: Race, Class, and Violence in a New South City.* Gainesville: University Press of Florida, 2005.

Momboisse, Raymond M. *Riots, Revolts, and Insurrections.* Springfield: Thomas, 1967.

Moore, Jacqueline M. *Booker T. Washington, W.E.B. Du Bois, and the Struggle for Racial Uplift*. Wilmington: Scholarly Resources Inc., 2003.

Moore, John Hammond. *Carnival of Blood: Dueling, Lynching, and Murder in South Carolina 1880–1920*. Columbia: University of South Carolina Press, 2006.

Moore, Jacqueline M. *Leading the Race: The Transformation of the Black Elite in the Nation's Capital, 1880–1920*. Charlottesville: University Press of Virginia, 1999.

Moore, Winfred B., Jr., Joseph F. Tripp, and Lyon G. Tyler, Jr., eds. *Developing Dixie: Modernization in a Traditional Society*. New York: Greenwood Press, 1988.

Morgan, William R. and Terry Nichols Clark. "The Causes of Racial Disorders: A Grievance-Level Explanation." *American Sociological Review* 38 (1973): 611–624.

Morris, Aldon. "Reflections on Social Movement Theory: Criticisms and Proposals." *Contemporary Sociology* 29 (2000): 445–454.

Moses, Wilson J. *Creative Conflict in African American Thought: Frederick Douglass, Alexander Crummell, Booker T. Washington, W. E. B. Du Bois, and Marcus Garvey*. New York: Cambridge University Press, 2004.

Moses, Wilson J. "The Lost World of the Negro, 1895–1919: Black Literary and Intellectual Life before the 'Renaissance.'" *Black American Literature Forum* 21 (1987): 61–84.

Myers, Daniel J. "Racial Rioting in the 1960s: An Event History Analysis of Local Conditions." *American Sociological Review* 62 (1997): 94–112.

Myrdal, Gunnar. *An American Dilemma: The Negro Problem and Modern Democracy*. New York: Harper, 1944.

National Association for the Advancement of Colored People. *Thirty Years of Lynching in the United States, 1889–1919*. Reprint of the 1919 edition. New York: Arno Press, 1969.

New York, New York. "Mayor LaGuardia's Commission on the Harlem Riot of March 19, 1935." *The Complete Report of Mayor LaGuardia's Commission on the Harlem Riot of March 19, 1935*. New York: Arno Press, 1969.

Nichols, Ronnie A. "Conspirators or Victims? A Survey of Black Leadership in the Riots." *Arkansas Review* 32 (2001): 123–130.

Niderost, Eric. "The Birth of a Nation." *American History* 40 (2005): 60–80.

Norwood, Stephen H. "Bogalusa Burning: The War against Biracial Unionism in the Deep South, 1919." *Journal of Southern History* 63 (1997): 591–628.

Oberschall, Anthony. *Social Conflict and Social Movements*. Englewood Cliffs: Prentice Hall, 1973.

Oklahoma Commission to Study the Tulsa Race Riot of 1921. "Tulsa Race Riot: A Report by the Oklahoma Commission to Study the Tulsa Race Riot of 1921." February 28, 2001. http://www.okhistory.org/trrc/freport.pdf.

Oliver, Lawrence J. "Writing from the Right during the 'Red Decade': Thomas Dixon's Attack on W. E. B. Du Bois and James Weldon Johnson in the Flaming Sword." *American Literature* 70 (1998): 131–152.

Oliver, Lawrence J. and Terri L. Walker. "James Weldon Johnson's 'New York Age' Essays on 'The Birth of a Nation' and the 'Southern Oligarchy.'" *South Central Review* 10 (1993): 1–17.

Olson, James S. and Sharon Phair. "The Anatomy of a Race Riot: Beaumont, Texas, 1943." *Texana* 11 (1973): 64–72.

Olzak, Susan. "Analysis of Events in the Study of Collective Action." *Annual Review of Sociology* 15 (1989): 119–141.

Olzak, Susan. *The Dynamics of Ethnic Conflict and Competition.* Stanford: Stanford University Press, 1992.

Olzak, Susan. "Labor Unrest, Immigration, and Ethnic Conflict in Urban America, 1880–1914." *American Journal of Sociology* 94 (1989): 1303–1333.

Olzak, Susan and Suzanne Shanahan. "Deprivation and Race Riots: An Extension of Spilerman's Analysis." *Social Forces* 74 (1996): 931–961.

Olzak, Susan, Suzanne Shanahan, and Elizabeth H. McEneaney. "Poverty, Segregation, and Race Riots: 1960 to 1993." *American Sociological Review* 61 (1996): 590–613.

Osofsky, Gilbert. *Harlem: The Making of a Ghetto: Negro New York, 1890–1930.* Chicago: Ivan R. Dee, 1996.

Ovington, Mary White. *How the National Association for the Advancement of Colored People Began.* New York: National Association for the Advancement of Colored People, 1914.

Palmer, Dewey H. "Moving North: Migration of Negroes during World War I." *Phylon* 28 (1960): 52–62.

Parikh, Sunita. *The Politics of Preference: Democratic Institutions and Affirmative Action in the United States and India.* Ann Arbor: University of Michigan Press, 1997.

Parikh, Sunita. "Religion, Reservations and Riots: The Politics of Ethnic Violence in India." Pp. 33–57 in Amitra Basu and Atul Kohli, eds. *Community Conflicts and the State in India.* New York: Oxford University Press, 1998.

Park, Robert E. and Ernest W. Burgess. *Introduction to the Science of Sociology.* Chicago: University of Chicago Press, 1921.

Petersen, Roger Dale. *Resistance and Rebellion: Lessons from Eastern Europe.* New York: Cambridge University Press, 2001.

Platt, Anthony M., ed. *The Politics of Riot Commissions: A Collection of Official Reports and Critical Essays.* New York: Macmillan Company, 1971.

Porter, Bruce and Marvin Dunn. *The Miami Riot of 1980: Crossing the Bounds.* Lexington: Lexington Books, 1984.

Potegal, Michael and John F. Knutson, eds. *The Dynamics of Aggression: Biological and Social Processes in Dyads and Groups.* Hillsdale: Lawrence Erlbaum Associates, Publishers, 1994.

Powell, A. Clayton, Sr. *Riots and Ruins.* New York: Richard R. Smith, 1945.

Powell, A. Clayton, Sr. "We Have Taken a City." Pp. 15–41 in *Democracy Betrayed: The Wilmington Race Riot of 1898 and Its Legacy.* David S. Cecelski and Timothy B. Tyson, eds. Chapel Hill: University of North Carolina Press, 1998.

Prather, H. Leon, Sr. *We Have Taken a City: Wilmington Racial Massacre and Coup of 1898*. Rutherford: Fairleigh Dickinson University Press, 1984.

Rabinowitz, Howard N. *The First New South: 1865–1920*. Arlington Heights: Harlan Davidson, Inc., 1992.

Rabinowitz, Howard N. "More Than the Woodward Thesis: Assessing the Strange Career of Jim Crow." *Journal of American History* 75 (1988): 842–856.

Rable, George C. *But There Was No Peace: The Role of Violence in the Politics of Reconstruction*. Athens: University of Georgia Press, 1984.

Rasler, Karen. "War, Accommodation, and Violence in the United States, 1890–1970." *American Political Science Review* 80 (1986): 921–945.

Rauchway, Eric. *Murdering McKinley: The Making of Theodore Roosevelt's America*. New York: Hill and Wang, 2003.

Rosenbaum, H. Jon and Peter C. Sederberg. "Vigilantism: An Analysis of Establishment Violence." *Comparative Politics* 6 (1974): 541–570.

Rosewood Investigative Team. *Documented History of the Incident Which Occurred at Rosewood, Florida, in January 1923*. http://mailer.fsu.edu/~mjones/rosewood/rosewood.html.

Rudwick, Elliot M. "The Niagara Movement." *Journal of Negro History* 42 (1957): 177–200.

Rudwick, Elliot M. *Race Riot at East St. Louis July 2, 1917*. Carbondale: Southern Illinois University Press, 1964.

Rule, James B. *Theories of Civil Violence*. Berkeley: University of California Press, 1988.

Rummel, Rudolph J. "Is Collective Violence Correlated with Social Pluralism?" *Journal of Peace Research* 34 (1997): 163–175.

Salert, Barbara and John Sprague. *The Dynamics of Riots*. Ann Arbor: Inter University Consortium for Political and Social Research, 1980.

Schaffer, Michael. "Lost Riot." *Washington City Paper*. April 3, 1998.

Schaich, Warren. "A Relationship between Collective Racial Violence and War." *Journal of Black Studies* 5 (1975): 374–394.

Schelling, Thomas C. *Micromotives and Macrobehavior*. New York: Norton, 1978.

Schelling, Thomas C. "The Process of Residential Segregation: Neighborhood Tipping." Pp. 157–184 in *Racial Discrimination in Economic Life*. A. Pascal, ed. Lexington: Lexington Books, 1972.

Schelling, Thomas C. *The Strategy of Conflict*. Cambridge: Harvard University Press, 1960.

Schneider, Mark Robert. *African Americans in the Jazz Age: A Decade of Struggle and Promise*. Boulder: Rowman & Littlefield Publishers, Inc., 2006.

Schneider, Mark Robert. *"We Return Fighting": The Civil Rights Movement in the Jazz Age*. Boston: Northeastern University Press, 2002.

Schuman, Howard, Charlotte Steeh, and Lawrence Bobo. *Racial Attitudes in America: Trends and Interpretations*. Cambridge: Harvard University Press, 1985.

Sears, David O. and John B. McConahay. *The Politics of Violence: The New Urban Blacks and the Watts Riot*. Boston: Houghton Mifflin, 1973.

Sears, David O. and T. M. Tomlinson. "Riot Ideology in Los Angeles: A Study of Negro Attitudes." Pp. 375–388 in *The Black Revolt: The Civil Rights Movement, Ghetto Uprisings, and Separatism*. J. A. Gerschwender, ed. Englewood Cliffs: Prentice Hall, 1971.

Senechal de la Roche, Roberta. *In Lincoln's Shadow: The 1908 Race Riot in Springfield, Illinois*. Carbondale: Southern Illinois University Press, 2008.

Seybert, Tony. "The Historic Black Press—Essay Overview." *The History of Jim Crow*. http://www.jimcrowhistory.org/resources/lessonplans/hs_es_black_press.htm.

Shapiro, Herbert. *White Violence and Black Response: From Reconstruction to Montgomery*. Amherst: University of Massachusetts Press, 1988.

Shoemaker, Robert B. *The London Mob: Violence and Disorder in Eighteenth-Century England*. New York: Hambledon and London, 2004.

Shogun, Robert and Tom Craig. *The Detroit Race Riot: A Study in Violence*. Philadelphia: Chilton Books, 1964.

Sitkoff, Harvard. "The Detroit Race Riot of 1943." *Michigan History* 53 (1969): 183–206.

Sitkoff, Harvard. *The Struggle for Black Equality, 1954–1992*. New York: Hill and Wang, 1993.

Smallwood, James. *The Struggle for Equality: Blacks in Texas*. Boston: American Press, 1983.

Smelser, Neil J. *Theory of Collective Behavior*. New York: Free Press, 1963.

Smith McKoy, Sheila. *When Whites Riot: Writing Race and Violence in American and South African Cultures*. Madison: University of Wisconsin Press, 2001.

Snow, David A. and Robert D. Benford. "Ideology, Frame Resonance, and Participant Mobilization." in *From Structure to Action: Comparing Social Movement Research Across Cultures*. Bert Klandermans, Hanspeter Kriesi, and Sidney G. Tarrow, eds. Greenwich: JAI Press, 1988.

Snow, David A. and Robert D. Benford. "Master Frames and Cycles of Protest." Pp. 133–155 in *Frontiers in Social Movement Theory*. Aldon D. Morris and Carol McClurg Mueller, eds. New Haven: Yale University Press, 1992.

Snow, David A. and Pamela E. Oliver. "Social Movements and Collective Behavior: Social Psychological Dimensions and Considerations." Pp. 571–599 in *Sociological Perspectives on Social Psychology*. K. S. Cook, G. A. Fine, and J. S. House, eds. Boston: Allyn and Bacon, 1995.

Snow, David A., E. Burke Rochford, Jr., Steven K. Worden, and Robert D. Benford. "Frame Alignment Process, Micromobilization, and Movement Participation." *American Sociological Review* 51 (1986): 464–481.

Somers, Dale A. "Black and White in New Orleans: A Study in Urban Race Relations, 1865–1900." *Journal of Southern History* 40 (1974): 19–42.

Southern, David W. *The Progressive Era and Race: Reaction and Reform, 1900–1917*. Wheeling: Harlan Davidson, 2005.

Spilerman, Seymour. "The Causes of Racial Disturbances: A Comparison of Alternative Explanations." *American Sociological Review* 35 (1970): 627–649.

Spilerman, Seymour. "The Causes of Racial Disturbances: Tests of an Explanation." *American Sociological Review* 36 (1971): 427–442.

Spilerman, Seymour. "Strategic Considerations in Analyzing the Distribution of Racial Disturbances." *American Sociological Review* 37 (1972): 493–499.

Spilerman, Seymour. "Structural Characteristics of Cities and the Severity of Racial Disorders." *American Sociological Review* 41 (1976): 771–793.

Staub, Ervin. "The Origins and Prevention of Genocide, Mass Killing, and Other Collective Violence." *Peace and Conflict* 5 (1999): 303–336.

Staub, Ervin. *The Psychology of Good and Evil: Why Children, Adults, and Groups Help and Harm Others.* New York: Cambridge University Press, 2003.

Staub, Ervin and Lori H. Rosenthal. "Mob Violence: Cultural-Societal Sources, Instigators, Group Processes, and Participants." Pp. 377–403 in *The Psychology of Good and Evil: Why Children, Adults, and Groups Help and Harm Others.* Ervin Staub, ed. New York: Cambridge University Press, 2003.

Steinberg, Marc W. "Tilting the Frame: Considerations on Collective Action Framing from a Discursive Turn." *Theory and Society* 27 (1998): 845–872.

Steverson, Leonard A. "Rosewood (Florida) Riot of 1923." Pp. 572–576 in *Encyclopedia of American Race Riots.* Walter Rucker and James Nathaniel Upton, eds. Westport: Greenwood Press, 2006.

Stockley, Grif. *Blood in Their Eyes: The Elaine Race Massacres of 1919.* Fayetteville: University of Arkansas Press, 2001.

Stockley, Grif. "The Legal Proceedings of the Arkansas Race Massacres of 1919 and the Evidence of the Plot to Kill Planters." *Arkansas Review* 32 (2001): 141–149.

Stohl, Michael. "War and Domestic Political Violence: The Case of the United States 1890–1970." *Journal of Conflict Resolution* 19 (1975): 379–416.

Sugrue, Thomas J. *The Origins of the Urban Crisis: Race and Inequality in Postwar Detroit.* Princeton: Princeton University Press, 1996.

Tambiah, Stanley J. *Leveling Crowds: Ethnonationalist Conflicts and Collective Violence in South Asia.* Berkeley: University of California Press, 1996.

Tarrow, Sidney. *Power in Movement: Social Movements and Contentious Politics.* New York: Cambridge University Press, 1998.

Taylor, Kieran. "'We Have Just Begun': Black Organization and White Response in the Arkansas Delta, 1919." *Arkansas Historical Quarterly* 58 (1999): 264–284.

Taylor, Verta and Nancy E. Whittier. "Collective Identity in Social Movement Communities: Lesbian Feminist Mobilization. Pp. 104–129 in *Frontiers in Social Movement Theory.* Aldon D. Morris and Carol McClurg Mueller, eds. New Haven: Yale University Press, 1992.

Thornbrough, Emma Lou. "The Brownsville Episode and the Negro Vote." *Mississippi Valley Historical Review* 44 (1957): 469–493.

Tilly, Charles. *From Mobilization to Revolution.* Reading: Addison Wesley, 1978.

Tilly, Charles. *The Politics of Collective Violence.* New York: Cambridge University Press, 2003.

Tolnay, Stewart E. and E. M. Beck. *A Festival of Violence: An Analysis of Southern Lynchings, 1882–1930*. Urbana: University of Illinois Press, 1995.

Tolnay, Stewart E., E. M. Beck, and James L. Massey. "The Power Threat Hypothesis and Black Lynching: 'Wither' the Evidence?" *Social Forces* 67 (1989): 634–641.

Tomlinson, T. M. "The Development of a Riot Ideology among Urban Negroes." *American Behavioral Scientist* 11 (1968): 27–31.

Turner, Ralph H. "Collective Behavior." Pp. 382–425 in *Handbook of Modern Sociology*. R. E. L. Faris, ed. Chicago: Rand McNally, 1964.

Turner, Ralph H. and Lewis M. Killian. *Collective Behavior*. Englewood Cliffs: Prentice Hall, 1957, 1972, 1987.

Tuttle, William M., Jr. "Contested Neighborhoods and Racial Violence: Prelude to the Chicago Riot of 1919." *Journal of Negro History* 55 (1970): 266–288.

Tuttle, William M., Jr. "Labor Conflict and Racial Violence: The Black Worker in Chicago, 1894–1919." *Labor History* X (1969): 408–432.

Tuttle, William M., Jr. *Race Riot: Chicago in the Red Summer of 1919*. Champaign: University of Illinois Press, 1996.

Tuttle, William M., Jr. "Violence in a 'Heathen' Land: The Longview Race Riot of 1919." *Phylon* 33 (1972): 324–333.

Tyson, Timothy B. *Radio Free Dixie: Robert F. Williams & the Roots of Black Power*. Chapel Hill: University of North Carolina Press, 1999.

Umfleet, LeRae. *1898 Wilmington Race Riot Report*. North Carolina Office of Archives and History, 2006. http://www.ah.dcr.state.nc.us/1898-wrrc/report/report.htm.

United States Bureau of the Census. *Fifteenth Census of the United States, 1930*. Washington, D.C.: Government Printing Office.

United States Bureau of the Census. *Fourteenth Census of the United States, 1920*. Washington, D.C.: Government Printing Office.

United States Bureau of the Census. *Seventeenth Census of the United States, 1950*. Washington, D.C.: Government Printing Office.

United States Bureau of the Census. *Sixteenth Census of the United States, 1940*. Washington, D.C.: Government Printing Office.

United States Bureau of the Census. *Thirteenth Census of the United States, 1910*. Washington, D.C.: Government Printing Office.

Upton, James N. "The Politics of Urban Violence: Critiques and Proposals." *Journal of Black Studies* 15 (1985): 243–258.

Upton, James N. *Urban Riots in the 20th Century: A Social History*. 2nd ed. Briston: Wyndham Hall Press, 1989.

Vela, Ramón G. "The Washington-Du Bois Controversy and African-American Protest: Ideological Conflict and Its Consequences." *Studies in American Political Development* 16 (2002): 88–109.

Voogd, Jan. "Longview (Texas) Riot of 1919." Pp. 369–371 in *Encyclopedia of American Race Riots*. Walter Rucker and James Nathaniel Upton, eds. Westport: Greenwood Press, 2006.

Voogd, Jan. *Race Riots & Resistance: The Red Summer of 1919*. New York: Peter Lang Publishing, 2008.

Waddell, Alfred M. "The Story of the Wilmington, North Carolina, Race Riots." *Collier's Weekly* November 26, 1898.

Wade, Wyn Craig. *The Fiery Cross: The Ku Klux Klan in America*. New York: Simon and Schuster, 1987.

Wanderer, Jules J. "An Index of Riot Severity and Some Correlates." *American Journal of Sociology* 74 (1969): 500–505.

Washington, Booker T. "The Atlanta Compromise." Pp. 128–131 in *Ripples of Hope: Great American Civil Rights Speeches*. Josh Gottheimer, ed. New York: Basic Civitas Books, 2004.

Waskow, Arthur I. *From Race Riot to Sit-In, 1919 and the 1960s: A Study in the Connections between Conflict and Violence*. Garden City: Doubleday, 1966.

Weaver, John Downing. *The Brownsville Raid*. New York: W. W. Norton, 1970.

Wells-Barnett, Ida B. *Crusade for Justice: The Autobiography of Ida B. Wells*. Alfreda M. Duster, ed. Chicago: University of Chicago Press, 1970.

Wetherington, Mark V. "Streetcar City: Knoxville, Tennessee, 1876–1947." *East Tennessee Historical Society's Publications* 54–55 (1982–1983): 70–110.

Whayne, Jeannie M. "Low Villains and Wickedness in High Places: Race and Class in the Elaine Riots." *Arkansas Review* 32 (2001): 102–119.

Whayne, Jeannie M. "Oil and Water: The Historiography of the Elaine Riots." *Arkansas Review* 32 (2001): 149–155.

Wheeler, Jared. "Prelude to Anarchy." *Texas Ranger Dispatch* 54 (1969): 4–14.

Whitaker, Robert. *On the Laps of Gods: The Red Summer of 1919 and the Struggle for Justice That Remade a Nation*. New York: Three Rivers Press, 2008.

White, Walter. *A Man Called White*. Reprint of the 1948 edition. New York: Arno Press, 1969.

White, Melvin Johnson. "Populism in Louisiana during the Nineties." *Mississippi Valley Historical Review* 5 (1918): 3–19.

Whites, LeeAnn. "Love, Hate, Rape, Lynching: Rebecca Latimer Felton and the Gender Politics of Racial Violence." Pp. 143–162 in *Democracy Betrayed: The Wilmington Race Riot of 1898 and Its Legacy*. David S. Cecelski and Timothy B. Tyson, eds. Chapel Hill: University of North Carolina Press, 1998.

Widick, B. J. *Detroit: City of Race and Class Violence*. Chicago: Quadrangle Books, 1972.

Wilkinson, Steven. *Votes and Violence: Electoral Competition and Ethnic Riots in India*. New York: Cambridge University Press, 2004.

Williams, John A. "The Long Hot Summers of Yesteryear." *History Teacher* 1 (1968): 9–23.

Williams, Lee E. II. *Post-War Riots in America, 1919 and 1946: How the Pressures of War Exacerbated American Urban Tensions to the Breaking Point*. Lewiston: E. Mellen Press, 1991.

Williams, Robin M., Jr. *Strangers Next Door: Ethnic Relations in American Communities*. Englewood Cliffs: Prentice-Hall, 1964.

Williams, R. Hal. *Years of Decision: American Politics in the 1890s*. New York: Wiley, 1978.

Williams, Lee E. and Lee E. Williams II. *Anatomy of Four Race Riots: Racial Conflicts in Knoxville, Elaine (Arkansas), Tulsa and Chicago, 1919–1921*. Hattiesburg: University and College Press of Mississippi, 1972.

Williamson, Joel. *The Crucible of Race: Black-White Relations in the American South since Emancipation*. New York: Oxford University Press, 1984.

Williamson, Joel. "Wounds Not Scars: Lynching, the National Conscience, and the American Historian." *Journal of American History* 83 (1997): 1221–1253.

Wood, Amy. *Lynching and Spectacle: Witnessing Racial Violence in America, 1890–1940*. Chapel Hill: University of North Carolina Press, 2009.

Woodward, C. Vann. *Origins of the New South, 1877–1913*. Baton Rouge: Louisiana State University Press, 1971.

Woodward, C. Vann. *The Strange Career of Jim Crow*. A Commemorative Edition. New York: Oxford University Press, 1996.

Woodward, C. Vann. *Tom Watson: Agrarian Rebel*. New York: Oxford University Press, 1963.

Wright, Richard. *Black Boy (American Hunger): A Record of Childhood and Youth*. New York: Harper Perennial, 1993.

Wright, Sam. *Crowds and Riots: A Study in Social Organization*. Beverly Hills: Sage Publications, 1978.

Wynne, Lewis N. "Brownsville: The Reaction of the Negro Press." *Phylon* 33 (1972): 153–160.

Yarborough, Richard. "Violence, Manhood, and Black Heroism: The Wilmington Riot in Two Turn-of-the-Century African American Novels." Pp. 225–251 in *Democracy Betrayed: The Wilmington Race Riot of 1898 and Its Legacy*. David S. Cecelski and Timothy B. Tyson, eds. Chapel Hill, N.C.: University of North Carolina Press, 1998.

Zunz, Olivier. *Making America Corporate, 1870–1920*. Chicago: University of Chicago Press, 1990.

PERIODICALS

The Atlanta Constitution
Boston Globe
Chicago Tribune
Christian Science Monitor
The Crisis
Los Angeles Times
New York Times
Oberlin Tribune
Wall Street Journal
Washington Post

INDEX

Precipitating events: definition, 8–9, 10, 118–20; in racial pogroms, 33, 70; during the Red Summer, 85
Press. *See* Newspapers
Pullman, Raymond, 92

Race riot: definition, xvi; model, 10; rational, xvii, 3–5; *See also* specific riots
Racial pogrom, 35–36, 69–70, 118
Radicalism, 2, 6–8, 10, 14, 17–20, 23, 25, 32–33, 42, 70, 77, 118, 129n14, 137n83
Randolph, A. Philip, 148–49n207
Red Scare, 84, 112
Red Shirts, 38, 142n13
Red Summer, 71, 87, 115, 118–19
Republican Party, 1, 14, 36, 38–39, 41, 42, 55–56, 73, 96, 109, 119, 139n93, 143n18, 160n77
Robertson, Curtis. *See* Charles, Robert
Robertson, James, 65–66
Robeson, Paul, 31
Roosevelt, Franklin, 16, 68, 77, 116, 148–49n207, 166n7
Roosevelt, Theodore, 60, 138–39n93
Rosewood, Florida, riot, 115, 123–24, 164n1
Rowland, Dick, 63–66
Rumors: 8–9, 33, 78, 85, 113, 118, 132n48; in Atlanta, 52; in Chicago, 95, 97; in Detroit, 116–17; in East St. Louis, 55, 58; in Harlem (1935), 165n4; in Houston, 157n91; in Knoxville, 101; in Longview, 89; in Omaha, 103; in Phillips County, 110; in Tulsa, 16, 63; in Washington, D.C., 92; in Wilmington, 38
Russell, Daniel, 36, 38

Schmeling, Max, 31
Secret Nine, 36, 37, 39, 70
Silent protest parade, 60–61

Simmons, Furnifold, 36–38
Smith, Edward, 103, 105
Smith, Hoke, 48, 54
Smith, Lillian, 22
Smyth, Ora, 100–101
Social Darwinism, 6, 17, 73
Southern Truth and Reconciliation, 123
Spanish-American War, 7, 17, 31–32, 73, 141n105
Special Committee Authorized by Congress to Investigate the East St. Louis Riots (1917), 60–61, 121–22
Springfield, Illinois, riot, 20, 30, 56, 139n95
Strike. *See* Labor strike
Strikebreakers, 55, 75–76, 95, 103
Structural factors: definition, 5–6, 10, 118–20; in racial pogroms, 13–17, 69; during the Red Summer, 72–77, 112
Sweet, Ossian, 74

Thompson, William Hale, 96, 99, 160n77
Thorne, Jack. *See* David Bryant Fulton
Tillman, Ben, 19, 30, 139n93, 142n13
Tipping point model, 4–5
Transportation strains, 5, 68, 116, 119
Tripp, Stephen Orville, 59
Trotter, William Monroe, 25, 29, 79
Tulsa, Oklahoma, riot, xv, 61–67, 115, 123–25
Turner, Henry M., 43, 47

Union. *See* Labor union

Vardaman, James, 18–19, 30, 137n83, 139n93

Waddell, Colonel Alfred Moore, 14, 37, 39–41
Walters, Lemuel, 88–89
Washington, Booker T., 7, 27–28, 53–54, 155n69

About the Author

ANN V. COLLINS is an assistant professor of political science at McKendree University in Lebanon, Illinois. She is a contributor to *Encyclopedia of American Race Riots* (Greenwood Press, 2007), *Encyclopedia of African American History* (ABC-CLIO, 2010), and *Oxford Encyclopedia of American Social History* (Oxford University Press, 2012).